Anthropologies and Histories

ANTHROPOLOGIES
AND
HISTORIES

Essays in Culture, History, and Political Economy

William Roseberry

RUTGERS UNIVERSITY PRESS

NEW BRUNSWICK AND LONDON

The author wishes to acknowledge permission to reprint revised versions of the following chapters:

Chapter 1, "Balinese Cockfights and the Seduction of Anthropology," was originally published in *Social Research* 49 (4): 1013–1028. Copyright © 1982 by the New School for Social Research, New York.

Chapter 2, "Marxism and Culture," was originally given as a lecture in the 1987 series "The Politics of Culture," sponsored by the Anthropological Society of Washington, D.C., and the Smithsonian Institution.

Chapter 3, "Images of the Peasant in the Consciousness of the Venezuelan Proletariat," was originally published in *Proletarians and Protest: The Roots of Class Formation in an Industrializing World,* edited by Michael Hanagan and Charles Stephenson, pp. 149–169 (Westport, Conn.: Greenwood Press). Copyright © 1985 by Michael Hanagan and Charles Stephenson.

Chapter 5, "European History and the Construction of Anthropological Subjects," was originally published in *Dialectical Anthropology* 10: 141–153. Copyright © 1985 by Elsevier Science Publishers, Amsterdam.

Chapter 6, "Anthropology, History, and Modes of Production," was originally published in *Anthropology, Capitalism, and the State,* edited by Benjamin Orlove, Michael Foley, and Thomas Love (Boulder, Colo.: Westview Press, 1988).

Library of Congress Cataloging-in-Publication Data

Roseberry, William, 1950–
    Anthropologies and histories : essays in culture, history, and political economy / William Roseberry.
        p.   cm.
    Bibliography: p.
    Includes index.
    ISBN 0-8135-1445-2 (cloth)   ISBN 0-8135-1446-0 (pbk.)
    1. Ethnology—Philosophy.   2. Economic anthropology.   3. Political anthropology.   4. Symbolism.   I. Title.
GNN345.R668   1989
306—dc19   89-30378
                                                                       CIP

British Cataloging-in-Publication information available

for Nicole, in my right mind

C O N T E N T S

P R E F A C E

My aim in this book is to explore some of the cultural and political implications of an anthropological political economy. In my view, too few of these implications have been explored, by those authors who dismiss the very *possibility* of a political economic understanding of culture as well as by many of the political economists themselves. Our ideas about culture and history never seem to confront each other. Within too many understandings of political economy, we may have sophisticated treatments of uneven development and of the formation of centers and peripheries, but when we come to consider culture and politics, we enclose profoundly contradictory social experiences within unproblematic and simplistic class or epochal labels. Within too many understandings of cultural anthropology, history is little more than a new terrain into which to extend anthropological practice. Anthropologists seldom let what they know about history affect what they think about culture. In this book, I have tried to place culture and history in relation to each other, in the context of a reflection on the political economy of uneven development.

In pursuing my argument, I ask the reader to accompany me through a discussion of Geertz's essay on the Balinese cockfight, Marx's postulation of Germanic and Asiatic and Ancient modes of production, Wolf's exploration of the formation of anthropological subjects in world history, Cardoso and Faletto's understanding of the "internalization of the external" in Latin America, Williams's concept of a selective tradition, and so on. I also ask the reader to consider these ideas in relation to politics and culture in contemporary Venezuela or processes of "Americanization" in Latin America. While I come to this book with large questions, my discussions are embedded within a consideration of particular texts and historical processes. The argument is carried by essays, a form that requires some preliminary discussion.

Clifford Geertz's observation that the essay has become the "natural genre" for anthropological writing (1973b: 25) finds apparent support from the number of recent books in anthropology that are based on essays. They are often more widely read than the ethnographic work that gives rise to or informs the essays, and they are generally published as part of an ongoing intellectual argument, as in Geertz's *Interpretation of Cultures* (1973a) or Marshall Sahlins's *Islands of History* (1985), so that the *book* makes a statement or pursues an argument that could not be found in any of the *essays,* taken individually or in their severalty. Essays and books of essays have become our principal means of communication.

What, then, are we to make of George Marcus's contention that the advantage of the essay is that it,

> opposes conventional systematic analysis, absolves the writer from having to develop the broader implications of his thought (while nonetheless indicating that there are such implications) or of having to tie loose ends together. The essayist can mystify the world, leave his subjects' actions open-ended as to their global implications, form a rhetorical posture of profound half-understanding, half-bewilderment with the world in which the ethnographic subject and the ethnographer live. This is thus a form well suited to a time such as the present, when paradigms are in disarray, problems intractable, and phenomena only partly understood. (1986: 191)

What is missing in this celebration of anthropological "play" is the very aspect of the essay that made it attractive to Geertz—the constant and sustained engagement with ethnographic subjects and the requirement that one embed one's observations, inferences, and interpretations within that engagement. How far this is from an anthropology that sets out to "mystify the world"!

Indeed, if we look at the way most essays have been written and read in anthropology, their importance lies in their attempt to *make sense*—of ethnographic encounters, of texts, of ideas, of processes—without enclosing that sense within totalizing models. They are, or should be, the means by which we develop our ideas, interpretations, and arguments rather than mere performances or rhetorical postures, demonstrations of an author's interpretive prowess or postmodern consciousness.

In my own case, I began working five years ago on a comparative history of the emergence of "family economy" in regions of Europe and Latin America. My object was to develop a critique of the notion of "domestic modes of production," especially those modes that treated domestic modes as quintessential precapitalist forms and projected them into a primordial human past. That book remains in progress, if such a phrase be permitted to describe the actual state of notes accumulated through two leaves and three years of bureaucratic post sitting (see Roseberry 1986b; 1988). Had I not begun that book, however, I would never have written the present one. In order to work through the historical materials, I found that I had to rethink some of my understandings of capitalism, of history, of peasantries. In order to develop the larger implications of the argument, I needed to think more clearly about culture, ideology, and politics and to link my emerging understandings of culture and politics to my perspectives on history and capitalism.

Rather than dealing with Culture or History or Capitalism in the abstract, however, I looked at what Geertz or Sahlins or Williams said about culture or history, what Marx or Wolf said about capitalism, and so on. At the same time, I continued to work with historical materials. I wrote essays, usually viewed as unwelcome digressions from The Project at hand. With time, two things became clear. First, the very structure or my argument for the family economy project was changing as my understandings of capitalism, history, culture, and politics changed.

Second, I began to see the outlines of an argument that informed the individual essays but had not been explicitly developed. My object in writing this book has been to develop that argument, first by writing new essays that would make the connections more explicit (Chapters 2, 4, 6, and 8, two of which are "old" essays that have been extensively rewritten here) and second by reworking some of the others.

In writing this book, I have contracted serious intellectual debts, some of which are evident in the pages that follow. In some cases, I have thanked particular individuals so often in the past that I prefer to let my discussion of their work in these pages stand as an acknowledgment of their influence. I concentrate here on another group of colleagues. First, I thank the members of the short-lived Raymond Williams reading group at the New School for Social Research in 1981–82 (Richard Blot, Mary Fallica, Thomas Hardy, Francine Moccio, and Julie Niehaus) for helping me set out in a new direction. Second, I thank a more recent group of people who have influenced me in conversations in my office or over beers, who have asked uncomfortable questions or suggested books or articles that had to be read—Gus Carbonella, Kim Clark, Lindsay DuBois, Chandana Mathur, Mary McMechan, Patricia Musante, Nicole Polier, and Susan Suppe.

I have also benefitted from discussions and a collaboration with Jay O'Brien, who read an early version of Chapter 8 that was focused on the concept of domestic modes of production and suggested that the historical and political issues involved needed to be more broadly considered and stated. This book is one response to that suggestion; our collaborative work is another (O'Brien and Roseberry, eds., forthcoming). As the manuscript neared completion, I presented the final chapter at a session on "Confronting Capital" organized by Ashraf Ghani for the 1987 meeting of the American Anthropological Association. I thank the discussants in that session—Derek Sayer, Gavin Smith, and Joan Vincent—for their criticism and encouragement. I also thank Garth Green, who took on the thankless task of serving as discussant for the book manuscript in my course on culture and political economy in the spring of 1988. My relationship with

Rutgers University Press has been thoroughly satisfying, from the initial contacts with Marlie Wasserman through the review process, the graceful copy editing of Eve Pearson, and production. I thank the Press's reviewers, especially Jane Schneider and "Reader #3," for their helpful suggestions.

Most of the essays were written during two academic leaves, during which I was supported by the John Simon Guggenheim Memorial Foundation (1983–84) and the Social Science Research Council's Committee on Latin America and the Caribbean (1986–87). They thought I was working on the family economy project, and I promise that I was.

Above all, I thank my ally, Nicole Polier, without whom this book could not have been imagined. Any attempt to elaborate on that statement is necessarily incomplete: she helped me to see the pieces whole; she brought her enthusiasm, skepticism, and critical intelligence to our many conversations and discussions; she has consistently acted as this manuscript's first reader and best critic. With her, I once again enjoy anthropology, and much else.

Anthropologies and Histories

The temptation is to reduce the historical variety of the forms of interpretation to what are loosely called symbols or archetypes: to abstract
even these most evidently social forms and to give them a primarily psychological or metaphysical status. This reduction often happens when we
find certain major forms and images and ideas persisting through periods of great change. Yet if we can see that the persistence depends on
the forms and images and ideas being changed, though often subtly,
internally and at times unconsciously, we can see also that the persistence
indicates some permanent or effectively permanent need, to which the
changing interpretations speak. I believe that there is indeed such a
need, and that it is created by the processes of a particular history. But if
we do not see these processes, or see them only incidentally, we fall back
on modes of thought which seem able to create the permanence without
the history. We may find emotional or intellectual satisfaction in this, but
we have then dealt with only half the problem, for in all such major
interpretations it is the coexistence of persistence and change which is
really striking and interesting, and which we have to account for without
reducing either fact to a form of the other.

—Raymond Williams, *The Country and the City*

INTRODUCTION

On a June night in Tepoztlán in 1987, a brass band led a procession from the chapel of La Santísima toward the house of the *mayordomo*. Preparations for the barrio fiesta had begun the evening before with a small Mass, with fireworks, and with music from La Michoacana—a band hired especially for the festival—that lasted late into the night while women wove garlands to decorate the chapel. The next day, Sunday, would be the actual festival, with small processions from other barrios passing the busy market on the plaza to place their own barrio banners at the altar alongside the banner for La Santísima. A Mass would be held, followed by fireworks, mariachi music played by another band, as well as marches and waltzes from La Michoacana, and drunken revelry. But tonight the celebrants were leaving the chapel to drink *aguardiente* and to socialize at the home of the mayordomo or festival sponsor. The procession included the band, men and women who had been preparing for the fiesta, and the requisite fireworks. About a block and a half from the mayordomo's house, however, the band stopped playing while the procession passed the house of a wealthy merchant, where a party was in progress celebrating the fifteenth birthday of the merchant's daughter. The gates to the merchant's courtyard were open, and all were welcome to attend and dance to the lively mixture of American rock, Caribbean salsa, and Mexican pop being played by a Mexico City band. La Michoacana could not compete, and the crowd at the birthday party easily outnumbered the group making its way to the mayordomo's house. But the dominance of the merchant's party was not limited to the few moments when the procession passed his house: the merchant had set up a stage for his musicians in such a way that their loudspeakers pointed directly at the mayordomo's house.

In this conflict of fiestas is concentrated a conflict of anthropologies. In a sense it is fitting that our setting is Tepoztlán, since one of our most famous controversies concerns life in that highland village in Morelos. Robert Redfield saw in Tepoztlán an expression of the folk society, based in communitarian values and celebrating a fully developed calendar of village-wide and barrio festivals through which community solidarity might be expressed (1930). Oscar Lewis, on the other hand, saw a village torn by conflicts that were rooted in differential access to land as well as a history marked by profound and at times bloody political struggles (1951). The two points of view serve as central texts for two traditions in Mexican anthropology, both of which can point to a rich literature. Indeed, the literature on village politics in Mexico is so large that the conflict witnessed during the barrio fiesta in La Santísima should not surprise.

This book does not begin with a description of that conflict in order to say something new about Tepoztlán or about Mexican anthropology. The description is offered because it allows us to think through certain problems in contemporary anthropological theory.

Anthropologists are fond of presenting their most important disagreements in oppositional terms, the very statement of which implies the "correct" position—from Harris's opposition of cultural materialism vs. idealism or mentalism (1979), to Geertz's opposition of a semiotic approach vs. a predictive science (1973a), to Sahlins's opposition of a cultural account vs. vulgar materialism (1976), to, more recently, the postmodernists' opposition of a literary turn vs. a naive and unreflective realism (Clifford and Marcus 1986). At first glance, it might appear that all of these oppositions revolve around a single disagreement, one that has been expressed most forcefully by Marshall Sahlins:

> The alternatives in this venerable conflict . . . may be broadly phrased as follows: whether the cultural order is to be conceived as the codification of man's actual purposeful and pragmatic action; or whether, conversely, human action in the world is to be understood as mediated by the cultural design, which gives order at once to practical experience, customary practice, and the relationship between the two. The difference is not trivial, nor will it be resolved by tha happy academic conclusion that the answer lies somewhere in between. (1976: 55)

The divide to which Sahlins points is important, and this book is offered as a commentary upon it. Nonetheless, proper understanding of the issues involved and of the work of particular authors requires that the divide itself be presented in less sharply defined and provocative terms. As I argue more fully in Chapter 2, the several oppositions that characterize anthropological discussions are not simply variations on a single antinomious theme. The differences among those who pursue a "cultural account" are significant, as are the differences among those who pursue what Sahlins would call "practical reason." The arguments used to criticize a Marvin Harris cannot be recycled to criticize an Eric Wolf; nor can the same arguments be used against Marshall Sahlins and Clifford Geertz. The many attempts to do so represent allegiance to a convenient opposition rather than engagement with actual texts.

This book offers commentaries on a number of recent anthropological texts as part of an argument for a political economic approach to history and culture. To better understand that approach and its relation to other views of history and culture, we begin by returning to the birthday celebration in the merchant's courtyard.

———

To understand the competing fiestas, we would need to know something about the structural relations within and among

barrios in Tepoztlán, the place of La Santísima within those
structural relations, the place of this relatively minor barrio
fiesta within the round of fiestas in Tepoztlán, and so on. For
this, a whole body of literature from Redfield through Lewis to
Bock (1980) and Lomnitz-Adler (1982) is helpful. A number of
other questions need to be asked as well, however. Such questions could begin with the mayordomo and the merchant. Who
were these people, and how did their actions fit within their
particular life courses? How long had the mayordomo been
preparing himself for sponsorship? What had it cost him and
what had he hoped to gain from it? How did he make a living?
What kinds of economic, social, and political relations did he
have with others in the barrio and in Tepoztlán? What materials
did the merchant deal with, and what were his economic, social,
and political relations with others in the barrio and beyond?
Would he ever aspire to sponsorship of barrio or village-wide
fiestas, or did he consider all of that beneath him? Was there a
history of enmity between the mayordomo and the merchant,
or between the families of the mayordomo and the merchant,
or between the merchant and other residents in the barrio?
What was the merchant thinking about when he scheduled the
birthday party for the weekend of the barrio fiesta? Did he
consider holding it another weekend? How was the merchant's
party received—both in anticipation and in the event—by the
mayordomo, by others preparing for the barrio fiesta, by the
celebrants crowding into the merchant's courtyard? What, if
anything, did people say about the two fiestas or about the
merchant and the mayordomo and their relations with each
other? What consequences might the competing fiestas have—
over the coming weeks, the coming months, the coming years—
for relations between these two men, or for relations within the
barrio and within Tepoztlán?

To understand the conflicts, we need to know something
about the long-term structure and meaning of this particular
barrio fiesta within a cycle of fiestas, but we also need to know
something about how specific individuals are acting within
those structures, using a particular meaningful occasion to say
something about their relationships with each other, their rela-

tive standing in the barrio and village, their history or their prospects.

To understand what people are saying and hearing in particular situations, we need to turn to history. Each of our questions about the fiestas is historical—how did the actions fit within the life histories of particular individuals? How did those life histories relate to family histories? How did those life and family histories fit within recent and not so recent events and trends in the barrio and village? How had the barrio festival changed over the decades?

At this moment in the development of anthropological thought, such questions do not surprise. Anthropologists of various persuasions are discovering history these days, but as they do so they create two kinds of problems. First, they may write a partial history of the relationship *between* anthropology and history. In the most restricted understanding, there was no relationship at all until Clifford Geertz published *The Interpretation of Cultures* (1973a), and historians at Princeton and elsewhere discovered and appropriated a particular version of cultural anthropology (see Silk 1987). But this ignores a much longer tradition and argument, one that has often remained "subterranean" (Vincent 1989), not only within anthropology from Boas to some of his students and colleagues (see Mintz 1987) but also among anthropologists and historians involved in area studies in more recent decades.

Second, anthropologists may "turn to history" without specifying what kind of history they have in mind. I am not referring simply to the life, family, barrio, village, and national histories mentioned in our discussion of Tepoztlán, though the relationships among these remain important. Of more immediate consequence for our discussion here is the fact that anthropologists mean rather different things when they talk about history. The different understandings of history are, in turn, related to different positions within anthropological debates. We have, in short, a variety of anthropolog*ies* appropriating a variety of histor*ies*, making any one-sentence invocation of the intersection of anthropology and history simplistic and naive. Indeed, we can better understand the issues that divide anthropologists if we move beyond the oppositions encountered earlier and ask what particular anthropologists mean when they talk about history. Rather than presenting an exhaustive survey, I concentrate on three major authors who have contributed to "anthropology's" engagement with "history" and, through that engagement, have outlined the most important issues facing anthropologists today—Clifford Geertz, Marshall Sahlins, and Eric Wolf.[1]

As expressed in *The Interpretation of Cultures* (1973a), *Negara* (1980), and other works, Geertz's understanding of history is rooted in the neo-Kantian distinction between the natural and historical sciences, in which the latter are associated with the study of human society and culture. The invocation of history, given such usage, is tied to an epistemological and methodological critique of positivist social science. For Geertz, history cannot be understood by means of elaborately constructed theoretical formulas or by reference to general laws. A search for such laws misses the creative capacity and consequence of human activity, which occurs within the context of sets of "historically" derived symbols, to which human actors attach meaning. Geertz thus regards positivist attempts at historical explanation as incapable of addressing the problem of meaning and action. Accordingly, the anthropologist's or historian's task must be to interpret the meanings humans assign to their actions. In such a scheme, the terms "history" and "culture" are at least interrelated when they are not viewed as synonymous. And in much of Geertz's work, the two are indeed synonymous. To say that a problem or practice is historical is to say that it is culturally situated, and vice versa. Geertz makes this most clear in his reconstruction of the nineteenth-century Balinese state, which he sees as an explicit critique of certain styles of historical writing. In his introduction, he observes:

> The history of a great civilization can be depicted as a series of major events—wars, reigns, and revolutions—which, whether or not they shape it, at least mark major changes in its course.

Or it can be depicted as a succession not of dates, places, and prominent persons, but of general phases of sociocultural development. An emphasis on the first sort of historiography tends to present history as a series of bounded periods, more or less distinct units of time characterized by some special significance of their own. . . . The second approach, however, presents historical change as a relatively continuous social and cultural process, a process which shows few if any sharp breaks, but rather displays a slow but patterned alteration in which, though developmental phases may be discerned when the entire course of the process is viewed as a whole, it is nearly always very difficult, if not impossible, to put one's finger exactly on the point at which things stopped being what they were and became instead something else. This view of change, or process, stresses not so much the annalistic chronicle of what people did, but rather the formal, or structural, patterns of cumulative activity. (1980: 5)

One might think, on the first statement of difference, that Geertz is contrasting history seen as string of events, "one damn thing after another," with more structural readings of history. As he develops the contrast, however, it is clear that both styles of historical writing involve some sort of "structural" account. In the former, however, the writer sees history as a material social process ("the annalistic chronicle of what people did"); in the latter, the writer sees history as cultural pattern. Though Geertz suggests that both styles are valid, he clearly prefers the cultural, offering it as a critical alternative to the "annalistic" and suggesting that it is the style most appropriate for the non-Western societies most anthropologists study (ibid.: 6).

In one respect at least, Sahlins's approach to culture and history might appear similar. In *Culture and Practical Reason* (1976), he too tended to treat culture and history as virtually synonymous. Indeed, in a book that criticizes a variety of materialist styles of thought for their lack of a culture concept, one can generally replace his numerous references to "history" and "historical" with the words "culture" and "cultural" with no loss of meaning. Both history and culture are used as critical counterpoints to materialist styles that are seen to reduce human variety to positivist law. Yet Sahlins differs from Geertz in this 1976 book in important ways. With respect to culture, Sahlins is less concerned with meaning or action than with conceptual scheme, and his approach to that scheme depends less on Weber than on Lévi-Strauss. His analyses of structural oppositions and transformations within various conceptual schemes may be more or less sophisticated, but the basic point in *Culture and Practical Reason* was an opposition between a conceptual scheme and "praxis," with the conceptual scheme being seen as both prior to activity and mediator of activity. Culture, as conceptual scheme, was not seen as the product of past activity and concept.

This left Sahlins with an important problem: ethnographic and "historical" evidence presented numerous examples of profound transformation of conceptual schemes, and an anthropology that set up the opposition of praxis and culture in such an extreme fashion could be seen as sophisticated, erudite, and out of touch. In his more recent work, then, Sahlins has paid more attention to the complex interaction of conceptual scheme and activity. As he has done so, the relationship between culture and history in his work has altered. Sahlins still does not pay much attention to meaning: he continues to see culture as conceptual scheme to be subjected to structural analysis. Indeed, the two terms that are now seen as synonymous would appear to be "culture" and "structure." (Remarkably and humorously, if one looks up the word "culture" in the index of his recent *Islands of History* [1985], one reads, "see structure."[2]) But history is now seen as a process in which conceptual scheme informs practice and practice transforms the conceptual scheme. As he observes at the beginning of *Islands of History:*

> History is culturally ordered, differently so in different societies, according to meaningful schemes of things. The converse is also true: cultural schemes are historically ordered, since to a greater or lesser extent the meanings are revalued as they are practically enacted. The synthesis of these contraries unfolds in the creative action of the historic subjects, the people concerned. For on the one hand, people organize their

projects and give significance to their objects from the existing understandings of the cultural order. . . . On the other
hand, then, as the contingent circumstances of action need
not conform to the significance some group might assign
them, people are known to creatively reconsider their conven-
tional schemes. And to that extent, the culture is historically
altered in action. We can speak even of "structural transformation," since the alteration of some meanings changes the
positional relations among the cultural categories, thus a
"system-change." (1985: vii)

One might note that the definition of structural transformation as change in "positional relations among the cultural categories" is rather partial and limited, given the antimaterialist
stance of Sahlins's recent work. Granted that definition, however, his approach to history is no longer one that reduces it to
context. He now uses it to characterize the "transformations"
associated with the relation and interaction of structure and
event, or structure and practice. As this perspective is applied to
examples from Polynesian history, however, the overwhelming
emphasis remains fixed on the incorporation of "event" within
structure—the structural (cultural) reading of new events within
preexisting codes and relations. We are treated to entertaining
and enlightening discussions of the ways in which Hawaiians or
Maoris or Fijians interpreted the actions of Westerners in terms
of preexisting categories, incorporating event within myth. But
we learn relatively little about transformation—except in the
narrowly structuralist terms Sahlins sets for himself. The most
important case of transformation to which Sahlins directs our
attention is the set of events associated with early Western
contact with Hawaii, events that led to what anthropologists
have long recognized as a "cultural revolution" (Davenport
1969). But much of Sahlins's attention is still directed to the
attempt, finally unsuccessful, to incorporate these events within
preexisting conceptual schemes. The political and economic
transformation that accompanied contact receives mention, especially in *Historical Metaphors and Mythical Realities* (1981), but it
serves as backdrop and is not itself the subject of analysis. The

anthropological reading of history is seen as focused on other, cultural, questions. "The problem now," Sahlins tells us, "is to explode the concept of history by the anthropological experience of culture" (1985: 72).

Despite their differences, both Sahlins and Geertz use a concept of history that is tied to a concept of culture. It can be used to criticize more scientific or materialist approaches: reference to history, like reference to culture, is a recognition of human difference. As Sahlins expresses it, "The different cultural orders studied by anthropology have their own historicities" (ibid.: 53). While such understandings of culture and history may be viewed as attempts to grasp an "actor-centered point of view" or as contributions to an emerging "practice theory" (Ortner 1984), the most significant aspect of both of these approaches is that they are several steps *removed* from action. As Geertz stresses, his interest lies not in "the annalistic chronicle of what people did, but rather the formal, or structural, patterns of cumulative activity" (1980:5). In Sahlins's case, while we read much about the "structure of the conjuncture," about the interrelation of structure and practice, the emphasis remains on practice *as a theoretical category* rather than the practice*s* of differently situated and positioned actors within contradictory social relations. In this view (or in this momentary conjunction of two distinct views), culture is *enacted* rather than *acted*.

If we were to return briefly to Tepoztlán, we might find that anthropologists working within, say, a structuralist framework would have much to say about the symbolic and structural relationships that exist among barrios—the division between those from above and those from below, the pairing of individual barrios from above with individual barrios from below, the analogous links between animal symbols attached to paired barrios, the importance of the number three in the link between the barrios of Los Reyes (The Three Kings) and La Santísima (The Holy Trinity) (see Bock 1980). They would have much more to say about the symbolism of La Santísima than about the symbolism of the loudspeakers.

A different understanding of history can be used to criticize the cultural assumptions of a Sahlins or Geertz. Within anthropology, this perspective has been developed most importantly by Eric Wolf. Here history is seen as a material social process, one characterized by economic and political inequality and domination, and by transformations not only of the relations among cultural terms but of entire social orders. History in this sense is not simply the marking of different cultural contexts— though it includes that. It is also the attempt to trace the connections among various cultural orders within a global, unevenly developing but unified, social process. The critical project to which this understanding of history is attached is one that rejects those anthropological styles that draw analytical boundaries around particular villages, regions, or "cultures" and then treat those analytical entities as different by definition. In a comment on the uncritical use of the Human Relations Area Files by some anthropologists, Wolf makes an observation that can easily be extended to other understandings of culture and history:

What, however, if we take cognizance of *processes* that transcend separable cases, moving through and beyond them and transforming them as they proceed? Such processes were, for example, the North American fur trade and the trade in native American and African slaves. What of the localized Algonkin-speaking patrilineages, for example, which in the course of the fur trade moved into large nonkin villages and became known as the ethnographic Ojibwa? What of the Chipeweyans, some of whose bands gave up hunting to become fur trappers, or "carriers," while others continued to hunt for game as "caribou eaters," with people continuously changing from caribou eating to carrying and back?. . . . What, moreover, of Africa, where the slave trade created an unlimited demand for slaves, and where quite unrelated populations met that demand by severing people from their kin groups through warfare, kidnapping, pawning, or judicial procedures, in order to have slaves to sell to the Europeans? In all such cases, to attempt to specify separate cultural wholes and distinct boundaries would create a false sample. These cases exemplify spatially and temporally shifting relationships, prompted in all instances by the effects of European expansion. If we consider, furthermore, that this expansion has for nearly 500 years affected case after case, then the search for a world sample of distinct cases is illusory. (1982: 17–18)

A few points require clarification here. First, although the anthropological project Wolf envisions might be called a global and historical political economy, it has little in common with some forms of global social science with which readers may be familiar. Most popular versions, especially the "world-system" theory of Immanuel Wallerstein (1974; 1979), tend to obliterate cultural difference and interpret social processes in various parts of the world in terms of processes occurring in the developed centers of the world economy. As an anthropologist, Wolf starts with the multiform and various societies studied by other anthropologists and attempts to explore their histories in a way that connects them with processes occurring elsewhere. Second, although Wolf's is a view of history as material social process and therefore fits within materialist approaches to anthropology, it has nothing in common with evolutionist attempts to subsume cultural variety within general, lawlike explanatory schemes (see below, Chapter 2). Wolf is attempting to place various cultures within the context of a global, but uneven, history; he is not attempting to produce a science of universal history.

Both historical styles—history as cultural difference and history as material social process—have important critical things to say to a more traditional, "ahistorical" anthropology. It might be comforting to assert that there is room for both histories within anthropology; alone, each perspective offers a partial and necessarily distorting perspective. Comforting but insufficient: room for both remains within an expansive and eclectic discipline, but their partial and distorting visions do not necessarily complement one another. Although I approach this book with the conviction that the oppositions between apparently antinomious terms like "meaning" and "action," or "meaning" and "power," can be mediated, I do not think that mediation consists of cooking a stew with a little bit of Wolf, a little bit of

Geertz, and a little bit of Sahlins. Some foods do not complement each other; some anthropologies are incompatible. The
incompatibility here rests with basic attitudes toward cultural
others, which in turn rests on fundamentally different understandings of history. The one sees the Other as different and
separate, a product of its own history and carrying its own historicity. Connections with a larger history may not be denied,
but authors within this tradition contend that one must understand culture (as meaning or as structure) by setting that larger
history aside (see Ortner 1984). The second sees the Other as
different but *connected,* a product of a particular history that is
itself intertwined with a larger set of economic, political, social,
and cultural processes to such an extent that analytical separation of "our" history and "their" history is impossible. In this
view, there are no cultures-outside-of-history to be recon-
structed, no culture without history, no culture or society "with
its own structure and history" to which world-historical forces
arrive. The *concept* of culture that emerges from such a project
is fundamentally different from the concept of culture with
which a Geertz or Sahlins might begin; the anthropological
project that emerges is different as well.

———

   This book bases itself in Wolf's understanding of an anthropological history and devotes its argument to an examination of
the implications of this understanding of history for our analyses of culture and politics. My argument is as follows:
   Geertz and other anthropologists who have been influenced
by Weber are fundamentally correct when they point to culture as the central concept of anthropological practice and
when they situate that centrality within a call for studies of
meaningful action. That is, cultural meaning is important because social and political actors, and their actions, are formed
in part by preexisting understandings of the world, of other
people, of the self. Their approach to meaning is inadequate,
however, because they pay insufficient attention to cultural
differentiation, to social and political inequalities that affect
actors' differential understandings of the world, other people,

and themselves, and to the historical formation of anthropological subjects within processes of uneven development.

Sufficient attention to such questions requires a concern for political economy. I therefore explore the assumptions and practices of anthropological political economy, indicate the kinds of problems that should be central to such an approach, and review some of the inadequacies of many anthropological studies of politics and economics.

Although I trust that the argument is coherent, I do not develop it in a step-by-step, linear fashion. The book is divided into two parts, "Culture" and "Political Economy," which are linked by a particular understanding of history. The essays in each part follow a similar pattern. I begin with a consideration of a particular text—Geertz's essay on Balinese cockfights in Part One and Wolf's study of the historical formation of anthropological subjects in Part Two. Discussion of central texts then leads to a more general discussion of theoretical issues and problems—Marxism and culture in Part One and anthropological approaches to political economy in Part Two. The last two essays in each section address more specific problems suggested by the theoretical essays. In Part One, I turn to historical analyses—of politics and culture in modern Venezuela and of a more wide-ranging reflection on the "internalization of the external" (Cardoso and Faletto 1979) in Latin American history. In Part Two, I explore more specific theoretical problems within anthropological political economy—our understandings of the positions, roles, and fates of peasantries within modern Latin America, and our understanding of politics and culture within processes of uneven proletarianization. In the final chapter, I essay a statement of the kinds of understandings of culture and politics that emerge from an approach to the formation of anthropological subjects in terms of uneven development. Central to this argument is a return to the concept of community, seen not as a given society- or culture-outside-of-history but as a political association formed through processes of political and cultural creation and imagination—the generation of meaning of contexts of unequal power.

CULTURE

The starting-point of critical elaboration is the consciousness of what one really is, and is "knowing thyself" as a product of the historical process to date which has deposited in you an infinity of traces, without leaving an inventory. . . .

Philosophy cannot be separated from the history of philosophy, nor can culture from the history of culture.

—Antonio Gramsci, *The Prison Notebooks*

Balinese Cockfights and the Seduction of Anthropology

Few anthropologists in recent years have enjoyed wider influence in the social sciences than Clifford Geertz. Sociologists, political scientists, and social historians interested in popular culture and *mentalités* have turned increasingly to anthropology, and the anthropologist most often embraced is Professor Geertz.

A number of factors can be adduced to account for this trend. In the first place, Geertz's position at the Institute for Advanced Study has allowed him to transcend the disciplinary and subdisciplinary involution that characterizes anthropology and other social sciences. At the Institute, he is able to attract scholars from a variety of disciplines, adopting an antidisciplinary mood and focus that is rare in current academic practice. Second, Geertz is an excellent ethnographer who writes with an eloquence and sophistication uncommon for the social sciences. His cultural essays can be read with profit by introductory students or graduate students in advanced seminars. And his descriptions of life in Bali or Java or Morocco call to mind one of the aspects of anthropology that has always been so seductive: the lure of distant places and other modes of being. Thus, in part, the title of this essay. But the title is intended to suggest another aspect of Geertz's work as well, for there is a sense in which anthropologists—and other social scientists— have been seduced by Geertz's writings on culture.

To explore this claim, we must first examine a third aspect of Geertz's prominence: his participation in anthropological debates between materialists and idealists. Although the apparent antinomies between explanation and interpretation, science and history, and materialism and idealism have served as constant themes in anthropological debates over the years, the discourse became increasingly acrimonious during the 1960s and 1970s. Over a period of approximately twenty years after World War II, many American anthropologists turned away from Boasian relativism and toward more scientific, explanatory approaches to culture and society. With this trend, a type of materialism dominated anthropological discussions, especially through the cultural ecology of Julian Steward and the cultural evolutionism of Leslie White. By the late 1960s, however, increasing numbers of social scientists were rejecting explanatory accounts as positivist and were rediscovering German historicism and the interpretive sociologies that had influenced the early Boasians. Yet, at approximately the same time, the position of public dominance in anthropological materialism passed to Marvin Harris upon the publication of his *Rise of Anthropological Theory* (1968). With that book and subsequent volumes, most notably his *Cultural Materialism* (1979), Harris mapped out a materialist terrain that was resolutely scientific, although it exhibited much less caution regarding what we can know about social and cultural processes than did the cultural ecology of Julian Steward.

In such a context, Geertz's prominence is hardly surprising. The 1973 publication of a collection of his essays, *The Interpretation of Cultures* (1973a), and especially an essay entitled "Thick Description: Toward an Interpretive Theory of Culture" (1973b), written especially for that volume, provided a persuasive text for those anthropologists who were dissatisfied with the vision of a science of culture offered by Harris. Given Geertz's background in Weberian perspectives and his familiarity with the phenomenological and hermeneutic literature that Harris dismisses as "obscurantist," Geertz can, with a short discussion of winks and blinks, call into serious question Harris's unmediated understanding of social and cultural facts.

And he is able to make a persuasive case for an anthropology that is "not an experimental science in search of law but an interpretive one in search of meaning" (ibid.: 5).

The difference between Harris and Geertz, and their particular versions of explanation and interpretation, can be demonstrated with a discussion of their approaches to culture. For Harris,

> The starting point of all sociocultural analysis for cultural materialism is simply the existence of an etic human population located in etic time and space. A society for us is a maximal social group consisting of both sexes and all ages and exhibiting a wide range of interactive behavior. Culture, on the other hand, refers to the learned repertory of thoughts and actions exhibited by the members of social groups. (1979: 47)

Harris goes on to make rigid distinctions among infrastructure, structure, and superstructure and tells us that "The etic behavioral modes of production and reproduction probabilistically determine the etic behavioral domestic and political economy, which in turn probabilistically determine the behavioral and mental emic superstructures" (ibid.: 55–56). Note that culture is reduced to a set of ideas, or, less imaginatively, a "learned repertory of thoughts and actions." Culture is seen as a product; it is not seen simultaneously as production. There is, then, no concern in Harris's work with *meaning* —the socially constructed understandings of the world in terms of which people act. But as long as we are working with such an ideational view of culture, whether from a materialist or idealist perspective, we remove it from human action and praxis and therefore exclude the possibility of bridging the anthropological antimony between the material and ideal. We may explore this assertion by turning to Clifford Geertz.

The promise of Geertz's project, especially as elaborated in "Thick Description," is that he seems to be working with a concept of culture as socially constituted and socially constituting. He explicitly criticizes ideational definitions of culture,

concentrating on symbols that carry and communicate meanings to social actors who have created them. Unfortunately, at
no point does he say what he means as clearly and rigorously as
does Harris. Instead, he places his definitions in a more elegant
and elusive prose. For example: "Believing, with Max Weber,
that man is an animal suspended in webs of significance he
himself has spun, I take culture to be those webs . . . " (1973b:
5). Or: "culture consists of socially established structures of
meaning in terms of which people do such things as signal
conspiracies and join them or perceive insults and answer
them . . . " (ibid.: 13). Or: "The culture of a people is an ensemble of texts, themselves ensembles, which the anthropologist
strains to read over the shoulders of those to whom they properly belong" (1973c: 452). The last quote comes from the well-
known essay, "Deep Play: Notes on the Balinese Cockfight," to
which more attention is devoted here. It was noted earlier that
Geertz *seems* to be working with a concept of culture as socially
constituted and socially constituting. We must now question
whether he has realized this promise. This essay compares
Geertz's claims for himself in "Thick Description" with one of
his own pieces of description. Because Geertz's ethnographic
work is voluminous, and the aims of this chapter are modest, we
shall concentrate on his essay on Balinese cockfights.[1]

———

Geertz's essay is at once an attempt to show that cultural
products can be treated as texts and an attempt to interpret
one such text. The metaphor of the text is, of course, a favor-
ite of the practitioners of both structuralism and hermeneu-
tics, though Geertz takes his lead from Ricoeur rather than
Lévi-Strauss. The reference to culture as a text, given Geertz's
project, calls for an exercise in interpretation. Geertz interpretation must be summarized before we can ask some questions
of it. "Notes on the Balinese Cockfight" begins with an account
of the Geertzes' difficulties when first arriving in the field,
their response to a police raid on a cockfight, and their final
acceptance, given that response, by the villagers. The essay
then moves into a description of the cockfight itself, including

a discussion of the psychological identification of men and cocks, the procedures associated with cockfights and wagers, and so on. Preliminaries out of the way, Geertz moves toward an interpretation of the fight itself. He begins with Jeremy Bentham's notion of deep play, or games in which the consequences for losers are so devastating that participation in the games is irrational for all concerned. Noting that the central wagers in Balinese cockfights seem to correspond to such a high stakes game, he then counters:

> It is in large part *because* the marginal disutility of loss is so great at the higher levels of betting that to engage in such betting is to lay one's public self, allusively and metaphorically, through the medium of one's cock, on the line. And though to a Benthamite this might seem merely to increase the irrationality of the enterprise that much further, to the Balinese what it mainly increases is the meaningfulness of it all. And as (to follow Weber rather than Bentham) the imposition of meaning in life is the major and primary condition of human existence, that access of significance more than compensates for the economic costs involved. (1973c: 434)

Geertz then looks to two aspects of significance in the cockfight. Both are related to the hierarchical organization of Balinese society. He first observes that the cockfight is a "simulation of the social matrix," or, following Goffman, a "status bloodbath" (ibid.: 436). To explore this, Geertz mentions the four descent groups that organize factions in the village and examines the rules involved in betting against the cocks owned by members of other descent groups, other villages, rivals, and so on. Although he has not yet referred to the cockfight as a text, as Geertz moves toward the second aspect of significance, he begins to refer to it as "an art form" (ibid.: 443). As an art form, it "displays" fundamental passions in Balinese society that are hidden from view in ordinary daily life and comportment. As an atomistic inversion of the way Balinese normally present themselves to themselves, the cockfight relates to the status hierarchy in another sense—no longer as a status-based organization of the cockfight but as a commentary on the existence of status differences in the first place. The cockfight is "a Balinese reading of Balinese experience, a story they tell themselves about themselves" (ibid.: 448). What they tell themselves is that beneath the external veneer of collective calm and grace lies another nature. At both the social and individual level, there is another Bali and another sort of Balinese. And what they tell themselves they tell in a text that "consists of a chicken hacking another mindlessly to bits" (ibid.: 449).

After this basic interpretation of the Balinese cockfight in terms of status organization and commentary, Geertz closes with a discussion of culture as an ensemble of texts. He notes that their interpretation is difficult and that such an approach is not "the only way that symbolic forms can be sociologically handled. Functionalism lives, and so does psychologism. But to regard such forms as 'saying something of something,' and saying it to somebody, is at least to open up the possibility of an analysis that attends to their substance rather than to reductive formulas professing to account for them" (ibid.: 453).

Accepting this criticism of reductive formulas, we must question whether Geertz's analysis has sociologically handled the Balinese cockfight or paid sufficient attention to its substance. In what follows, no fundamental reinterpretation of the Balinese cockfight is attempted. Such a reinterpretation is the task of a writer more familiar with Bali and Indonesia than is the present one. This essay simply points to a few elements present in Geertz's essay but omitted from the interpretive exercise that should form a part of a cultural and sociological interpretation of the cockfight. Although Geertz might regard reference to these elements as a form of functionalist reductionism, no attempt is made here to account for or explain the existence of the cockfight. Rather, by pointing to other aspects of Balinese society and history with which the cockfight may be involved, this essay calls into question the metaphor of culture as text (cf. Keesing 1987).

Accepting for a moment that metaphor, we might briefly turn to three aspects of Balinese society not included in the interpretation. The first has to do with the role of women. In a footnote early in the article, Geertz notes that while there is little apparent public sexual differentiation in Bali, the cockfight is one of the few activities from which women are excluded (1973c: 417–418). This apparent anomaly may make sense in terms of Geertz's interpretation. As with status differences, so with sexual differences. The cockfight, and betting on the cockfight, are the activities of men, serving as commentaries on the public denial of difference. But sex cannot be subsumed so simply within status. The sexual exclusion becomes more interesting when we learn in another footnote that the Balinese countryside was integrated by rotating market systems that would encompass several villages and that cockfights were held on market days near the markets and were sometimes organized by petty merchants. "Trade has followed the cock for centuries in rural Bali, and the sport has been one of the main agencies of the island's monetization" (ibid.: 432). Furthermore, in yet another footnote in his more recent *Negara,* Geertz tells us that the traditional markets, which were "staffed almost entirely by women," were held in the morning, and that the cockfights were held on the same afternoon as the market (1980: 199).

Aside from sexual differentiation and the connection with markets, Geertz also notes throughout the early part of the essay (1973c: 414, 418, 424, 425) that the cockfight was an important activity in precolonial Balinese states (that is, before the early twentieth century), that it was held in a ring in the center of the village, that it was taxed and was a significant source of public revenue.[2] Further, we learn that the cockfight was outlawed by the Dutch and later by Indonesia, that it is now held in semisecret in hidden corners of the village, and that the Balinese regard the island as taking the shape of a "small, proud cock, poised, neck extended, back taut, tail raised, in eternal challenge to large, feckless shapeless Java" (ibid.: 418). Surely these matters require some interpretive attention. At the very least they suggest that the cockfight is intimately related (though not reducible) to political processes of state formation and colonialism. They also suggest that the cockfight has gone through a significant change in the past eighty years, that if it is a text, it is a text that is being written as part of a profound social, political, and cultural *process*.

This, finally, brings us to the third point, which is less an aspect omitted from the interpretation than one that is not sufficiently explicated. Geertz refers to the cockfight as a "status bloodbath" and tells us that as a commentary on status, the cockfight tells the Balinese that such differences "are a matter of life and death" and a "profoundly serious business" (ibid.: 447). Yet, in this essay at least, we learn very little about caste and status as material social process and the connection that process does or does not have with cockfighting. In *Negara*, Geertz turns his attention to elaborate cremation ceremonies and sees them as an "aggressive assertion of status" (1980: 117). Comparable in spirit to the potlatch, the cremation is "conspicuous consumption, Balinese style" (ibid.: 117) and is one of various rituals that elaborately tell the Balinese that "status is all" (ibid.: 102). In this case, we are dealing in part with political competition among high-caste lords and princes. But lords are also communicating to their commoners that the hierarchy is divinely ordained. Status in Bali has to do with inherited caste but also with positions achieved in life through various forms of political maneuver—most clearly among lords but also among low-caste Sudras. With so much maneuver, and with so many cultural "texts" relating to status, some attention should be paid to the different messages of these texts and to their construction in the context of status formation as a historical process.

These three problems lead to a basic point. The cockfight has gone through a process of creation that cannot be separated from Balinese history. Here we confront the major inadequacy of the text as a metaphor for culture. A text is written; it is not writing.[3] To see culture as an ensemble of texts or an art form is to remove culture from the process of its creation.[4] If culture is a text, it is not everyone's text. Beyond the obvious fact that it means different things to different people or different sorts of people, we must ask who is (or are) doing the writing. Or, to break with the metaphor, who is doing the acting, the creating of the cultural forms we interpret. This is a key question, for example, in the transformation of the cockfight after the arrival of the Dutch. In a recent essay, Geertz has pointed to the separation of the text from its creation as one of the strengths of the metaphor. Referring to Ricoeur's notion of "inscription," or the separation in the text of the said from the saying, Geertz concludes:

> The great virtue of the extension of the notion of text beyond things written on paper or carved into stone is that it trains attention on precisely this phenomenon: on how the inscription of action is brought about, what its vehicles are and how they work, and on what the fixation of meaning from the flow of events—history from what happened, thought from thinking, culture from behavior—implies for sociological interpretation. (1983: 31)

The reader should not assume that I am calling for the reduction of culture to action (see Chapter 2). Geertz correctly points to meanings that persist beyond events, symbols that outlast and transcend the intentions of their creators. But neither should culture be separated from action; otherwise we are caught in yet another of anthropology's antinomies. Unfortunately, the text as metaphor effects precisely this separation.

———

The emphasis on cultural creation brings out two aspects of culture that are missing from Geertz's work. The first is the presence of social and cultural differentiation, even within an apparently uniform text. Reference to differentiation is, in part, reference to the connections between culture and relations of power and domination, as implied in the previous comments on state and status. Some might think that to refer to culture and power is to reduce culture to power, to treat values as "glosses on property relations" (Geertz 1973c: 449) or to "run on about the exploitation of the masses" (1973b: 22). But there are reductions, and then there are reductions. And the denial of such connections is but one of many classical reductions in American anthropology. The second aspect that is missing is a concept of culture as material social process. Without a sense of

culture as material process or creation—as writing as well as
what is written—we once again have a conception of culture as
product but not as production.[5] The reference to culture as
material social process is not intended to take us back to the
anthropological materialism of Marvin Harris. Indeed, the criticism I have directed at Clifford Geertz is similar to the criticism
I directed at Marvin Harris: both treat culture as product but
not as production. There the similarity ends, of course. But
both have removed culture from the process of cultural creation and have therefore made possible the constant reproduction of an antinomy between the material and the ideal.

The resolution of the antinomy, and the concept of culture
that emerges from that resolution, must be materialist. But the
materialism invoked in this essay is far removed from the reductive scientism that has come to dominate materialism in American anthropology. Rather, what is needed is something close to
the "cultural materialism" of Raymond Williams (1977; cf.
1980; 1982), who notes that the problem with mechanical materialism is not that it is too materialist but that it is not materialist
enough. It treats culture and other aspects of a presumed "superstructure" simply as ideas. It therefore makes room for,
indeed requires, idealist critiques that share the ideational definition but deny the material connection or, as in the case of
Geertz, that reject the ideational definition in favor of one that
sees a socially constructed text that is, nonetheless, removed
from the social process by which the text is created. In contrast,
Williams suggests that cultural creation is itself a form of material production, that the abstract distinction between material
base and ideal superstructure dissolves in the face of a material
social process through which both "material" and "ideal" are
constantly created and recreated.

Yet Williams does not leave his analysis at this elementary
assertion. He also pays attention to the socially constructed
meanings that inform action. He does this in part by means of a
revaluation of the idea of tradition, defining it as a reflection
upon and selection from a people's history (1961; 1977). The
process of selection is political and is tied to relations of domination and subordination, so that Williams can talk of a dominant

culture, or hegemony, as a selective tradition. Although this dominant culture is related to and supports an order of inequality, Williams does not view it simply as a ruling-class ideology imposed upon the dominated. Rather, as a selection from and interpretation of a people's history, it touches aspects of the lived reality or experience of the dominant and dominated alike. It is, in short and in part, "meaningful." But Williams also notes that no order of domination is total. There are always relationships and meanings that are excluded. Therefore, alternative meanings, alternative values, alternative versions of a people's history are available as a potential challenge to the dominant. Whether such alternative versions are constructed depends upon the nature of the cultural and historical material available, the process of class formation and division, and the possibilities and obstacles presented in the political process. Williams's concept of culture, then, is tied to a process of class formation but is not reduced to that process. Dominant and emergent cultures are formed in a class-based social world, but they are not necessarily congruent with class divisions.

The themes of culture as material social process and of cultural creation as (in part) political action are further developed in an article by Peter Taylor and Hermann Rebel (1981; cf. Rebel 1988). In a masterful analysis of culture in history, the authors concentrate on four "texts"—four of the Grimm's folk tales that deal with common themes of inheritance, disinheritance, family dissolution, and migration. After criticizing psychological interpretations, they place the tales in the late-eighteenth- and early-nineteenth-century context in which they were collected. They then take two innovative methodological steps that are of great importance for the concept of culture. First, they ask who is telling the tales and in what context. They also note that while the tales are *traditional,* they are not *timeless;* that is, the form and content of the tales may change in the telling. The question of who is telling the tales and in what context therefore becomes important. Taking a form of culture as a text, the authors take the first step toward an analysis of text as writing, as material social process. Second, they assume that the peasant women who are telling the tales form a "peasant intelligentsia" that is trying to intervene in the social process. That is, the tales are commentaries on what is happening to them and their families that call for particular forms of action to alter the situation. This is a crucial methodological step in the construction of a concept of culture not simply as a product but also as production, not simply as socially constituted but also as socially constituting. Given this framework, the authors then embark on a detailed symbolic analysis of the tales and, finally, suggest that the tales were attempts by peasant women to respond to the disruption of families and the drafting of their disinherited sons. The suggested response: inheriting daughters should renounce their inheritance, move from the region, marry elsewhere, and offer a refuge for their fleeing brothers. Taylor and Rebel show that such a response is in accord with demographic evidence from late-eighteenth-century Hesse, although it cannot yet be demonstrated whether the process they suggest actually occurred. Nonetheless, the authors have produced a cultural analysis that goes significantly further than does Geertz's in his "Notes on the Balinese Cockfight." To ask of any cultural text, be it a cockfight or a folk tale, who is talking, who is being talked to, what is being talked about, and what form of action is being called for, is to move cultural analysis to a new level that renders the old antinomies of materialism and idealism irrelevant.[6]

It might be argued that this is precisely what Geertz does. As one of our most able ethnographers, he is one of the few anthropologists who can provide detailed ecological, economic, and political information at the same time that he engages in sophisticated symbolic analysis. His examination of the theater state in nineteenth-century Bali is an example of this: we find treatments of political and social structure at hamlet, irrigation system, and temple levels, of caste divisions, of trade, and of the rituals of hierarchy. That Geertz sees all of these as necessary for a cultural argument, and that he sees his inclusion of these elements as rendering an "idealist" charge absurd, is clear from his conclusion to *Negara*. Although all the elements are presented and connected in a fashion, they are never fully joined. Culture as text is removed from the historical process that shapes it and that it in turn shapes. When we are told that in Bali "culture came

from the top down . . . while power welled up from the bottom"
(1980: 85), the image makes perfect sense given the analysis of
state structure that precedes it. But the image implies separation,
a removal of culture from the wellings-up of action, interaction,
power, and praxis.

We return, then, to the comparison of Geertz's promise with
his practice. Although this essay already contains more quota-
tions than it can easily bear, it closes with yet another. The
quotation returns us to the promising approach to culture expressed in "Thick Description," and it is a statement of connection rather than separation. The passage establishes a standard
for cultural interpretation that is in accord with the premises of
this essay. That it also serves as a standard in terms of which
Geertz's cultural analysis can be criticized should be apparent.

> If anthropological interpretation is constructing a reading of
> what happens, then to divorce it from what happens—from
> what, in this time or that place, specific people say, what they
> do, what is done to them, from the whole vast business of the
> world—is to divorce it from its applications and render it
> vacant. A good interpretation of anything—a poem, a person,
> a history, a ritual, an institution, a society—takes us into the
> heart of that of which it is an interpretation. When it does not
> do that, but leads us instead somewhere else—into an admira-
> tion of its own elegance, of its author's cleverness, or of the
> beauties of Euclidean order—it may have its intrinsic charms;
> but it is something else than what the task at hand . . . calls for.
> (1973b: 18)

Interpretation cannot be separated from what people say, what
they do, what is done to them, because culture cannot be so
separated. As long as anthropologists are seduced by the intrin-
sic charms of a textual analysis that takes such separation as a
point of honor, they will continue to do something other than
what the task at hand calls for.

CHAPTER TWO

Marxism and Culture

The history of anthropology can be written in terms of a series of theoretical oppositions, or antinomies—evolutionism and particularism, science and history, explanation and interpretation, materialism and idealism, and so on. Such expressions are useful in that they help us to organize a mass of material and quickly see what was at issue at a particular moment. They point to areas of tension, irresolvable conflicts between mutually exclusive sets of assumptions—between, for example, those who take a science of society as their goal and seek precise explanations of social processes and those who deny that such an explanatory science is possible and seek instead interpretive understanding of social life.

But antinomious thinking carries its own problems as well. Most obviously, the presentation of theory in terms of opposed paradigms may oversimplify the actual movement of social thought. More complex or problematic work may be lost or underemphasized, while work that more easily fits the oppositional scheme becomes a part of officially remembered histories. Thus, an Alexander Lesser might be forgotten while a Leslie White is easily remembered. Less obviously but more importantly for the development of anthropological thought, presentation of our history in oppositional terms may reproduce or recreate the antinomies, fortifying the appearance of mutually exclusive sets of assumptions and foreclosing the possibility of mediation. For Marshall Sahlins, for example, the opposition, which he expressed as a "conflict between practical activity and constraints of the mind," is seen as "an original, founding contradiction, between the poles of which anthropological theory has oscillated since the nineteenth century . . . " (1976: 55). His conclusion that mediation of this conflict is impossible, that one must choose sides and get on with it, its hardly surprising given the way he has set out the terms of discourse.

The problem with the "founding contradiction" view is that it collapses the various oppositions to which one might point into a single grand opposition. To take the examples used earlier, we could present them on a grid of analogous oppositions, thus:

evolutionism	particularism
science	history
explanation	interpretation
materialism	idealism

On the one side we find the materialists, or those who promote "practical reason"; on the other side we find those who seek a cultural account. The arguments used to criticize one of the poles in one of the pairs can then be used to criticize all of the analogous poles in the other pairs. An argument against evolutionism can be seen as an argument against science, explanation, and materialism because they are all part of a single founding contradiction.

The title of this essay would seem to fit well within such a contradiction, giving us another pair for the list, with Marxism on the left and culture on the right. That I want to suggest ways in which the apparent antinomy can be mediated, that I want to sketch out the possibility of a Marxist understanding of culture and a cultural reading of Marx would seem, for some, to pursue the impossible; for others, a gross form of theoretical pretension. But my goals are more modest: I do not pretend that the personal and idiosyncratic understanding sketched here will become some grand synthesis that will finally destroy all of the antinomies of anthropological thought. Many Marxists would find the framework presented here too far from an original vision to be Marxist; many cultural theorists would find the concept of culture explored here too social and material to be meaningful. Grand synthesis is neither promised nor possible.

Yet mediation is possible if we reject the analogous positioning of the pairs. Before exploring that possibility, let us introduce a more recent opposition—that between political economy and symbolic anthropology. Both are rather loose terms used to categorize heterogeneous movements, but most of us have some general understanding of the sort of work that might be given one or the other label. On the whole, there is some room for dialogue between political economists and symbolic anthropologists, and the level of discourse seems to have improved from the time when charges like "reductive" and "mentalist" were thrown around with ease. Some political economists and symbolic anthropologists share certain apparent interests—in history, in the study of particular social groups, in the interpretation of social action and movements. Yet they may understand each of these terms differently, and their anthropological projects are finally, and fundamentally, different. We can easily point to literature on each side that dismisses the work of the other.

Let us concentrate, however, on a recent criticism of political economy from a broadly conceived interpretive side. In a survey of recent anthropological history, George Marcus and Michael Fischer contend that three internal critiques emerged in anthropology during the 1960s—interpretive anthropology, critiques of the practice of fieldwork, and critiques of the ahistorical and apolitical nature of anthropological work. The first movement "was the only one . . . that had an early and important impact on changing the practice of anthropologists." The latter two "were mere manifestos and polemics, part of the highly politicized atmosphere of that period"(1986: 33). Of work in political economy, Marcus and Fischer assert that it "tended to isolate itself from cultural anthropology's concurrent development of a more sophisticated ethnographic practice on interpretive lines. It retreated into the typically Marxist relegation of culture to an epipheonomenal structure, dismissing much of cultural anthropology itself as idealist" (ibid.: 84).

By this view, political economy and symbolic anthropology would fit neatly on the grid outlined above, with political economy on the left and symbolic anthropology on the right. We could therefore repeat the grid with all of the terms thus far presented:

evolutionism	particularism
science	history
explanation	interpretation
materialism	idealism
Marxism	culture
political economy	symbolic anthropology

Recent work within a loosely conceived political economic literature, however, suggests a much richer interconnection between the concerns of political economy and those of symbolic anthropology than is recognized by those critics who repeat facile dismissals based on old-fashioned antinomies. Let us briefly consider four rather different and interesting books: Benedict Anderson's *Imagined Communities* (1983), William Sewell's *Work and Revolution in France* (1980), Sidney Mintz's *Sweetness and Power* (1985) and Gerald Sider's *Culture and Class in Anthropology and History* (1986). Only two of the authors are anthropologists, and at least one might well reject a connection with political economy. That is not the point; the point is an intersection of the *concerns* of political economy and symbolic anthropology, an intersection that is based on an emphasis upon meaningful action and recognizes that action is shaped by the meanings people take to their action even as meanings are shaped by people's activities.

Anderson's book is an attempt to grasp the importance of nationalism in the modern world. It views nationalism as a kind of "imagined community" and analyzes the rise of this type of imagined community in the context of the world-historical demise of other types (e.g., religious communities, monarchical realms). The rise of nationalism is also situated in the emergence of what he calls "print-capitalism," a rather nice welding of a political economic and a cultural argument. Given this world-historical understanding of nationalism as a general phenomenon, he then examines the emergence of particular kinds of nationalism in their more specific historical contexts—nation building in the nineteenth-century Americas, nationalism in dominated regions of nineteenth-century European empires, late-nineteenth-century "official" and reactive nationalism at the centers of the empires themselves (e.g., Prussia), and, more recently, nationalism in post-colonial states.

Sewell's book is a reflection on the origins of the concept of a proletariat in France from the eighteenth century to 1848. In pursuing his study, this historian calls upon the cultural anthropology of Clifford Geertz (indeed, the book was written at the Institute for Advanced Study), but he deals with a set of issues and a political process of profound interest to political economists. He traces the continuities in certain forms of association and a certain language for describing association from old regime to revolutionary France. Of particular interest were the corporations and confraternities that linked journeymen and workers within particular trades but maintained rigid divisions between the trades, thus making class forms of association difficult. Despite such continuities in language and association, the meanings of the terms and associations were extended in fundamentally new directions during the first half of the nineteenth century, so that the image emerged of a union of workers as a class, a confraternity of proletarians despite differences in trade. This fundamental shift in meaning and action is in turn understood in terms of the political movements and events from the French Revolution to the revolution of 1848.

Mintz's book is an important contribution to political economy and social history, one that links the transformation of Caribbean islands into a series of plantation economies with changing diet and increasing sugar consumption in England, from the seventeenth to nineteenth centuries. He begins with an outline of the place of sugar in the creation of a world economy, the creation of plantation economies in the Caribbean, and the increasingly powerful position of England in the sugar trade and in the colonization of the islands. Though his study is explicitly placed in this context, the focus is on the changing structure of consumption. Here he traces changing uses of sugar from late-medieval to industrial contexts, from differentiated uses as medicine, spice, decorative substance, sweetener, and preservative to more widespread and less differentiated use as sweetener. He also examines the transition from exclusively upper-class use to more general, population-wide use. The change of diet, and of the place of sugar in the diet, are explicitly connected with the change in class structure—the proletarianization of working people and consequent changes in domestic groups, work and eating habits, and forms of sociality within and between households. Although the data on diet are not presented in terms of regional and social differentiation, Mintz makes a powerful case for understanding cultural change in terms of changing circumstances of class, work, and power.

Sider's book reflects upon a series of traditions and forms of interaction in the "traditional" outport fisheries of Newfoundland, especially in the nineteenth century. He connects a theoretically sophisticated analysis of work, merchant capital, and the social relations between fishermen and merchants with a series of telling vignettes, drawn from a variety of documentary sources, that illuminate the psychological consequences of those social relations. Of special interest and importance is Sider's examination of a number of "new" or recent traditions (Christmas mumming, scoffing, and cuffing) that simultaneously express sociality and isolation. If the connection between these fine-grained analyses and some of Sider's more important cultural arguments (e.g., on hegemony) is not always clear or direct (see Rebel 1989b), the book is nonetheless an important contribution. Among its most important innovations is a stress on the role of merchant capital in creating social relations that dissolve relations of kinship and community among small producers and tie individualized producers to particular merchants. Sider stresses the importance of such social relations for both political economic and symbolic analyses. The many implications of this insight can be explored more fully in Newfoundland and in a number of other settings.

These books are not, strictly speaking, comparable. They deal with separate problems in distinct historical periods and

settings, and they adopt different strategies to do so. But they
also have certain common aspects. They all approach the relation of meaning and action in a context of unequal power. That
is, there is a political element to all of these books: if power is to
a certain extent shaped by meaning, meaning is also shaped,
quite profoundly, by power. They are also deeply historical.
They place their reflections within precise historical contexts
and examine the shaping of meaning and power over time. It
should also be noted that none of the books can be made to fit
on a grid of founding oppositions in anthropological theory
without the loss of all that is special and distinctive about their
contributions.

Let us return, then, to the terms in the antinomious grid and
sketch a framework for the consideration of Marxism and culture that could include the work of Anderson, Sewell, Mintz,
and Sider. I do not mean to suggest that any of these authors
would agree with the framework to be sketched. Indeed, I
would expect disagreement. Nonetheless, I think that it is a
framework that will allow us to come to an appreciative reading
of their work and move beyond the "founding contradiction"
view of anthropological theory. We begin by removing the
Marxism/culture opposition from the list, precisely because it is
the relationship between the two that we are attempting to explore. I also remove the science/history opposition because it is
based on a special, and especially narrow, understanding of
history and can only be understood in terms of the anthropological oppositions between evolutionism and particularism,
and explanation and interpretation. My approach is historical,
but not in the sense implied by a science/history opposition.
The approach suggested here would then be one that is materialist and one that is simultaneously political economic and symbolic. It rejects evolutionism and particularism, and it tries to
place itself between the extreme versions of explanatory scientism and interpretive self-absorption. That is, it rejects the goal
of an explanatory science that postulates a set of transhistorical
laws of history or evolution. Yet it is also resolutely materialist: it
sees ideas as social products and understands social life as itself
objective and material. Its approach to public symbols and cul-

tural meanings would therefore place those symbols and meanings in social fields characterized by differential access to political and economic power.

———

The materialism called for here is not the sort that comes from a quick reading of Marx's well-known "Preface" to the *Contribution to the Critique of Political Economy:*

> In the social production of their existence, men inevitably enter into definite relations, which are independent of their will, namely relations of production appropriate to a given stage in the development of their material forces of production. The totality of these relations of production constitutes the economic structure of society, the real foundation, on which arises a legal and political superstructure and to which correspond definite forms of social consciousness. The mode of production of material life conditions the general process of social, political and intellectual life. It is not the consciousness of men that determines their existence, but their social existence that determines their consciousness. (1970 [1859]: 20–21)

This is the classic and most influential statement of Marx's materialism. While there are aspects of it with which most any Marxist would agree, it has had unfortunate consequences. First, although it seems to begin with people ("men"), it moves quickly to structure: relations of production, economic structure of society, mode of production. These structures then act upon, or "condition," other structures (the political superstructure and consciousness), which are seen as secondary or derivative. Whether one's approach to the relationship between these structures is mechanical or "dialectical," the structural hierarchy remains intact. Later passages of the "Preface" then apply this structural hierarchy to an explanation of the evolutionary movement from one mode of production to another. Thus, a pervasive and tenacious version of Marxism, rooted in the words of Marx, would amply justify the inclusion of an opposition between Marxism and culture on the grid of analogous oppositions as part of a founding contradiction.

In other passages, however, Marx offers a different starting point for his materialism. One could begin this approach in *The German Ideology* (a text with its own problems, as Sahlins [1976] and others have shown). There the basic premise offers more possibilities for an understanding of culture:

> The premises from which we begin are not arbitrary ones, not dogmas, but real premises from which abstraction can only be made in the imagination. They are the real individuals, their activity and the material conditions under which they live, both those which they find already existing and those produced by their activity. . . .
>
> This mode of production must not be considered simply as being the production of the physical existence of the individuals. Rather it is a definite form of activity of these individuals, a definite form of expressing their life, a definite *mode of life* on their part . . . (Marx and Engels 1970 [1846]: 42)

A number of aspects of this materialism, as expressed in this passage and later in *The German Ideology,* deserve mention.

First, it is a materialism that starts not with nature or with a postulated economic structure but with a human population. It begins not with matter but with the social, conceived as material.

Second, it is a materialism that is active. People enter into definite relations with others and with nature, but as they enter into those relations they transform both nature and themselves. Nature and the social world, then, are always socially constructed, historical.

Third, in his conception of activity, the most fundamental activity is that associated with production. But Marx never has a narrow conception of production, as, for example, the production of subsistence. Rather, it is "a definite form of activity of these individuals, a definite form of expressing their life, a definite *mode of life* . . . . "

Fourth, the materialism here presented is historically situated, the forms of activity and modes of life being the products of prior forms of activity and modes of life:

"History is nothing but the succession of the separate generations, each of which exploits the materials, the capital funds, the productive forces handed down to it by all preceding generations, and thus, on the one hand, continues the traditional activity in completely changed circumstances and, on the other, modifies the old circumstances with a completely changed activity" (ibid.: 57).

It is only in light of the previous points that we can suggest an interpretation of the fifth aspect of the materialism presented here: the approach to consciousness. In *The German Ideology*, Marx and Engels constantly contrast their approach to that of classical German Philosophy, and they express the contrast in the starkest possible terms: "we do not set out from what men say, imagine, conceive, nor from men as narrated, thought of, imagined, conceived, in order to arrive at men in the flesh. We set out from real, active men, and on the basis of their real life-process, we demonstrate the development of the ideological reflexes and echoes of this life-process" (ibid.: 47). Any materialist must start with an assertion of a connection between being and consciousness, but there are two unfortunate aspects of Marx and Engels's conception of this connection here. The first is in the "reflexes and echoes" expression here and elsewhere, which places us once again in the realm of hierarchical structures with primary forces and derivative products. The second is in the expression of consciousness as arising *directly* from material activity. This is a consequence, in part, of their attempt to tie their statement of premises to an evolutionary speculation, so that consciousness is introduced as part of a discussion of the first supposedly genuine human acts. Yet if we understand material activity in the more broad sense suggested above—production as production of a whole way of life that is itself part of a historical process—then we need a more historical and less derivative understanding of consciousness.

Two suggestions from Marx's work in other contexts point to his use of this more historical and less derivative understanding. The first comes from the well-known passage in *Capital* in

which Marx talks about the specifically human character of productive labor:

> A spider conducts operations which resemble those of the
> weaver, and a bee would put many a human architect to
> shame by the construction of its honeycomb cells. But what
> distinguishes the worst architect from the best of bees is that
> the architect builds the cell in his mind before he constructs it
> in wax. At the end of every labour process, a result emerges
> which had already been conceived by the worker at the begin-
> ning, hence already existed ideally. (1977 [1867]: 284)

At the least, this would suggest a simultaneity or unity of activity
and consciousness, hand and brain, thus challenging the derivative view expressed in *The German Ideology*. But here consciousness is still tied to a direct material activity or object. For a more
historical understanding, we can turn to another well-known
passage from yet another work.

At the beginning of *The Eighteenth Brumaire*, Marx makes his
famous observation that "Men make their own history, but not of
their own free will; not under circumstances they themselves
have chosen but under the given and inherited circumstances
with which they are directly confronted" (1974 [1852]: 146).
Most people who cite and think about this passage use it as part of
a reflection on the relationship between structure and agency, or
historical determination and human activity (to call up some
more antinomies). It is seldom noted that the observation introduces a comment on the weight of ideas in a historical process:

> The tradition of the dead generations weighs like a nightmare
> on the minds of the living. And, just when they appear to be
> engaged in the revolutionary transformation of themselves
> and their material surroundings, in the creation of something
> which does not yet exist, precisely in such epochs of revolu-
> tionary crisis they timidly conjure up the spirits of the past to
> help them; they borrow their names, slogans and costumes so
> as to stage the new world-historical scene in this venerable
> disguise and borrowed language. . . . In the same way, the

beginner who has learned a new language always retranslates
it into his mother tongue. (ibid.: 146–147)

This text, and the larger work it introduces, are instructive for
Marxists who could reduce their Marxism to a set of formulas,
or rules for pedants. *The Eighteenth Brumaire* is an attempt to
analyze the political events surrounding the movement in
France from a republican revolution in February 1848 to the
Bonapartist coup in December 1851. One sees here the engagement of Marx's method with actual political and historical materials. The materials are not made to fit into some narrow and
preconceived scheme: the two great classes of capitalist society
give way to a series of competing and combating class fractions.
The particularities of the French case—the history and structure of the state, the relative lack of industrial development, the
social position of the peasantry, the role of Bonaparte—are all
included in Marx's analysis. The epochal or evolutionist materialism of the "Preface" or *The German Ideology* has given way to a
historical materialism that starts with "real individuals, their
activity and the material conditions under which they live, both
those which they find already existing and those produced by
their activity."

More to the point, among the material conditions under
which they live is included a set of ideas, or sets of ideas, themselves historical products, that serve as material forces. Here,
culture itself is made material. The kind of materialism pro-
posed here, then, is not one that appropriates and subsumes
culture and consciousness within an expanding material base
but one that starts with a given population and the material
circumstances that confront it and includes culture and consciousness among the material circumstances to be examined.
This approach to symbolic analysis is one that most cultural
theorists in anthropology would not accept. It seems to grant
culture no autonomy and to reduce it to a derivative product of
human activity. But the assertion of autonomy can only be understood in terms of a structural hierarchy. In this sense,
mechanical materialism and a cultural theory that denies the
materiality of culture are complementary reflections of each

other. Each starts in a structural universe removed from "real individuals, their activity and the material conditions under which they live" and directs questions to relationships (or the presumed lack of relationship) among structural levels.

The "autonomy" of culture, in my view, comes not from its removal from the material circumstances of life but from its connection. As one of many products of prior activity and thought, it is among the material circumstances that confront real individuals who are born in a concrete set of circumstances. As some of those circumstances change, and as people attempt to conduct the same sorts of activities under new circumstances, their cultural understandings will affect the way they view both their circumstances and their activities. It may imbue those circumstances and activities with an appearance of naturalness or of order, so that the utterly new may appear to be a variation on a theme. In this sense, people's activities are conditioned by their cultural understandings, just as their activities under new circumstances may stretch or change those understandings. Culture's autonomy, and its importance, rest on this dual character: although meanings are socially produced, they may be extended to situations where a functionalist might say they do not fit, or they may be applied even after the circumstances and activities that produced them have changed. This is not to call up the old notion of "cultural lag," which would imply that the lack of fit is temporary and that at some point functional correspondence will be regained. Here Geertz's notion of inscription (1983), or the removal of cultural meaning from the *immediate* circumstances of its creation, is especially appropriate. Because action takes place in meaningful contexts—that is, because people come to their actions with prior understandings and act in terms of them—a materialism that saw consciousness arising solely and directly out of activity would be especially impoverished. Culture is at once socially constituted (it is a product of present and past activity) and socially constitutive (it is part of the meaningful context in which activity takes place).

For example, a white boy growing up in a Southern city in the 1950s and 1960s would be coming of age in a situation of ferment, of changing economic, political, and social circumstances.

Yet he might experience these circumstances in the context of a family that is trying to raise him in a certain way, to reproduce a certain style of life and set of values. He might be learning what it is to be a boy or young man, to be white, to be an American, to be a Southerner (or an Arkansan, or a Georgian), to be a Methodist, and so on at a time when what it means to be all of these things is changing. He will learn these things in changing institutional settings—schools, churches, his family—each of which has developed a particular form of discourse for talking about the world and each of which is undergoing rapid change. His ideas about race, or sex, or class, or nation will be conditioned by events, but the events will be interpreted in terms of a religious language that emphasizes justice, morality, giving unto Caesar that which is Caesar's, or a high school civics language that emphasizes ideas about equality, democracy, or freedom. Yet the attempt to talk about new events with old language and meanings stretches the language and develops new meanings.

It should be stressed that this understanding of action and meaning is not akin to Sahlins's discussion of the "structure of the conjuncture" (1985) and the dialectical relation of structure and event. It differs in that (a) its understanding of culture is much less structural and systemic; and (b) it sees this concatenation of structure and event as a constant process, one in which culture is constantly being shaped, produced, reproduced, and transformed by activity rather than one in which culture encapsulates activity until the structure of culture can no longer hold. Thus the *meaning* of being a Southerner will be different for a Southern white boy who grew up in the thirties and forties than for one who grew up in the fifties and sixties, which in turn will be different for one who grew up in the seventies and eighties. In each case people would be trying, through families and institutions, to reproduce a way of life during a time in which local, national, and global events (we could produce a superficial list) altered the *experience* of life in the South in profound and intimate ways.

But there is, of course, more. The experience of a Southern white boy of the thirties or fifties or seventies will be different from that of a Southern white girl, or a black boy or girl, or one

from the country or one from the city, one from a sharecrop-
ping family or one from a cotton planter's family. Or, more to
the point, some of their experiences and the events to which
they respond will be common (let us say shared), and some will
be utterly different.

———

The attempt to understand these commonalities and differences takes us from the experience of persons (though we must
return) to the analysis of institutions and structures. It takes us
to political economy, first as an analysis of social relations based
on unequal access to wealth and power. Thus far our discussion
of the material nature of ideas and meanings and of the relationship between activity and consciousness has not taken this dimension into account. Yet if ideas and meanings are themselves
material products and forces, they too are caught up in hierarchical relations based on differential access to wealth and
power. Let us return to *The German Ideology* and another well-
known passage:

> The ideas of the ruling class are in every epoch the ruling
> ideas, i.e. the class which is the ruling *material* force of society,
> is at the same time its ruling *intellectual* force. The class which
> has the means of material production at its disposal, has con-
> trol at the same time over the means of mental production, so
> that thereby, generally speaking, the ideas of those who lack
> the means of mental production are subject to it. The ruling
> ideas are nothing more than the ideal expression of the domi-
> nant material relationships, the dominant material relation-
> ships grasped as ideas; hence of the relationships which make
> the one class the ruling one, therefore, the ideas of its domi-
> nance. The individuals composing the ruling class possess
> among other things consciousness, and therefore think. Inso-
> far, therefore, as they rule as a class and determine the extent
> and compass of an epoch, it is self-evident that they do this in
> its whole range, hence among other things rule also as think-
> ers, as producers of ideas, and regulate the production and
> distribution of the ideas of their age: thus their ideas are the
> ruling ideas of the epoch. (Marx and Engels 1970 [1846]: 64)

This passage is at once suggestive and problematic. Let us begin with one of the suggestive aspects and connect it with Gramsci's notion of hegemony (1971 [1929–35]) or Raymond Williams's concept of dominant culture (1977). The concept refers to a complex set of ideas, meanings, and associations, and a way of talking about or expressing those meanings and associations, which present an order of inequality and domination as if it were an order of equality and reciprocity, which give a product of history the appearance of natural order. A powerful element in such a dominant culture will be a particular and highly selective version of a people's history, what Williams calls a selective tradition. Such a tradition or history will be taught in schools or expressed in television programs. Thus differential access to power is crucial in the determination of control over the means of cultural production, the means for the selection and presentation of tradition.

But what makes this hegemony *culture* and not simply ideology is that it appears to connect with the experience and understanding of those people who do not produce it, people who lack access, or have sharply diminished access, to wealth and power. Here, paradoxically, it is important to return to Geertz's notion of inscription, to the removal of meaning from direct experience and activity, not as part of an argument for the removal of culture from relations of inequality and domination but as an essential part of our understanding of its connection. With hegemony, traditions, meanings, and forms of discourse are being produced and extended, with apparent success, to situations and groups who could not have experienced those events or who would have experienced them in profoundly different ways. In the process a common set of assumptions and selections from "our" tradition can emerge despite the fact of differentiation. Thus the Statue of Liberty, which can only serve as a meaningful symbol for a fraction (although sizeable) of the population, is, in the process of official celebration, transformed into a symbol of the nation, a nation in which "we all" were immigrants. Or, as part of the official celebration of Martin Luther King's birthday, his actual activities and the struggles in which he participated disappear from view. He becomes not the black man who struggled for racial justice, who upset the status quo and was murdered, but the Reverend Doctor who died for peace—a kind of mid-twentieth-century black Jesus who lived an exemplary life and died for our sins and can be elevated to a place in our pantheon of civil-religious heroes.

This notion of hegemony is important for any political economic understanding of culture, and one that requires much more analytical attention. Here I differ from these Marxist and socialist writers who are uncomfortable talking about hegemony because it seems to rule out resistance or because it seems to suggest a consensus view of a society based on shared values. In the first place, such authors romanticize working-class and other subaltern forms of experience and culture, granting them a heroism that makes it difficult to understand "unheroic decades" (Williams 1979). Second, they make too direct a connection between class and culture, so that the working class can be seen to have their own culture, based on their own experience of work and community. There are two problems with such a view. First, it implies much too direct a connection between meaning and experience and ignores the political implications of cultural inscription, the separation of meaning from experience in the context of domination. Second, it ignores the ambiguous and contradictory nature of experience itself (or, more properly, ongoing and confusing experiences), an ambiguity that can only produce a contradictory consciousness. As Gramsci expresses it, the "man-in-the-mass"

> has a practical activity, but has no clear theoretical consciousness of his practical activity, which nonetheless involves understanding the world in so far as it transforms it. His theoretical consciousness can indeed be historically in opposition to his activity. One might almost say that he has two theoretical consciousnesses (or one contradictory consciousness): one which is implicit in his activity and which in reality unites him with all his fellow-workers in the practical transformation of the real world; and one, superficially explicit or verbal, which he has inherited from the past and uncritically absorbed. But this verbal conception is not without consequences. 1971 [1929–35]: 333)[1]

Nonetheless, simply to describe hegemony or dominant culture as it has thus far been sketched in this presentation would be insufficient, for it grants to culture much too coherent and systemic a quality. To understand its lack of coherence and system, we can return to two passages from the Marx and Engels passage on ruling ideas. Let us begin with the sentence, "Insofar, therefore, as they rule as a class and determine the extent and compass of an epoch . . . they do this in its whole range. . . ." In their language, Marx and Engels have rendered problematic a relation that many Marxists treat as automatic. There are lines of cleavage and conflict among elements of a dominant class. Such a class is seldom so united or homogeneous as to "determine the extent and compass of an epoch." Even within a dominant culture, then, there will be elements of tension and contradiction. Aspects of a selected tradition may be rejected or differently valued by different groups among those who control the means of cultural production—witness the conflicts over funding policies of the National Endowments for the Humanities or the Arts, or over interpretations of the Vietnam War on public television.

Neither, however, should our understanding of hegemony be limited to those who produce dominant culture, ignoring those who appear to consume it. To do a slight turn on one of Marx and Engels' phrases, "The individuals composing the subordinate class possess among other things consciousness, and therefore think." If culture is inscribed, if meaning can be removed from direct experience, such inscription and removal can never be total. If some meanings produced by the dominant culture seem to connect, or at least not contradict, the experience of ordinary people, other meanings may directly conflict with lived experience. In normal circumstances, that may not matter, or not matter deeply. In less ordinary circumstances, such disjunction may be the focal point for the production of new and alternative meanings, new forms of discourse, new selections from tradition or conflicts and struggles over the meaning of particular elements within tradition. Martin Luther King's birthday again provides the example here: first the struggle over the designation of the day as a holiday and the inclusion of a black man as a national hero, and more recently and crucially, the struggle over the meaning of his life for "us"—the official attempt to sanitize his life and other attempts to make King a symbol of opposition and struggle. The outcome of this movement is by no means obvious, and the most important arena for struggle will be in public schools, the central forum for the production and modification of a selected tradition. "The line between dominant and subordinate cultures," Jackson Lears notes, "is a permeable membrane, not an impenetrable barrier" (1985: 574).

Let us return to our original example. We now have a framework for talking about—but not for reducing to neat formulas—culture and experience in the southern United States. It requires, first, the recognition of differential experience: the differential experience of persons—white and black, male and female, rural and urban, sharecropper and planter, and so on; of particular generations in particular times and places—and the understanding of that differential experience in terms of individual life courses but also in terms of structures of inequality and domination. Yet it also requires a recognition that across this differential experience, and to a certain extent across time, some common understandings emerge, along with common forms of language and modes of interaction, common sensibilities of self and place and history. The burden of the discussion of political economy has been to stress that these commonalities are produced through a variety of institutions and means of cultural production (which also vary across time)—churches, schools, 4-H clubs, county and state fairs, state celebrations of centennials and sesquicentennials, books, magazines, television, and the like—and that the production or shaping of culture occurs in the context of unequal access to power. But I have also tried to stress that these common understandings and modes of interaction can never encompass all of differential experience. Cultural production is not limited to those who control the means of cultural production. Experience constantly intrudes. Despite the apparent inscription of common understandings and modes of interaction, then, "Southern culture" in the thirties was different from what it had become by the fifties or from what it had become in the seventies. And in each of these decades, the *experience* and *meaning* of "Southern culture" would be quite different for specifically situated individuals. This discordant experience had direct effects on events in the South, e.g., the civil rights movement of the fifties and sixties, which in turn had a profound effect on "Southern culture." The attempt to constantly place culture in time, to see a constant interplay between experience and meaning in a context in which both experience and meaning are shaped by inequality and domination requires a much less structured and systemic understanding of culture than that prescribed by our most prominent cultural theorists.

―――――――

But there is another aspect to political economy, at least as it has emerged in anthropology over the past two decades, and that is its historical aspect, its attempt to understand the emergence of particular peoples at the conjunction of local and global histories, to place local populations in the larger currents of world history. Thus the different shape of Southern experience in the thirties, fifties, and seventies would be understood, in part, in terms of the national and global events and movements that had affected it. The social relations of differential access to wealth and power, then, are understood in world-historical terms. To discuss this aspect of political economy, we must leave behind our consideration of meaning and experience, not because the relationship is irrelevant but because the structure of experience is so much more complex than has thus far been indicated. Just because the word and concept of "culture" is not obviously present in what follows, this does not mean that what follows is irrelevant to an understanding of culture. The same basic framework for talking about culture would be in place, but the more complex structure of experience would require an even more complex approach to the production, shaping, and inscription of meaning.

Historical political economy does not simply assert that particular societies are part of world history. It also asserts that the attempt to draw rigid cultural boundaries around, say, the South, or Navajo or Ojibwa or Tsembaga or Nambiquara or Chamula is to reify culture. Because populations are not formed in isolation, their connections with other populations and, perhaps, with the larger currents of world history, require attention. To ignore these connections is to treat societies and cultures like "billiard balls," in Eric Wolf's telling words (1982: 6).

This political economic perspective on history, and the connection of apparently distinctive anthropological subjects within that history, provide us with our rejection of both poles of the antinomy between evolutionism and particularism. Both sides of this dispute took the billiard-ball view of culture as a starting point. The particularists argued that each billiard ball had its own history, which could be understood on its own terms. Evolutionists, on the other hand, placed the billiard balls in an evolutionary game that followed certain rules (laws) that the scientist could use to explain the direction of the balls themselves. Historical political economy shares the sense that the particular is part of a world-historical process, but it differs from evolutionists' understanding of that process in key respects.

First, the evolutionists' view is not radical enough to the extent that it still accepts the boundaries around particular cultures and seeks generalization by fitting the particular into specific points on an evolutionary ladder. Such a view ignores the constant shaping of the particular by the evolutionary process itself, the remaking of the "folk" in the civilizational process, the creation of (perhaps egalitarian) peripheries in the process of state formation. In recent years, two attempts to reinterpret Edmund Leach's analysis in *Political Systems of Highland Burma* (1964 [1954]) demonstrate this difference quite nicely. That both reinterpretations are avowedly Marxist and come from two rather different understandings of Marxism make the example all the more interesting. In 1975, Jonathan Friedman applied his systems theory Marxism to an attempt to use Leach's material as a meditation on state formation. Looking at a variety of populations in highland Burma, he tried to view the movement from *gumlao* to *gumsa* to Shan as an example of the process and problem of state formation. In doing so, however, he took all of the populations as distinct units with direct relations with an ecosystem, without examining the interconnections of the presumed units. More recently, David Nugent (1982; cf. Friedman 1987) has tried to interpret the *gumlao/gumsa* cycle in terms of the incorporation of the Kachin Hills in long-distance trade routes, their apparent relation to the opium trade, colonial attempts to cut the routes or remove the Kachin Hills from them, and so on. That Leach dismisses both reinterpretations is not so important for the current point. We have here two rather different attempts to place the particular in a larger context, one that fits the particular in a putative evolutionary scheme and another that attempts to understand the shaping of the particular by a larger historical process.

Historical political economy would view evolutionism as *too* radical, however, in another sense. From the perspective of historical political economy, we now have world history, and we must understand the particular, at least in part, in terms of that history. But we have not always had world history, which is itself a historical product. Or, better said, there has been a series of world histories, centered in civilizational focuses, the vast majority of which have not been truly global. If populations generally live in webs of relationships, in complex connection and interconnection with other populations, those webs are not necessarily and have not always been global. Global history comes with the expansion of the world market, which "produced world history for the first time" (Marx and Engels 1970 [1846]: 78), and the subsequent incorporation of regions within colonial empires or spheres of capitalist investment, a history that has been nicely sketched by Wolf (1982). The incorporation of local populations within that market or within empires, and the effect of such incorporation upon those populations, differ (or are "uneven") in space and time. Thus, world history of this sort came to Latin America sooner than it came to China, and is only being extended to some other regions (e.g., parts of Melanesia) in our lifetime. Any attempt to view particular populations in terms of historical political economy must take this unevenness into account as we attempt to explore the formation of populations in terms of local and global histories. As any careful reading of Wolf would indicate, incorporation within

the world market or the introduction of capitalist social relations does not set a local population en route to an unalterable
or predictable series of social or cultural changes.

It should be noted, however, that historical political economy
is not without its important anthropological critics, especially in
its approach to culture. One widespread view is best expressed,
perhaps, in Sherry Ortner's concern that the attempt to write a
political economic history reduces other cultural realities to
Western experience and Western historicities. Noting various
strengths in a political economic perspective, she finds its major
weakness in its "capitalism-centered worldview," its attempt to
place a variety of societies and social relations within a capitalist
world economy. She writes:

> The problems derived from the capitalism-centered world-
> view also affect the political economists' view of history. His-
> tory is often treated as something that arrives, like a ship,
> from outside the society in question. Thus we do not get a
> history *of* that society, but the impact of (our) history *on* that
> society. The accounts produced from such a perspective are
> often quite unsatisfactory in terms of traditional anthropologi-
> cal concerns: the actual organization and culture of the society
> in question. . . . . The political economists, moreover, tend to
> situate themselves more on the ship of (capitalist) history that
> on the shore. They say in effect that we can never know what
> the other system, in its unique, "traditional," aspects, really
> looked like anyway. 1984: 143)

While Ortner has isolated a genuine problem in political economic (as well as other) approaches to history, her statement of
the problem precludes a resolution of it. The dilemma for anthropologists is to view the people they study as *in some way*
connected with a wider world that includes capitalist relations
without reducing social and economic processes within those
societies to processes of world history or capital accumulation.
The resolution of that dilemma cannot be to set aside, even
temporarily, the wider world, to reassert the disjunction between "us" and "them" and claim that, "A society, even a village,
has its own structure and history, and this must be as much part

of the analysis as its relations with the larger context" (ibid.). If the rejection of an overly capitalism-centered and deterministic view leads to the contention that one can isolate a society or a history or a culture from its larger context, understand it "on its own terms," and *then* place it in context, one has replaced one simplistic view with its opposite extreme. Yet this seems to be what Ortner is proposing, and the evocative imagery of ship and shore supports such a vision. It perpetuates a disjunction between "our" history and "their" history that finally, regardless of which extreme one starts from, is reductive. And it returns us to a grid of anthropological antinomies.

But if we consider again the four books mentioned earlier, we see examples of work that is sensitive to the issues we have discussed and that render Ortner's objection moot. These books consider the shaping of social meanings in specific historical situations and in the context of relations of power. Each of the specific historical situations is seen in world-historical terms, most clearly, but not exclusively, in the work of Mintz and Anderson. Mintz carefully links the creation of Caribbean plantation economies with changing patterns of consumption and sociality in England, while Anderson sees nationalism arising at particular moments in global history. Yet each of these studies is sensitive to the particular, and none of them attempts to reduce the particular to a variation on a single capitalist theme. The way in which they link the global and particular makes the ship and shore, us and them, our history and their history imagery used by Ortner especially inappropriate. They point, then, toward an understanding of culture as historical product and historical force, shaped and shaping, socially constituted and socially constitutive.

Like the works considered here, historical political economy does not fit well within a scientist search for transhistorical laws. Nonetheless, the perspective outlined here does have a strong sense of determination. Because its materialism rejects the hierarchy of structures and takes as its starting point real individuals and the conditions in which they live, the determination here adduced is not one that concerns the shaping of superstructure by base, even in the putative last instance. Rather, I have in mind a historical determinism, the determination of action and the consequences of action by the conditions in which that action takes place, conditions that are themselves the consequences of prior activity and thought. Real individuals and groups act in situations conditioned by their relationships with other individuals and groups, their jobs or their access to wealth and property, the power of the state, and their ideas—and the ideas of their fellows—about those relationships. Certain actions, and certain consequences of those actions, are possible while most other actions and consequences are impossible.

These determinative pressures and limits are quite powerful, especially at present. If we step back from the activity of actual individuals and consider the formation and action of institutions, we can see a definite shape and direction in the historical process. But the shape and direction of history, and the determinative pressures and limits that give it that shape, are not predictable in a scientistic sense. The starting point is always conditioned activity, and if a large range of actions and consequences is ruled out, there is still a range of actions and consequences that is possible, some of which cannot even be imagined, either by the actors or by those who attempt to understand their action. We need to allow for the creative and sometimes surprising activity of human subjects, living conditioned lives and acting in conditioned ways with results that have a determined and understandable shape, and sometimes, under conditions not of their choosing and with results that cannot be foreseen, creating something new—whether that be the concept of the nation or of a proletariat, or the practice of Christmas mummery.

Images of the Peasant in the Consciousness of the Venezuelan Proletariat

In an influential and controversial book, James Scott suggested that peasants have a "moral economy" by which they evaluate the destructive effects of capitalist expansion and the increasing exactions of the colonial state. Based on a subsistence ethic, the moral economy demands that those who appropriate peasant surpluses offer guarantees for the continued survival of the peasant household. Although precapitalist orders may be seen as exploitative in a Marxist sense, they may be based on patron-client relations that offer survival guarantees and may not be perceived as exploitative by the peasants who enjoy the guarantees. The intrusion of capitalism or the formation of a colonial state may break the social ties of the old moral economy, erode survival guarantees, appear exploitative to the peasantry, and provoke rebellion (Scott 1976; cf. his 1977; Popkin 1979; Adas 1980).

Scott's analysis of peasant politics in Southeast Asia explicitly draws upon the work of E. P. Thompson and others who have emphasized the moral economy of peasants, artisans, and proletarians in eighteenth- and nineteenth-century England and France. This literature has emphasized the active presence of precapitalist traditions, values, and communities in the early working class—traditions that were transformed with the Industrial Revolution and in terms of which the industrial experience was evaluated, criticized, and resisted (Thompson 1963: 63; 1971; cf. Hobsbawm 1959; Rudé 1964). The literature has served an important corrective function with relation to Marxist and non-Marxist economic history, in which the history of capitalism is often considered the history of the capitalists, the history of those who won. Even more important than its recapturing of the history of those who lost, however, the moral economy literature has created the basis for a new theory of consciousness. It has renewed the notion of tradition, not as the dead weight of the past, but as the active, shaping force of the past in the present.

Although the moral economy literature, particularly that dealing with the European experience, must be regarded as advancing our historical understanding, there is an unfortunate tendency to treat the peasant or artisan past in unambiguous, uncritical terms. For example, when Thompson analyzes traditional notions of time in his essay "Time, Work-Discipline, and Industrial Capitalism" (1967), he freely draws on examples from the Nuer and other primitive societies without carefully distinguishing among these societies, the nature of their traditions, values, experiences, and communities, and the traditions of the peasants and artisans who were to experience the Industrial Revolution in England. In *Work, Culture and Society in Industrializing America* (1976), Herbert Gutman lumps together under the single label "preindustrial" a wide variety of peasant and artisan traditions from different parts of Europe and North America and at different historical moments. And James Scott (1976) has a tendency to overstate his case, romanticizing the precapitalist past and ignoring the forces of disorder and exploitation that preceded capitalism and the colonial state.

One must, then, question the distance from modernization theory traveled by these theorists. Although they adopt a much more critical stance toward the capitalist transformation than do the classical theorists of modernization, they have remarkably similar starting points for their historical trajectories—a relatively homogeneous, undifferentiated traditional order. More important for our purposes, this weakness has unfortunate consequences for their understanding of consciousness. Although they are correct to point to the active force of the past in the present, their uncritical approaches to the past leave them in poor positions to understand the contradictory images, values, and feelings presented to the emerging proletarian.

In *The Country and the City*, Raymond Williams notes the difficulty in dating the disappearance of an idyllic rural past. For whatever century, it always seems to have recently disappeared or to be in the process of disappearing. In a passage that has special relevance to the moral economy literature, he observes:

> Take first the idealisation of a "natural" or "moral" economy on which so many have relied, as a contrast to the thrusting ruthlessness of the new capitalism. There was very little that was moral or natural about it. In the simplest technical sense, that it was a "natural" subsistence agriculture, as yet unaffected by the drives of a market economy, it is already doubtful and subject to many exceptions; though part of this emphasis can be readily accepted. But the social order within which this agriculture was practiced was as hard and as brutal as anything later experienced. Even if we exclude the wars and brigandage to which it was commonly subject, the uncountable thousands who grew crops and reared beasts only to be looted and burned and led away with tied wrists, this economy, even at peace, was an order of exploitation of a most thoroughgoing kind: a property in men as well as in land; a reduction of most men to working animals, tied by forced tribute, forced labour, or "bought and sold like beasts"; "protected" by law and custom only as animals and streams are protected, to yield more labour, more food, more blood; an economy directed, in all its working relations, to a physical and economic domination of a significantly total kind. (1973: 37–38).

But, some might argue, the "moral economy" need not have existed in the past; it may be *perceived* in the past from the perspective of a disordered present. The images of a moral economy may be a *meaningful* image even if "what actually happened" was less idyllic. But as Williams suggests, the perceptions of the past will depend upon the relative positions of the perceivers; different idealizations and evaluations will emerge depending on distinct experiences of a "physical and economic domination of a significantly total kind."

In a commentary on Frank R. Leavis and Denys Thompson's *Culture and Environment* (1977 [1933]), Williams turned this point about the past toward an evaluation of consciousness in the present: "What is true, I would argue, is that a number of new kinds of unsatisfying work have come into existence; a number of new kinds of cheap entertainment, and a number of new kinds of social division. Against these must be set a number of new kinds of satisfying work; certain new kinds of social organization. Between all these and other factors, the balance has to be more finely drawn than the myth allows" (1960: 279). In pointing to these passages, I do not mean to suggest, just as Williams does not mean to suggest, that the industrial capitalist order represented, on balance, progress for humankind and advances for working people. My point has to do with our approach to consciousness. Too often moral economy theorists, while pointing out the importance of the past in the present, analyze a relatively unambiguous transition from an ordered past to a disordered present. We instead need to view a movement from a disordered past to a disordered present. With such a starting point we can assess the contradictions inherent in the development of working-class consciousness and appreciate that the past provides experiences that may make the transition seem positive as well as experiences that may make it seem negative. Only then can we see the moral economy as a source for protest and accommodation, despair and hope.

With this in mind, I turn to the social history of a segment of the Venezuelan peasantry. Unlike peasantries with which anthropologists are more commonly familiar, the peasantry I examine has relatively shallow historical roots. It formed in the nineteenth century with the emergence of a coffee economy and underwent a proletarianization process in the twentieth century with the rise of Venezuela's petroleum economy. This short historical existence, intimately related to the cyclical development of the world market, corresponds to another basic point of *The Country and the City:* that both country and city (and

I would add peasant and proletarian) are ever-changing qualities and, as qualities, are to be understood in the context of capitalist history (Williams 1973: 302 et passim).

———

Before turning to specifics, I offer some introductory comments. First, I do not pretend to analyze the Venezuelan peasantry as a whole. The Venezuelan peasantry never existed as an identifiable whole but only in its regionally differentiated parts. I concentrate on the coffee-producing peasantry of the Andes, which exhibits a number of unique features. My own personal knowledge of the Andean peasantry is dependent on field research in a smaller, specialized region—the Boconó District of Trujillo State (Roseberry 1983).[1] Second, despite such limitation, I do not give a detailed account of the peasantry's history. Such detail can be found elsewhere. Here I simply summarize those aspects of its history that are necessary for cultural analysis. Third, my analysis of peasant and proletarian consciousness is not based upon my presentation of ideas, opinions, or conceptions that were expressed to me by individuals; nor is it based upon the behavior of peasants and proletarians in elections, unions, or related political events and movements. This is, rather, an attempt to outline the cultural possibilities presented to Venezuelan peasants and proletarians in their social history—the constitutive elements of political consciousness.

I examine these cultural possibilities with four symbolic sets that, in deference to a fashion in cultural analysis, are presented as opposed pairs: coffee and petroleum, backwardness and development, country and city, and dictatorship and democracy. This is hardly an esoteric group of images, but the meanings attached to them are constitutive elements of political consciousness. In discussing each set, I first trace the political and economic history that produces and connects the images. I then concentrate on the images themselves and discuss how they are presented to Venezuelans, without distinguishing among different class perceptions. In the process, I attempt to outline the raw materials available for cultural analysis.

COFFEE AND PETROLEUM

The Andean peasantry emerged in the nineteenth century with the growth of a coffee economy. At independence, the Andes were not central to Venezuela's economy, which was based on lowland plantation production of cacao for export. Cacao-producing areas were devastated by the War of Independence, and coffee soon displaced cacao as Venezuela's principal export. Such a shift did not immediately involve major political, economic, or demographic upheavals. Plantation owners in the central and coastal lowlands could expand their holdings into surrounding highlands, planting coffee and displacing the garden plots (*conucos*) of their dependent tenants and slaves. Only in the late nineteenth century did the Andes—which had been relatively depopulated and which produced primarily for regional markets during the colonial period—emerge as an important coffee-producing region. By the end of the century, Maracaibo, which served the Andes, was a major port, the Andes produced more than half of Venezuela's exports, and Andeans captured national power in Caracas (Lombardi and Hanson 1970; Carvallo and Hernandez 1979; Rangel 1968; 1969; Roseberry 1983).

Because the Andes were not densely populated during the colonial period, the formation of the coffee economy could not proceed without an intense migration process. Peasants and merchants from other parts of Venezuela (especially the cattle-producing *llanos* to the south, in decline throughout the nineteenth century), as well as migrants from southern Europe, settled on vacant national lands or in the new towns and cities in the temperate zone where coffee was planted. The migrants entered some areas that were virtually unpopulated and other areas that had a long colonial history. The interaction of migrant and resident, coffee economy and colonial economy, is important for understanding regional differentiation in the Andes and the nineteenth-century political battles between liberals and conservatives. Such detail is not crucial for the present analysis, however. More important is an emphasis on the relatively small scale of production throughout most

of the temperate coffee-producing zone. Regional differentiation must be stressed here as well, but with the dissolution of
colonial forms of landed property, a property-owning peasantry was created. These property-owning peasants, along with
those who owned no property but occupied national lands,
became the principal coffee producers. For the most part, they
entered into direct relations with merchants who loaned them
the funds necessary to start a coffee farm and to maintain
themselves until the first harvest, and who thus established a
claim to most of the product of the coffee farms. The Andean
peasantry was therefore unique in many respects. Unlike other
parts of Venezuela, where large farms and dependent tenants
predominated, a relatively independent peasantry was established in the Andes. Unlike other regions, where landlords
were politically and economically dominant, merchants controlled the coffee-producing Andes. This is not to say that
landlords were nonexistent; it is to say that the merchant-
peasant relationship defined the Andean economy (Rangel
1968; 1969; Roseberry 1980; 1983).

The bright historical possibilities that faced pioneers who had
established their own farms and passed them on to their children began to dim in the twentieth century. The coffee economy reached its spatial limits around the turn of the century.
Indebtedness became a problem, especially during periodic
world market depressions, for example, in the market's virtual
closure during the World War I and especially during the 1930s
crisis. The depression could be seen as one of a series of cyclical
crises in the coffee economy. Two aspects of the Venezuelan
situation made the 1930s unique, however. First, the fact that
the effective spatial limits to coffee production had been
reached meant that the favored response to crisis—increased
production through spatial expansion—was available only by
expanding on to less productive land. Second, by the 1930s
coffee had been displaced by petroleum as the dominant Venezuelan export. Economic displacement was accompanied by political displacement, even while Andeans continued to hold
formal positions of state power. Farmers and merchants facing
foreclosure, poverty, and in some cases starvation abandoned

the coffee economy. Nearby petroleum camps in the Maracaibo basin attracted some Andean migrants, but most of them went to cities such as Caracas and Maracaibo to participate in the commercial and governmental expansion accompanying Venezuela's transformation. This is not to say that the coffee economy disappeared. Indeed, land area planted with coffee increased in the Andes during the decades following the crisis, even as productivity and total production declined, indicating expansion on to less and less favorable land. Except for growing urban centers in the Andes that participated in Venezuela's commercial and governmental expansion, however, most Andean districts either lost population from one census to the next or maintained extremely low levels of population growth. Sons and daughters left the area, aggravating the situation for those coffee farmers who remained.

The nature of the petroleum transformation is discussed in the next section. Here I concentrate on the coffee economy, the peasantry that characterized it, and the images it presented for a moral economy. First, the relative independence of the Andean coffee-producing peasantry must be stressed. Yet it is remarkable to note the disappearance of this peasantry from the political consciousness of contemporary Venezuela. In both the official versions of Venezuelan history and alternative left-wing versions, the rural landscape has been reduced to a relatively undifferentiated opposition between landlords and dependent tenants, with a peonage relationship defining the social existence of the peasantry. There is some debate about the relative importance of *latifundia* in the Andes, in part due to a tendency to ignore regional differentiation and to aggregate state-level statistics. Nevertheless, one would think that the coffee-farming peasant of the nineteenth century would serve as one basis for the construction of a moral economy pointing to an ordered past. A number of factors operate against this alternative historical memory, but I mention only those directly related to the coffee economy and the peasantry. The most important is the process of development of the coffee economy. The expansion and hopes of the late nineteenth century gave way to relative stasis in the early twentieth century and finally to the crisis and collapse of the 1930s. During a price crisis in the early twentieth century, a local Andean newspaper struck a note of despair:

> With rare exceptions, what is the capital which has been formed among coffee producers, even when prices were as high as thirty-six or forty pesos for one hundred kilos? None. And when the market presented low prices, our fields were inexplicably and painfully neglected. Many of our *hacendados* had to abandon their farms to go look for another way to survive; others stay on their *haciendas* in a languid, heavy life, with no strength to move themselves. (*El Renacimiento,* Boconó, Venezuela, 4 March 1904).

The people who experienced the years of collapse were the sons and daughters, grandsons and granddaughters of the nineteenth-century pioneers. During the years of crisis, their debt obligations were leading to foreclosures. Their consciousness and memories would not be of independence but of abject dependence.

This leads us to the crucial characteristic of the Andean peasantry that separates it from those peasantries analyzed in the moral economy literature. The moral economists consider peasantries that seem to have deep historical roots. Capitalist development or colonialism intrudes upon that peasantry and disrupts its traditions and forms of organization. There is no sense, however, in which the Andean peasantry was precapitalist. Rather, it emerged in the nineteenth century as the region was incorporated into the world market. It was not oriented toward subsistence but toward commodity production. From the beginning, its fate was tied to the cyclical development of the world market. Because of internal differentiation within the peasantry, some producers could prosper, take advantage of periods of high prices, establish debt relations with poorer farmers, and create a protective cushion to absorb the shock of periods of low prices. Their less fortunate fellows could get by during periods of high prices but suffered at other times. Given their relations with merchants—relations that were essential if the family was

to grow coffee—their establishment as a peasantry was simultaneously the establishment of a relationship with a form of capital. While one might legitimately argue about whether that relationship was capitalist or *non*capitalist, there is little historical
sense in labeling it *pre*capitalist. The coffee economy presented
some raw material for a moral economy that could point to an
ordered past, but it also presented raw material for a consciousness that could point to a disordered past.

BACKWARDNESS AND DEVELOPMENT

Were it not for petroleum, Venezuela would have fit the stereotypic model of an underdeveloped country—exporting one
or two agricultural raw materials and importing manufactured
products. At one level, petroleum extraction and export simply
replaced an agricultural raw material by a mineral one without
affecting the basic import-export model. Indeed, Venezuela became more dependent on a single product than had ever been
the case with coffee or cacao. A number of things were, however, different about petroleum. In the first place, it brought in
far greater returns than were possible with agricultural products. During the decade in which petroleum replaced coffee as
the principal export, the portion of total export value to which
coffee contributed dropped to a minuscule level *before* actual
production declined. Second, unlike agricultural and most
other mineral products, petroleum was less subject to cyclical
fluctuations in demand and price on the world market, at least
during these long decades of expansion. Finally, it was a re-
source on which the developed world was so dependent that
producing countries could occasionally exercise some pressure
and control in the international market, as demonstrated by the
success of the Organization of Petroleum Exporting Countries
in the 1970s. In short, more things became possible with petroleum than would have been possible with coffee.

While petroleum extraction made an escape from typical
forms of underdevelopment possible, it would be a mistake to
automatically link coffee to backwardness and petroleum to

development. The petroleum economy simultaneously symbol-izes Venezuela's backwardness and its development. The cof-fee economy was never under foreign control. Import-export houses in port cities were owned by resident foreigners—Germans and English—and their Venezuelan-born children, but local production rested in Venezuela hands. Even when a foreigner controlled some aspect of production or marketing, the foreigner was not a corporation; the Venezuelan patri-mony had not been sold. In contrast, the granting of conces-sions to Anglo-Dutch Shell or the Standard Oil Corporation introduced a wholly new chapter in Venezuela's underdevelop-ment. The early laws governing the concessions were written by representatives of the companies themselves and called for a modest royalty to be paid to the Venezuelan government, but the vast majority of the oil wealth was extracted by foreign companies to feed foreign capital accumulation. In short, the rise of the petroleum economy meant the insertion of Venezu-ela within the imperialist system.

A kind of development nevertheless occurred in Venezuela. In the previous section, I referred to the "commercial and governmental expansion" of Venezuela's economy. We must now give some content to that phrase. Venezuela's oil wealth has been distributed primarily by the state. Even in the early years, when foreign companies paid modest royalties to the state, the sums generated allowed for an enormous expansion of the governmental apparatus. As production and the per-centage of royalties owed to the state increased over the de-cades, this apparatus grew even larger. To serve the members of the growing bureaucracy and their families, merchants of consumer goods proliferated. One remarkable result of the petroleum transformation, then, was the growth of an urban middle class, dependent on incomes from government or com-merce. Venezuela's industrial structure, however, was weak. It was only with efforts starting in the 1940s to "sow the petro-leum" that the growing state began to turn its resources to-ward stimulating diversified production. Industrial investment and development were promoted by import-substitution poli-cies starting in 1959. The state began in 1974 to encourage

basic industry (e.g., petrochemicals) in public and mixed public and private enterprises. But even with these recent attempts
to stimulate industrial development, Venezuela has become an
urban, essentially nonindustrial country.[2]

This is reflected in statistics on the distribution of gross domestic product (GDP) and population among primary (agriculture,
mining), secondary (manufacture, construction, utilities), and
tertiary (commerce, transportation, service) sectors. Distribution
of GDP among sectors has been relatively stable because of the
importance of petroleum earnings in the primary sector. From
1950 to 1969, nevertheless, there was significant slippage in the
primarily sector (down from 38 percent to 28 percent of GDP), a
minor proportional increase in the secondary sector (up from 17
percent to 20 percent), and a larger proportional increase in the
tertiary sector (from 45 percent to 52 percent) (Venezuela,
Banco Central 1971). If we divide the economically active population among these same sectors, however, a more dramatic change
appears. In 1950, 46 percent were working in the primary sector; by 1971, only 22 percent were. The secondary sector has
remained relatively stable (rising from 17 percent to 20 percent),
and the percentage of the population working in the tertiary
sector increased from 34 percent to 42 percent. The major increase was in a group that confounded the census takers and that
will be discussed later. the residual "others" increased from 3
percent to 16 percent. The decline in the percentage of people
engaged in the primary sector can be explained by the decline in
the agricultural sector, which dropped from 43.0 percent to 20.3
percent of the economically active population (Venezuela, Ministerio de Fomento 1971).

The statistics tell us that a dramatic change has occurred in
the structure of the Venezuelan population; one aspect of that
change is discussed in the next section. Statistics also indicate
the skewed structure of Venezuela's economy—the overwhelming weight of petroleum in the primary sector and of government services and commerce in the tertiary sector. They can
only hint, however, at the quality of life that allows Darcy
Ribeiro to write of "the 'Puerto-Ricanization' of Venezuela"
1972: 288). He refers in part to the historical importance of the

petroleum companies and in part to the increased importance of multinationals in Venezuelan industry and commerce since 1959. He refers as well to a cultural transformation that—especially in urban areas such as Caracas and Maracaibo—affects language, dress, social relations, art, cinema, and other cultural manifestations.

The sketch of economic evolution in this century and of macrolevel statistics also does not indicate the struggles that have been waged around the petroleum sector. Efforts to "sow the petroleum" in the 1940s, increased royalties assessed by the state, import substitution and industrialization in the 1960s and 1970s and, finally, the nationalization of the petroleum companies in 1976 are associated with a series of political movements that are best assessed in our discussion of dictatorship and democracy. These struggles give social content to images of backwardness and development. Venezuela has been defined as a petroleum economy for most of this century. In the selling of Venezuela's patrimony, in the dominance of multinationals, in the cultural influence of New York, Miami, or Paris, the petroleum sector stands for Venezuela's backwardness. In the early labor struggles in the petroleum camps, in the attempts to redefine the relationship between the state and the corporations, in the nationalization of iron and petroleum, in the attempt to promote industrial development, and in the attempt to create and maintain democracy, the petroleum sector is made to stand for the possibility of Venezuela's development. With petroleum embodying both development and backwardness, coffee and the agricultural past occupy an ambiguous position. They are relegated to a relatively ahistorical tradition, largely devoid of social content and the positive and negative valuations that are placed on petroleum. This allows for rather contradictory attitudes toward the countryside.

COUNTRY AND CITY

There is perhaps no more visible marker of Venezuela's transformation than urbanization. In 1936, 35 percent of all Venezuelans lived in urban areas; by 1971, the figure was 77 percent. Much of the urban concentration has been in Caracas, but the phenomenon is not limited to the capital. Even the Andean states, once predominantly rural and one of many sources of migrants for Caracas and other urban centers, have become primarily urban. Although the Andean states have been major sources of migrants, they are not the only sources. Migrants to the city come from various regions and a variety of rural experiences. One factor in the urbanization process has been the stagnation of the rural sector, of which the coffee economy is only the most visible example. Another factor concerns the transformation of Venezuela's political economy and the expansion of government services and commerce mentioned earlier.

People who move from rural areas to the city may move into these growing spheres. This is less true for peasants and their sons and daughters than it is for the sons and daughters of the middle class from towns and cities in the interior. Such opportunities are not, however, entirely closed to the peasant. The first urban experience for such a person may be living with a relative in a provincial center while attending secondary school. This can open doors in the educational establishment or for low-level positions elsewhere in the bureaucracy, as a person with a high school degree and modest political connections can become a grade school teacher. For a young daughter, the first urban experience may, however, be living in a provincial center or in Caracas with a family that has hired her as a domestic servant. Or the move for a young man may involve a series of stays with relatives and searches for work during the agricultural dead season. He may eventually stay in the city. The work he finds, if he finds it, probably will not be in industry. It may be in commerce; it may be in petty trades servicing the growing urban population of unemployed; it may be a series of short jobs in construction, commerce, and petty trades. This last group makes up the "other" category that so confuses the census takers. A growing literature on these migrants in other parts of Latin America tells us that their "marginality" is a myth (e.g., Perlman 1976; Lomnitz 1977). This is particularly clear as we pay more attention to the petty trades that elude macrolevel statistics. Just as we cannot glibly label them "marginal," however, we also cannot subsume them within a "proletariat" in the sense of a working population integrated within an industrial economy. The move from country to city is not, in most cases, a move from peasant to proletarian but from peasant to "other." The industrial sector is too constricted to absorb the working population, and the portion of the population it absorbs is not, again for the most part, right off the farm.

Physical evidence of unemployment and underemployment of migrants can be found in the *ranchos* or slums that climb the hillsides and cling to the walls of riverbeds in towns of modest size and in major cities. The existence of the ranchos is not to be understood solely in terms of the economic condition of their residents. Some have a rather long history. With time, the cardboard houses give way to concrete tiles and zinc roofs; with time, water and electrical services, as well as public health and educational facilities, may be introduced. (Or the rancho may disappear in a landslide. Or it may be displaced by a government-sponsored housing project that rancho dwellers cannot afford to live in.) In addition to offering evidence of unemployment and underemployment, then, the rancho is also indicative of disordered urban growth. More migrants arrive than a city can absorb, and they find a place by creating one. City services follow at a slower pace and are constantly stretched beyond their capacity.

Even so, no discussion of a city like Caracas is adequate unless one mentions that it is an exciting place. This is obviously true for those who can afford to enjoy its restaurants and clubs, who can buy the latest New York or Paris fashions, or who can while away an afternoon discussing Marxism at a sidewalk *cafetín* — but these people and their historical memories are not central to our analysis. The city can also be an exciting place for those whose possibilities are more limited. Even if urban employment is limited, there is always a chance one will get a job. That chance may not exist in a stagnating countryside. Moreover, the petty trades can offer some opportunity for modest wealth. The city also offers other opportunities. For example, a young woman may find schooling in a place like Barquisimeto or

Caracas a necessary step in liberating herself from her family of orientation without getting married.

This brief discussion has indicated something of the contradictory images presented by notions of country and city. In the section on coffee and petroleum, I indicated that the image of the peasant and countryside emerging from the coffee economy is that of a disordered past, but the migrant moves from a disordered countryside to a disordered city. The city that presents itself as a symbol of modern Venezuela also creates its critical opposite: the pastoral countryside. Coffee, the countryside, and the peasant, which serve as symbols of an agricultural past, are also countersymbols to the present. They evoke a half-remembered prepetroleum, preurban, premodern Venezuela. This symbol is less effective for the recent migrant for whom the backwardness of the countryside is part of his or her lived experience. For someone born in the city, perhaps with parents who grew up in the countryside, or for someone who has lived in the city for a number of years, however, the country may be given a positive valuation. The countryside is able to carry this weight because, as noted previously, petroleum and the city that is a product of the petroleum economy simultaneously symbolize backwardness and development. The countryside, purged of its own history, comes to represent the true Venezuela.

This is evident in Venezuelan popular music. Protest music seldom celebrates the city. When it refers to the city at all, it is to the ranchos, the "houses of cardboard." The city is an object of protest along with imperialism, the petroleum economy in general, the state, and similar institutions. The countryside, however, has numerous referents. It too may be the object of protest, as songs call attention to the exploited position of the peasant, in the past and in the present, but it can also serve as a counterpoint to the present with the evocation of the simplicity of peasant life, the positive virtues of agricultural labor, and the daily life and interactions of the rural family. In addition to protest music, the production of folklore as an industrial commodity recalls the rural past as well. Recent folk music may nostalgically recall the "streets of my childhood." More importantly, traditional themes of folk music—love, nature, and the family—are placed in a rural setting and are presented in distinctive regional styles, such as the *tonada* (tone poem) of the llanos and the waltz of the Andes. On record albums or on television programs they celebrate a past when the regions mattered. In one sense, disordered urbanization creates an image of a homogenized countryside stripped of history and regional differentiation. In another sense, especially in popular music, regional affiliations are reasserted as differences in style and temperament.

I do not mean to enter into an extended discussion of popular music in Venezuela, but simply to indicate that the disordered nature of Venezuelan development, including the urban disorder of a city like Caracas, calls up the image of a Venezuelan past without disorder. This image can gain expression because most urbanites have some connections with the countryside where they or their parents grew up. Kinship ties connect them with rural regions, and they return to their or their parents' childhood home for Christmas or Holy Week. Some provincial towns organize reunions in which former residents are asked to return for a day-long celebration. While there, the urban resident can go to a country house for a *paseo* (picnic), where a *sancocho* (soup) is prepared, much rum is drunk, and the ideal of rural order is confirmed.

DICTATORSHIP AND DEMOCRACY

The final symbolic pair requires that we move in a different direction from that implied by our discussion of country and city. It is an essential direction, however, if we are to tie together the various threads of this discussion. The main lines of twentieth-century Venezuelan political history are fairly well known and can be found in literature widely available in North America.[3] I simply indicate a few key features and draw some conclusions important for our cultural analysis.

Coffee was displaced by petroleum during the dictatorship of Juan Vicente Gómez, who ruled from 1908 to 1935 and who, paradoxically, first came to prominence as a coffee grower in

the Andean state of Táchira. He oversaw the transformation
that removed coffee from its privileged position in the economy. Despite the fact that Andeans held positions of authority
in the army or the administration, the entire period of Andean
rule represents a progressive loss of political and economic
power by Andeans and the coffee economy. The transformation, and the emergent middle class that accompanied it, created an incipient democratic movement. Its first expression was
in student protests at the Central University, the most famous of
which occurred in 1928 and was led by men who later founded
the social democratic party Acción Democrática (AD), which later became the dominant political party. A series of political
parties emerged after Gómez's death, although political power
continued until 1945 to rest with Andeans who granted more
democratic freedoms than did Gómez. Acción Democrática
came to power in a coup that members continue to refer to as
the Revolution of '45. The party then organized the first Venezuelan presidential election based on universal suffrage, from
which the novelist Rómulo Gallegos emerged victorious. His
administration was overthrown by a military coup in 1948,
shortly after a number of progressive measures were passed—
among them a series of agrarian reform laws and a law requir-
ing the petroleum companies to pay 50 percent royalties. Pérez
Jiménez eventually became the strong man of the junta until
massive demonstrations in 1958 forced him to flee and ushered
in a democratic period that has lasted until the present.

Acción Democrática has dominated this period, although the
two major parties—AD and the Christian Democratic COPEI (Committee for Political Organization and Independent Elections)—
exchanged positions every five years in the general elections
from 1968 to 1988. When AD came to power in 1959, many in its
top leadership maintained their commitment to democracy, but
they had abandoned the radical perspectives of their youth.
Rómulo Betancourt and his followers defined their project in
nationalist terms. They would exact ever greater royalties from
the petroleum companies—from 60 percent to 80 percent
during the 1960s—and would assume control of the petroleum
sector by a series of steps that would culminate in 1976 with

nationalization. They would initiate and participate in the formation of OPEC. They would institute import-substitution policies to stimulate industrialization. Diversification—"sowing the petroleum"—had been a concern of AD since the mid-1940s, but diversification and industrialization did not exclude participation by multinationals. The direction of new foreign investment changed dramatically from petroleum and iron extraction to industry and commerce after 1959. Acción Democrática welcomed foreign investment as part of its attempt to alter the course of Venezuelan development.

A number of participants in Acción Democrática, as well as members of other parties including the Communist party, were disillusioned with AD's project and initiated a guerrilla movement in the countryside during the 1960s. The movement never attracted as much support as guerrilla leaders had hoped. One reason was that the movement romanticized and attempted to organize the peasantry during a decade when it was disappearing. By the end of the 1960s, the economically active population engaged in agriculture was only 20 percent of all Venezuelans. More importantly, however, many peasants were sympathetic to AD. This brings us to a point crucial to understanding Venezuelan culture and politics. The initial strength of AD was in popular organizations of peasants, workers, and others without representation in a backward, dictatorial Venezuela. There were two aspects to this. The party owed its existence and support to such organizations, and peasants and workers were first organized and first acted politically through Acción Democrática. These bases of support were not ignored by AD, even if they were not always well served. One of the first measures passed when AD came to power in 1959 was an agrarian reform law—weak, but nonetheless an apparent reform.

There is in the formation of Acción Democrática and the political history of which it is a part an aspect that too often eludes those on the Left who deride Venezuela's democracy. Three movements were symbolically united in AD: development, democracy, and the organization of working people. Acción Democrática gave particular and partial definitions to development and democracy, but it was able to impose those

definitions through its organizations. Images of backwardness
and development in the petroleum economy are associated with
the images of dictatorship and democracy. The backwardness
of the petroleum economy is seen as a legacy of the past, of the
dictators who sold the Venezuelan patrimony and who, as it
happens, were also associated with the coffee economy. The
struggle for development is simultaneously presented as a struggle for democracy.

This symbolic association has exercised enormous power in
the political consciousness of Venezuelan peasants, proletarians, and "others," but there are two sorts of weakness in that
association that require elaboration—the potential failure of
development and the potential failure of democracy. Given the
fact that the democratic period has lasted for three decades,
both sources of weakness have become apparent and have
given greater space to movements of the Left and Right than
existed in the early 1960s. The failure of democracy results in
part from the fact that the political leaders and spokesmen for
AD and other parties often pursue individual aims and individual careers. Parties and factions of parties may pursue their
own projects and candidacies by endlessly debating relatively
trivial matters in congress. There is a tremendous dissipation of
energy in Venezuela's democracy, and during periods of economic crisis, when the country's development seems imperiled,
"democracy" can seem a nonessential luxury. The failure by
leaders pursuing their own goals to attend to the country's "development" calls "democracy" into question and gives organizational space to the Right.

The failure of development results in part from the fact that
multiclass democratic parties like AD are nonetheless pursuing
class projects. Acción Democrática's class project is associated
with an incipient industrial bourgeoisie. The form of development they advocate closely approximates F. H. Cardoso's notion of associated dependent development—linkage between
sectors of local capital, state capital, and multinational capital
in the diversification and industrialization of the Venezuelan
economy (Cardoso 1973a; Cardoso and Faletto 1979). Unlike
other examples of this model, the linkage between develop-

ment and democracy is more than a symbol, and Venezuela has so far escaped the more authoritarian forms of government usually associated with this model. Much of the explanation for this rests with the petroleum sector. As indicated, petroleum wealth has been channeled by the state into the tertiary sector, and part of that expansion has been an expansion of social services, subsidies for agricultural producers, marketing organizations, and housing projects. The democrats therefore are simultaneously able to promote dependent development and to incorporate significant segments of the Venezuelan population into the state through social services. However, as the attempt to promote basic industry has in recent years encountered declining petroleum revenues, the state has diverted funds from social services. The results for the fortunes of the two major parties of this diversion are not clear. A class project may no longer be coterminous with a democratic project. The old linkage between democracy and development is therefore imperiled, giving organizational space to both the Left and Right.

Can we put these shifting and contradictory images of Venezuela's past, present, and future into a coherent picture? To address this question, I turn to the cultural analysis suggested by Raymond Williams in *Marxism and Literature* (1977: 108–127, et passim). Unlike much recent anthropology, Williams's notion of culture cannot be separated from political economy. As indicated in Chapters 1 and 2, Williams points to the construction of a "dominant culture" that is not a coherent integrated cultural system or structure but a rather inchoate set of lived experiences, feelings, and relationships within a political and economic order of domination. Because it is not a closed system, it is in a constant process of construction and reconstruction. Although many elements could be considered constitutive of a dominant culture, one that Williams points to is of particular relevance to the moral economy literature: tradition as a *selective* tradition—a version (indeed, the ruling version) of a people's history (see Chapters 1 and 2). Tradition as selective tradition is important when we consider one of Williams's central points about dominant culture—that no order of domination is total. There are always sets of relationships and experiences that are excluded and that may serve as points around which alternative, perhaps oppositional, cultural forms can emerge. With the creation of an alternative culture, a basic element must be an alternative tradition—a reinterpretation and rewriting of history, concentrating on events and relationships excluded from the ruling version and pointing to a different set of historical possibilities.

Williams is clearly suggesting a cultural analysis that goes beyond approaches to culture as symbolic systems or shared values or meanings. He has tied his notion of culture to a historical process and to class structures and relationships. Nevertheless, there is no sense in which dominant and emergent culture are coterminous with particular class positions. The images of Venezuela's tradition that have been discussed in this essay are not class specific. A class culture or class discourse is never given; it must be constructed from the cultural raw material presented by history, from the "tradition" that is used to construct both dominant and emergent forms of culture. It is in this sense that I refer in the title of this essay to the consciousness of a proletariat. I can, by analysis of Venezuela's history, indicate the kinds of images that have been used to create a hegemonic order or dominant culture. I can also indicate the kinds of images that are available for a counterhegemony. In both cases, cultural creation and the formation of consciousness are political processes. An emergent culture must be created by using elements of past and present that have been excluded in the dominant culture or by giving new meanings to elements that have not been excluded.

Thus the first point to be made about the dominant culture in Venezuela is that it is political. The linkage between development and democracy created by Acción Democrática is so profound that it sets the terms for all political debate. The principal opposition party, COPEI, accepts the linkage and contests particular policies. Most socialist parties also accept the linkage but argue that the dominant parties are not *really* democratic or that their form of development is not *really* development. To a certain extent, this linkage and associated aspects of dominant culture are consciously promoted and can be seen as constitutive of a ruling ideology. Professors of history sympathetic to AD write histories of Venezuela showing a movement from degradation to democracy and from backwardness to development. All history is a movement toward the progress enjoyed in the present. There is also a constant manipulation of emotions in the use of television, public rallies, and state occasions. For example, the contradictory images of the peasant and the countryside—images that stress an exploited past or that stress pastoral calm and independence—can be expressed simultaneously and played against each other. Official celebrations of the anniversary of the agrarian reform law romanticize the Venezuelan peasant even as they emphasize the exploitative "past." The dominant culture cannot, however, simply be dismissed as conscious manipulation or ruling-class ideology. When these histories are written, or when the past is unfavorably compared with the present, the ideologues are touching on one aspect of the lived experiences of peasants and proletarians. The move from country to city, from peasant to proletarian or "other," or from backwardness to development can be experienced as progress.[4]

Given the contradictory nature of Venezuela's development, the dominant culture can only touch on one aspect of that experience. It can point to Venezuela's progress; it cannot point to all that is troubling and contradictory in that disordered progress. To what extent does the past provide raw material for an emergent culture, a moral economy of protest? The past is certainly available, most obviously in the everyday comparison of present basic food and grain prices with those in effect of generation, a year, or even a month ago. By examining the symbols of coffee and petroleum, backwardness and development, country and city, I have traced the emergence of an image of an ordered rural past that serves as critical counterpoint to the disordered present. Can this image serve as the basis for an alternative emergent tradition? I think not. It represents not historical memory, but historical nostalgia. It has no connection

with the lived experience of most peasants or even most proletarians. It simply calls up an idealized past, and as an ideal it can
support the present order or, in the event of the failure of
Venezuela's models of development and democracy, a fascist
turn. Here it is interesting to note that most socialist historians
do not fundamentally differ from AD historians on large segments of Venezuela's past. Both stress the dependence and backwardness of the early petroleum economy. They differ on their
interpretations of the present and on some of the labels they
give to past and present. They differ, in short, in their valuations of Venezuelan forms of development and democracy.[5]

The construction of an emergent culture that can serve a
proletarian consciousness, then, cannot turn to an idealized
past but must begin with the lived experience of Venezuelan
proletarians. The starting point is the very linkage that proved
so powerful for the dominant culture—development and democracy. It must recognize and celebrate those aspects of progress in Venezuela's twentieth century that represent historic
gains: the emergence of forms of organization of popular
masses, the struggle to gain control over petroleum resources
and to turn the wealth created by the petroleum sector toward
national development, and the struggle for democracy. Because
these achievements have been progressive and because historically they are associated with Acción Democrática, they have
served as constitutive elements of the dominant culture, but the
contradictions inherent in the dominant parties' approach to
development mean that these same achievements can be turned
into constitutive elements of an emergent political culture. Development and democracy may still serve as the basis for
working-class consciousness, but the terms may be given fuller,
more critical, more demanding meanings. Workers may demand forms of organization they control, forms of development that exclude multinationals, forms of democracy that give
them greater control over their own destiny.

The moral economists argue that a first-generation proletarian or a peasantry first confronted with capitalist development
looks backward for its forms of response at the same time that it
looks forward. This is true in Venezuela; a less anthropologi-

cally inclined writer might argue that it is universally true. When Venezuelan peasants and proletarians look back, however, their view is not clear. Venezuelan peasants and proletarians are confronted with a disordered past that has given way to a disordered present. Their political and cultural task is to take aspects of the past and of the present that have offered promise and turn them into demands for the future.

Americanization in the Americas

It is understandable that the rational talents on this side of the world, exalted in the contemplation of their own cultures, should have found themselves without a valid means to interpret us. It is only natural that they insist on measuring us with the yardstick that they use for themselves, forgetting that the ravages of life are not the same for all, and that the quest of our own identity is just as arduous and bloody for us as it was for them. The interpretation of our reality through patterns not our own serves only to make us ever more unknown, ever less free, ever more solitary.

             Gabriel García Márquez, Nobel Prize Acceptance Speech, 1982

Writing a survey of the Americas in the 1960s, Darcy Ribeiro, in an essay on Venezuela, foresaw the possibility of "the 'Puerto-Ricanization' of Venezuela" (1972: 288). He did not say what he had in mind: his survey had little to say about Puerto Rico, and the phrase simply appeared without elaboration in a discussion of the political options facing Venezuelan elites. The attempt to preserve their own positions would lead to greater dependence, restriction of population growth, and, at the extreme, Puerto-Ricanization. Even in the absence of elaboration, however, the phrase produces strong images of economic and political dependence and cultural debasement: multinationals stripping the environment and exploiting cheap labor, beach resorts and casinos catering to North American tourists, shopping malls on the North American model, language that mixes English and Spanish, politics based on the U.S. party system and dependent on decisions made in Washington. In short, the phrase "Puerto-Ricanization" calls up a "first time tragedy, second time farce"[1] vision; we know what Ribeiro is talking about.

When we hear the word "Americanization," a similar set of images comes to mind. We think of office buildings for local outlets of multinationals, of McDonalds and Kentucky Fried Chicken, of shopping malls filled with products carrying labels from U.S. corporations even though they are *hecho en México*, of Exxon and Coca-Cola signs, of television stations carrying Spanish-language versions of "Dallas" or "Dynasty," of mass-market magazines carrying translations of articles from *People*, of stores selling plastic pumpkins and Halloween costumes and children going door to door saying, "Trick or treat, trick or treat, ¿tiene dulces para mí?" We think of debasement, of homogenization, of domination, of "the material apparatus of perfected civilization which obliterates the individuality of old towns under the stereotyped conveniences of modern life" (Conrad 1960 [1904]: 89). We are right, of course: the examples offered above could be elaborated at considerable length. But we are also wrong, and the burden of this essay is to explore both the accuracy and inaccuracy of such perceptions.

When I was first asked to address the topic of Americanization for a group of historians who did not specialize in Latin America,[2] I had the reaction most anthropologists would have: an automatic, almost instinctive, revulsion. We are accustomed to dealing with local populations, studying their histories, their forms of social organization, forms of adaptation and resistance, ritual practices, myths, beliefs, values—in short, their cultures. And we find the very notion of Americanization and the image of homogenization and debasement that it conjures up to be a form of ethnocentrism. We nod in assent to García Márquez's plea for a recognition of Latin America's "out-sized reality" (1983). But our automatic, almost instinctive, response cannot take the simple and naive form of a celebration of "our" people and "their" own history. (Indeed, the possessive

adjectives themselves indicate part of the problem.) Part of
Latin America's out-sized reality is a multistranded encounter,
stretching across nearly five hundred years, with Western powers, the most important of which, since the early twentieth
century, has been the United States.

An anthropologist interested in Latin America should have
something to say about Americanization, then. He or she
should be able to reject the homogenizing stereotype without
retreating into the equally stereotypic comfort of the distinctive-
ness of his or her "own people." To think carefully about Americanization, then, is to explore our ideas about history, culture,
power, America, and the Americas. What follows is not a history
of Americanization in the Americas. Instead, I want to suggest
ways in which we might think about processes such as Americanization, and the understandings of culture, history, and politics that are necessarily involved.

———

We might begin by returning to Darcy Ribeiro's phrase and
suggesting that his choice of "Puerto-Ricanization" rather than
the equally available "Americanization" is instructive. Let us
first admit that as an author Ribeiro simply chose the phrase
because it was effective, because it could produce a sharp and
shocking set of images. A critical consideration of the concept
of Americanization was not his object. But Ribeiro has something to tell us nonetheless.

First, although a North American might have looked at Venezuela in the 1960s and spoken of Americanization, a Brazilian
sociologist chose another term. Both would be trying to understand the impact of a powerful economic, political, and cultural
force on Venezuela, but where Americanization might imply a
kind of uniformity of experience and incorporation, Puerto-
Ricanization implies diversity. The phrase reminds us that we
are dealing with plural experiences, the Americas, not simply
(though importantly) in the sense that the United States is not
the only "American" country but also in the sense that there are
many Latin American countries with a variety of experiences of
dependence and incorporation. Ribeiro could look critically at

the experience of his own country and of Venezuela, and he explored U.S. domination in each case. He was writing a few years after a military coup that had been backed by the U.S. government in Brazil, and his account of Venezuela emphasized the domination of the Venezuelan economy by primarily North American petroleum companies. But whatever had happened in those countries, they had not yet approached the extreme of Puerto Rico. They were not colonies. Implicit in Ribeiro's phrase is the idea of a range of experiences of North American domination.

There are other lessons to be drawn from the shift in perspective provided by a view from Brazil. While an emphasis on Americanization might begin with processes emanating from a powerful center and expanding outward, and emphasis on Puerto-Ricanization begins with a specific dependent entity, explores the forces of domination coming from a powerful center, put places those forces in the context of specific local forces and experiences. Indeed, this was the intent of Ribeiro's book. Another Brazilian sociologist, Fernando Henrique Cardoso, has made a similar criticism of some North American approaches to imperialism and dependency in Latin America. Calling for an approach to economic and political dependence that would concentrate on specific cases and situations, he criticized the tendency among North American scholars to concentrate solely on North American forces and ignore specific Latin American responses and accommodations. He concluded:

> In the process of disseminating these studies in the U.S., however, the characterization of dependency acquired local color. There was a preoccupation with the denunciation of forms of "foreign aid"—the intervention of the CIA in foreign policy, the invisible and Machiavellian hand of the multinationals, etc.—a politically legitimate preoccupation that emphasized real aspects of the contemporary historical process. Little by little, however, this ended by reestablishing the priority of the *external* over the internal (which may be well-founded), and it led in the end to the elimination of the dynamic proper to dependent societies as a relevant explanatory factor (which is not acceptable). Once again, in metaphysical fashion, the two terms of the

> opposition—external and internal—were separated, and the
> opposition passed from dialectical to structural-mechanical,
> when it was not conceived of in terms of antecedent causes and
> inert consequences. (1977a: 14)

This problem in studies of political and economic dependence has its analogue in cultural theory. Beginning in the 1930s, studies of "acculturation" began to appear in American anthropology, gaining popularity in the forties, fifties and sixties before dropping out of fashion.[3] As the studies began to appear, they addressed certain perceived problems in anthropological studies concerning history, social and cultural change, and the impact of the Western world on anthropological subjects. Before acculturation studies became fashionable, anthropologists seldom attempted to place the people they studied in a contemporary context. They were "historical" in that they attempted to recover and recapture values, practices, and traditions of American Indians from the eighteenth and nineteenth centuries, but history stopped with conquest and the move to reservations. Indeed, fieldworkers might do their research in reservation settings without ever mentioning the reservation context in their published reports.

Acculturation studies were attempts to bring such populations into the present, to explore the settings in which they lived and the impact of those settings on their cultural practices and beliefs. Although early attempts met with resistance from an anthropological establishment—the *American Anthropologist* even declined to publish acculturation studies for a period in the 1930s because they went too far beyond traditional anthropological concerns—they were to go through a prodigious development, with theoretical elaboration (Redfield, Linton, Herskovitz 1936; SSRC Summer Seminar in Acculturation 1954) and empirical investigation.

In the theoretical statements on acculturation, the common assumption was that two "autonomous" cultures entered into contact. Anthropologists could think through the logical possibilities: they could envision different sorts of contact situation, situations of relative equality or relative inequality, and they could outline different outcomes—diffusion, cultural creativity, cultural disintegration, and "reactive adaptation" (i.e., rejection) (SSRC 1954). With regard to disintegration, the anthropologists' language might be full of references to "forced" change, "coercion," loss of "political freedom," and so on (ibid.: 986). But the two autonomous cultures were still referred to as "donor" and "receptor," analysis of colonialism and imperialism was avoided, and the *concept* of power was absent.

But most of the situations anthropologists were familiar with were those in which the donor was much more powerful than the receptor, in which the contact situation was one that produced a variety of forced and unforced economic, political, and social changes, and one in which the receptor might be expected in time to look a lot more like the donor. This became a problem even as anthropologists became much more willing to talk about colonialism and power, with effects that carried beyond the acculturation literature to the modernization literature of the fifties and sixties and even to the radical critiques of the sixties and seventies. At the heart of the approach was a problematic set of understandings of history, culture, and power that led to a linear understanding of cultural change.

The historical problem begins with the assumption of two "autonomous" cultures that are placed in contact. Eric Wolf (1982) suggests that anthropologists treated such cultures in contact as if they were billiard balls striking each other on a billiard table. One could then postulate a precontact base-line period or culture (a postulation that was quite popular in both the acculturation and modernization literatures) and analyze the effects produced by contact with another autonomus culture, effects that might be labeled acculturation, Westernization, modernization, Hispanicization, or whatever. For the present, it does not matter whether the analysis crudely lists and counts Western and non-Western traits or pursues a more sophisticated exploration of cultural webs of meaning. Nor does it matter whether the writer is willing to write about power, force, and colonialism. The more important problem is the denial of history to at least one of the cultures. What acculturationists called the donor culture—the colonial power or dominant center—might be seen to have a history, and we might be able to talk with some sophistication about the emergence of capitalism or the particular stage of capitalist development at which the center in question—the United States or England or Spain—began to enter a particular arena. But we might have much less to say about the so-called receptor. There we were more likely to postulate a historical base line. Yet this ignored the significant fact that the supposedly autonomous receptor cultures rarely existed in isolation, that they entered into multiple relations with other societies, that those relations might involve exchange and trade networks of some scope, that those trade networks might be implicated in the formation of regional and social inequalities or in processes of state formation, and that those trade networks might even involve a set of relations with the Western world. In short, the autonomous receptors had histories. The contact situation did not involve the establishment of a base line between two autonomus cultures but the intersection of at least two—and often more—historical processes, each of which was developing in contradictory and uneven fashion, each of which involved different and evolving forms, uses, and conceptions of social space and time, different and evolving modes of work and appropriation.

This has implications for our understanding of culture. Just as the historical assumptions of the acculturationists and their successors were overly simple and linear, their concept of culture was reified. Cultures were donors and receptors, "they" gave or received, adapted, responded, or disintegrated. Central to this reification was a sometimes implicit assumption of homogeneity. I stress the implicitness of the assumption because many contributors to the literature worked with concepts of pluralism and subcultural diversity. Unfortunately, such concepts seldom affected the way the authors conceived the contact situation itself. Indeed, pluralism was often seen to be an outcome of contact. But if we have a model that sees the intersection of two or more historical currents, each involving differential and changing occupation and use of space and time, then the cultural webs of meaning are also differential and changing. It becomes difficult to outline the "Hispanic" or "American" toward which a group or sector is Hispanicizing or Americanizing, and it becomes equally difficult to outline what is Mayan or Quechuan or, for more recent history, Mexican or Peruvian. In each case, images come to mind, and we think we know what we are talking about, just as clear images came to mind when we first used words like "Americanization" or "Puerto-Ricanization." But confidence fades when we begin to place cultures in time and space. If whole cultures do not enter into contact, the interaction involves individuals, groups, institutions, representatives of institutions, corporations, representatives of corporations, products such as books, movies, television programs consumed by individuals, and so on. Each of these people, institutions, and products is the bearer not of a whole culture or even of a "subculture" but of particular cultural traditions or emergent formations. The people may be Peace Corps volunteers or tourists (from rich and brash to poor, young [and brash], including Canadians, English, French, and German, all of whom will be labeled American) or anthropologists or retired couples or expatriates. The institutions will include Venezuelan-American Friendship Associations, protestant churches, and Disney World in Florida. The products will include movies such as *Rambo* or *One Flew Over the Cuckoo's Nest*, or books such as *Hollywood Wives* and *The Grapes of Wrath*. The encounter, then, is between two different but overlapping sets of cultural traditions and formations.

This brings us to power. To analyze cultural meanings in terms of power means that we cannot remove our discussion of cultural contacts and processes from a discussion of colonialism and imperialism. Our sense of Puerto-Ricanization cannot ignore Puerto Rico's colonial status. Nor can we ignore, if our concern is Americanization, the role of multinationals or of State Department Cultural Offices or of official programs such as the recent "Project Democracy." But we must also look beyond the obvious forms of economic and political power and examine the role of power in cultural production in other arenas as well. "To resort to the concept of cultural hegemony," Jackson Lears notes,

is to take a banal question—"who has power?"—and deepen
it at both ends. The "who" includes parents, preachers, teachers, journalists, literati, "experts" of all sorts, as well as advertising executives, entertainment promoters, popular musicians,
sports figures, and "celebrities"—all of whom are involved (al-
beit often unwittingly) in shaping the values and attitudes of a
society. The "power" includes cultural as well as economic and
political power—the power to help define the boundaries of
common-sense "reality" either by ignoring views outside those
boundaries or by labeling deviant opinions "tasteless" or "irre-
sponsible." (1985: 572)

Yet the concept of hegemony also carries with it a strong
sense of contradiction and tension, as we have seen in earlier
chapters. Relations of political and economic domination are
seen as contradictory and incapable of determining or encom-
passing all social life and activity; dominant culture based on
produced and disseminated shared values enters at several
points into problematic connection with a variety of individual
and group experiences that do not connect with dominant
meanings (see Gramsci 1971 [1929–35]; Williams 1977; Lears
1985).

When we connect the three dimensions—intersecting histories characterized by differentiation, heterogeneous cultural
relations and values, and relations of power that encompass
contradictions and tensions—we approach a more fruitful and
challenging set of understandings. As was evident in my earlier reference to anthropological instincts, our more automatic
and unreflective ways of thinking about the conjunction of
local and global historical processes are inadequate. We commonly refer to "internal" and "external" factors as if they
could be easily distinguished and identified. It is then simple
enough to criticize some anthropologists for "ignoring the importance of external factors" or world-system theorists for "ignoring internal factors." But the very terms of critique place
us back on the billiard table. The more important challenge is
to grasp, through a variety of historical processes, the "internalization of the external" (Cardoso 1977a: 13; see also Cardoso

and Faletto 1979: xvi). Cardoso and Falleto elaborate on such internalization as follows:

> The expansion of capitalism in Bolivia and Venezuela, in Mexico or Peru, in Brazil and Argentina, in spite of having been submitted to the same global dynamic of international capitalism, did not have the same history or consequences. The differences are rooted not only in the diversity of natural resources, nor just in the different periods in which these economies have been incorporated into the international system (although these factors have played some role). Their explanation must lie in the different moments at which sectors of local classes allied or clashed with foreign interests, organized different forms of state, sustained distinct ideologies, or tried to implement various policies or defined alternative strategies to cope with imperialist challenges in diverse moments of history. (1979: xvii)

Yet the problem can be extended more radically, for such differential encounters do not simply involve the encounter with capitalism but earlier relations with expanding mercantile empires and with Spain and Portugal. For example, when a petroleum company sets up shop in Maracaibo during the second decade of the twentieth century, this "external" force is encountering an "internal" force that already contains within it a particular sedimentation of prior encounters with the Western world—in this case, a group of German and English merchants operating import-export houses and running a thriving coffee trade buying up coffee from the Venezuelan and Colombian Andes. The fathers and grandfathers of these merchants, in turn, had encountered a local society just emerging from a colonial relationship with Spain. And so on. Thus, any moment of encounter between a particular agent of a global economy and a local population, between the "external" and the "internal," will necessarily intertwine with prior and ongoing encounters, each of which will have its own structure, its own "concentration of many determinations, hence unity of the diverse" (Marx 1973 [1857–58]: 101), its own internalization of the external.

Thus, if we have a more differentiated understanding of histories, cultures, and powers, we can analyze both the imposition of powerful economic, political, and cultural forces and the contradictory nature of such impositions. The lack of success of such forces (or, more properly, their success in some places and times and their lack of success in other places and times) would not be due necessarily or solely to the resilience of local populations or to the cultural resistance of precapitalist traditions and values (although both of these may sometimes be powerfully operative), but to the fact that one set of powers, containing and generating its own contradictions, is being imposed upon another set of powers, containing and generating its own contradictions, producing a variety of unintended consequences. And each of these sets of powers, forces, and contradictions will represent the sedimentation of particular historical moments and encounters.

A significant task for the person trying to understand such processes will be the attempt to map these powers, contradictions, and consequences in space and time. In this sense, an exploration of Americanization in the Americas provides an especially interesting challenge. In the first place, if what we have said about the specificity of historical experience has any validity, an adequate study could not deal with Latin America as a whole but rather with a particular country. And in the consideration of any country's experience of Americanization, we must recognize the intersection of two states, with two structures of political, economic, and cultural domination, each of which has its own set of histories. The encounter, or unfolding set of encounters, comes at particular moments in those histories, each of which must be understood. We can analyze the forces producing domination by exploring the social, economic, and political forces producing the encounters. What are the interests and motivations of the companies investing in this particular activity in this particular country at this particular time? What are the interests and motivations of state officials granting concessions to multinationals in that particular area? What are the interests and motivations of individual entrepreneurs entering into limited partnerships with multinationals for the establishment of enterprises in Mexico or Venezuela or Brazil? We can understand something of the unintended consequences and contradictions of such encounters by exploring the different sets of interests, but also by tracing the rather different histories into which such interests are inserted.

Our interpretation of Americanization, then, cannot begin with the first indication of North American influence. We must push our analyses back in time and examine the historical currents into which a variety of North American forces have been inserted. This means that any project studying Americanization is undertaking an enormously complex problem and that it will have to analyze a rich variety of subjects before it even gets to the Spanish-American War. But I know of no other way to avoid a billiard-ball approach.

Given what has been said, an analysis of Americanization would have to combine a history of the United States with histories of various Latin American countries. Such would be the task of many books, combining local histories with global perspective. What follows is a more modest effort to point to four moments within the ongoing, centuries-long process of the internalization of the external in Latin America: the conquest and establishment of colonial institutions, the process of state and nation building after independence in the nineteenth century, the period of outward expansion in the late nineteenth and early twentieth centuries, and the experience of the American century from the 1930s to the present. The argument is necessarily at a very general level and cannot possibly satisfy any specialist in the region. To sketch the map of powers, contradictions, and consequences for any one of these "moments" would be a major task. My purpose here is not to undertake such a task but to give it a certain shape, to sketch a context for the more detailed study of particular conjunctions of local and global histories. It is an invitation to an anthropological and historical examination of a variety of internalizations, one that would take our understanding of problems like Americanization off the billiard table.

To begin with, we state the obvious and elaborate upon it. Latin American nations had prior experiences with colonialism and imperialism before the United States began to exercise hegemony in the region. If we are interested in processes of "-ization," the peoples of Latin America had experienced processes of Hispanicization and Westernization, and even a bit of modernization of various sorts. Some of these processes overlapped with the kinds of processes we might associate with Americanization; others differed.

Spain encountered various sorts of societies in the New World of the sixteenth century. In Mesoamerica and the Central Andes, Spaniards found densely populated state societies with richly elaborated civilizations. On the margins of these civilizations and throughout much of the tropical lowlands and coasts, they found less densely populated but settled horticultural groups with emergent social and political hierarchies but without states. And in the extensive plains of the southern cone and of northern Mexico, they found nomadic hunting and gathering populations. These differences affected the nature and progress of conquest and continue to affect the nature of populations and social integration to this day. The states of Mesoamerica and the Central Andes were most quickly subdued. Upon conquest, Spanish entrepreneurs were able to incorporate preexisting forms of tribute and domination. Less densely settled and less hierarchical populations were not so easily conquered. Here the conquest was protracted, extending into the eighteenth century. Indeed, some areas (such as the Atlantic coast of Central America and vast stretches of the South American lowlands) never came under Spanish or Portuguese control during the colonial centuries. Where fringe areas were subdued and incorporated into the Empire, however, they often suffered more, and more radical, changes. Thus the areas where indigenous populations are concentrated today, and the areas that may seem most marginal to "Western" influence, are in parts of Mesoamerica and the Central Andes.[4]

This was partly due as well to the pattern of Spanish settlement and exploitation, which did not neatly overlay indigenous settlement and exploitation. For example, while indigenous populations were most densely settled in southern and central Mexico, Spaniards settled in central and northern Mexico, where their mining and hacienda complexes were concentrated. In Peru, Spaniards exploited the Andean mines at Potosi, but most of the population settled on the coast, the administrative and export center.

This is not to suggest that few changes occurred in those areas of indigenous concentration. Few have not heard of the extraordinary demographic collapse of the sixteenth and seventeenth centuries, the extent of which is debated by historians but the fact of which is beyond dispute. In addition, Spaniards were interested in collecting tribute and labor and introduced a variety of institutions to do so. The indigenous community, or *república de indios,* became a key colonial and indigenous institution. At once the mechanism for colonial exploitation and colonial protection, the community took on a corporate character, with certain obligations (taxes and tithes) and certain rights (to land) recognized by the Crown.[5]

Furthermore, indigenous populations were subject to missionization. Of the *intentions* of the missionaries, Nancy Farriss has commented:

> What distinguished Spain from other colonial powers was the concerted effort to impose their culture on their colonial subjects by force: to transform the Indians into shorter, darker versions of Spaniards. . . .
>
> The Spanish missionaries in the New World thought it not only necessary but possible . . . to transform the Indians into replicas of Spaniards—Spanish peasants, to be more precise, and a highly idealized peasantry at that. . . . For the Spanish clergy in America, the pursuit of this ideal was no more than a corollary to their Christian ministry. Any Catholic priest entrusted with the "care of souls" has the duty to keep watch over the faith and morals of those in his charge. The Spanish missionaries, with the full support of the Crown, interpreted this duty broadly as a mandate to supervise every aspect of the Indians' lives from birth to death and to modify them when necessary in accordance with the church's teachings. (1984: 91)

Scholars debate the extent to which such conversions were complete or successful, noting the persistence of a variety of indigenous beliefs and practices or the syncretic combination of indigenous and Christian symbols. Yet there were several areas in which Christianization had profound effects. One among many that could be mentioned was in the organization of family life. In New Spain, for example, missionaries imposed the ideal of the nuclear family, condemning and prohibiting a variety of forms and practices as concubinage, and prohibiting joint family residence as promoting incest. Here they coincided with Crown tribute policies, which imposed a modified head tax. Tribute was collected and paid by communities, but they were assessed on the number of heads of household resident in a community (see Farriss 1984: 165–174 passim; Ricard 1966 [1933]: 96–115 passim; Gibson 1964: 197–204 passim; Barnabas 1984).

By the end of the eighteenth century, Spanish colonialism had only partially occupied and transformed its territories. Core areas included mining and hacienda complexes, administrative centers and ports, and—increasingly, in the eighteenth century in formerly marginal zones such as Venezuela and the Caribbean—plantation zones producing sugar and cacao for export. Spanish settlement had concentrated in those complexes and in highland regions. Vast stretches of land were marginal to Spanish interests and had only been partially incorporated within Spanish spheres of control. Alexander von Humboldt's comment at the turn of the nineteenth century was telling:

> In every part of America, where civilization did not exist to a certain degree before the Conquest (as it did in Mexico, Guatimala [sic], Quito, and Peru), it has advanced from the coasts toward the interior, following sometimes the valley of a great river, sometimes a chain of mountains, that afforded a temperate climate. Concentrated at once in different points, it has spread itself as by diverging rays. The union into provinces and kingdoms was effected at the first immediate contact between civilized parts, or those at least subject to a

permanent and regular sway. Lands deserted, or inhabited by savage nations, now surround the countries, which European civilization has subdued. They divide its conquests like arms of the sea difficult to pass, and neighboring states are often connected with each other only by strips of cultivated land. It is less difficult to acquire a knowledge of the configuration of coasts bathed by the ocean, than of the sinuosities of that interior shore, on which barbarism and civilization, impenetrable forests and cultivated land, touch and bound each other. It is from not having reflected on the early state of society in the New World, that geographers so often disfigure their maps, by tracing the different parts of the Spanish and Portugueze [*sic*] colonies, as if they were contiguous at every point in the interior. (1818, 3: 421–422)

One need not accept his language of civilization and barbarism to recognize that when Humboldt wrote of "that interior shore" he was outlining a problem that all of the newly independent states were to face in the nineteenth century—the problem of occupying and controlling territory, of extending "civilization," and of turning states on a disfigured map into nations.

All of these problems involved struggles between liberals and conservatives, and it was in these nation-building struggles that the United States first entered, as actor and example. Let us first note that liberal/conservative splits pitted two elites against each other, although both could call upon peasants, artisans, and other common people for support. Conservatives wanted to preserve the benefits and protections of Spanish civilization. Such benefits and protections included the central role of the Catholic Church, in addition to the maintenance of corporate rights and privileges (*fueros*) that had been transferred from the Spanish old regime to the New World. Such privileges included the right of the Church to own land and collect tithes without state interference and control, and they included the structurally subordinate position of Indians, owing special taxes but holding the right, as corporate indigenous communities, to own land. Conservatives also wanted to preserve their own privileged position in the old colonial economy. The old activities were to be continued if possible, the commercial relationship with Spain was to be continued if possible, and privileged ports and cities were to retain their privileged position if possible.

Liberals, on the other hand, wanted to open their new nations to wider economic, political, and intellectual currents. They were anticlerical, often anti-Spanish, and opposed to corporate and other forms of privilege. They wanted either to abolish Church landholdings or to treat the Church like any other landholder. They wanted all persons to be equal citizens under the law. Indians should therefore not be subject to degrading special taxes, but neither should they hold land in common. The basis for a good citizenry was individual private property—all property and all persons subject to a common set of laws. Likewise, the old monopolies and privileges attached to administrative and port cities should be abolished. Formerly marginal regions should be allowed free access to world markets; free trade should reign.

The battles between these two sets of elites and their ideas were profoundly implicated in the processes of nation building. They might take the form of centralism (conservatives) versus federalism (liberals), which could results in the disintegration of polities (e.g., Gran Colombia into Venezuela, Colombia, and Ecuador; Central America into five states) or separatist movements in particular regions. They also set in motion a series of social transformations (e.g., indigenous loss of lands) that are beyond the scope of this essay.

It should be evident that many of these ideas had their European and North American antecedents. Certainly their free trade doctrines were profoundly influenced by Manchester liberalism. In addition, Charles Hale (1968) has argued persuasively that the most important influences on Mexican liberalism were French, partly because French revolutionary thinkers were addressing an analogous set of problems. They too were confronting an old regime based on corporate privilege, and they provided powerful arguments against such privileges. The United States could be and was admired and emulated for its War of Independence, and its constitutional structure served as a model for many nineteenth-century Latin American constitutions. But the United States had not had to shake off a feudal legacy. For liberals, the thinkers who gave them the most insight on social questions were French (Hale 1968). This is not to suggest that the liberals' approach to social questions was necessarily thoroughgoing. They were trying to shake free of conservative and corporate restraints; they were not trying to free their own dependents. In this the United States may have served as a model. As Marco Palacios suggests, Latin American liberals admired the United States model because in the United States the elite had won their independence, established the equality of citizens, and kept their slaves (1986).[6]

———

As Latin American states entered what Cardoso and Faletto (1979) call the period of "outward expansion" (roughly, from the mid-nineteenth century until 1930), however, their primary contacts were with European capitalists and powers, most importantly England, but also—especially in some of the coffee regions—Germany. Such ties became important in the last half, and especially the last quarter, of the nineteenth century, when liberals came to power in many Latin American countries. As they did so, they sought out new markets for new and old products. Coffee was important in Brazil, Venezuela, Costa Rica, and, as the century closed, Colombia, Guatemala, El Salvador, and Nicaragua.[7] As liberal governments attempted to stimulate economic activity and establish close ties with European centers, they also turned their attention to longstanding projects of nation building. The liberal/conservative wars had given some liberals state power in many regions, but the liberal program remained an uncompleted project. Disamortization laws made the dissolution of indigenous landholdings possible, but they were enforced unevenly. In some regions, the laws simply legalized prior dispossessions; in others, the laws were never enforced because of indigenous resistance, elite hesitance to undermine a secure labor supply, or the marginality of the region. Likewise, whole regions remained undeveloped and unincorporated. To develop them, states might encourage immigration schemes, both to settle new areas and "whiten" the population so that it could become more like the "civilized" world. They also undertook public works projects. For example, in Central America, Hispanic settlement had concentrated in the highlands along the Pacific coast. As the Central American states developed stronger export economies, the Pacific location of their ports presented problems. For states such as Guatemala and Costa Rica, the establishment of Atlantic ports remained a dream, prompting various unrealized road, and later railroad, projects across the lowlands to shallow Atlantic ports. Such projects would, it was thought, incorporate new lands and establish a closer and firmer link to European markets and with it the possibility of wealth and development. In these and other projects of railroad building and public works, Latin American states entered into contracts with European companies, banks, and states (Woodward 1985; McCreery 1976; C.F.S. Cardoso 1986).

This is not to suggest that the United States played no role at all in this period. For the most part, the United States was in the midst of its own westward expansion and consolidation. That very expansion had its effects, most obviously on Mexico, which lost vast territories to the United States and was the first and most important object of North American investment in the late nineteenth century, but also on Central America after the mid-nineteenth century, when more rapid communication and trade between the east and west coast became important and Vanderbilt established coach and then train lines across the isthmus (Woodward 1985: 137–140). It was only toward the end of the nineteenth century, however, with the close of the frontier and the maturation of North American industrial capitalism, that it became both possible and desirable for particular investors and corporations to directly challenge English and German investors in Latin America.

For all practical purposes, the American century proper begins with the Spanish-American war in 1898 and the annexation of Puerto Rico and Cuba. From this point, U.S. domination in some areas was exercised most clearly in military terms (as in the Gunboat Diplomacy of Roosevelt and the actual occupations of Haiti [1915–34], the Dominican Republic [1916–24], and

Nicaragua [1912–33], the interventions in the Mexican Revolution at Veracruz and in northern Mexico, and the creation of Panama in 1903 and the subsequent building and administration of the canal, in addition to a variety of other, not so subtle, diplomatic pressures). The spirit of such interventions was captured most forcefully in T. Roosevelt's 1904, "corollary" to the Monroe Doctrine:

> If a nation shows that it knows how to act with reasonable efficiency and decency in social and political matters, if it keeps order and pays its obligations, it need fear no interference from the United States. Chronic wrongdoing, or an impotence which results in a general loosening of the ties of civilized society, may in America, as elsewhere, ultimately require intervention by some civilized nation, and in the Western Hemisphere the adherence of the United States to the Monroe Doctrine may force the United States, however reluctantly, in flagrant cases of such wrongdoing or impotence, to the exercise of an international police power. (Cited in R. F. Smith 1986: 101–102)

It was also during this period that U.S. capitalYwas invested in Latin America in growing volume, especially in minerals and agricultural enclaves (sugar in Cuba and Puerto Rico, bananas in Central America and Colombia, copper in Mexico and Chile, petroleum in Mexico and Venezuela). By the beginning of World War I, many Latin America republics were already importing more from the United States than from Britain; by the end of the war, the United States had become the dominant trader and investor in the region. This position was consolidated during the so-called "Dance of the Millions" in the 1920s, in which unprecedented amounts of U.S. capital flowed into Latin America, both in the form of direct investments and indirect investments (setting up banks, making public loans to national and provincial governments, etc.).[8]

We are now in a position to explore the advent of Americanization per se. Economically and politically, U.S. dominance was established during the period of outward expansion and was to continue into subsequent periods. One important implication of the foregoing should be stressed at this point, however. What some might regard as a cultural *consequence* of the American presence actually *preceded* it, at least among those liberals holding state power and their supporters. There was a remarkable coincidence between the liberal and positivist ideology of Latin American powerholders and North America investors at the turn of the century. Peace depended on progress, and progress depended on outwardly focused development. There were to be no major barriers to private enterprise and initiative, and the greatest good for the greatest number could be achieved by risk-taking entrepreneurs trying to enrich themselves. Yet neither liberalism nor positivism were North American imports to Latin America.[9]

This vision was not shared by all; it generated its own opposition. Some of that opposition came from conservatives who had long been suspicious of non-Hispanic civilization and had articulated critiques of economic openness and free trade in the nineteenth century. Some of the opposition came from fellow liberals as well. Here it is important to consider the nature of liberal rule in late-nineteenth-and early-twentieth-century states in the context of the transformations that were wrought as companies and entrepreneurs from the United States began to invest in Latin America.

In the first place, it was seldom the case that "the liberals" came to power. Rather, a group of liberals came to power, coalescing around the leadership of a single person. The struggle for power might involve wars with conservatives, but it would also involve battles with fellow liberals as well. In Mexico, for example, Porfirio Díaz had fought for Benito Juarez but came to oppose him. After Juarez's death, he fought fellow liberal Sebastiano Lerdo de Tejada for control of the state. The person who captured state power might have a liberal agenda, but he had regionalist and personalist agendas as well. Díaz was a liberal, but he was also a Oaxacan and a military hero. Cipriano Castro and Juan Vicente Gómez in Venezuela were liberals, but they were also Andeans, the political and military expressions of a vibrant coffee economy. Liberal ideology and politics were never undiluted expressions, then. They involved a collection of conflicting, and sometimes contradictory, ideas, attitudes, ambitions, alliances, struggles, and dreams.

As powerholders entered into relations with foreign states, corporations, and banks, they were acting on one or all of these ideas and struggles. They might be seeking development. In Costa Rica, for example, Guardia acted on a longstanding liberal and national dream of opening an outlet to the Atlantic and incorporating the Atlantic lowlands into the Costa Rican economy and polity when he contracted with Henry Meiggs in 1871 to build a railroad from San José to Limon. The deal was to lead to the establishment of vast banana plantations owned by United Fruit (formed in 1899), but Costa Rican liberals gained access to the Atlantic. Guatemala and Honduras eagerly followed suit (Woodward 1985). Powerholders might also be attempting to consolidate their rule. In Mexico, Díaz was most interested in developing a network of railroads, which facilitated commerce, improved communications, and allowed him to build a mobile army (Coatsworth 1981; Bazant 1977). Or powerholders might simply be attempting to enrich themselves. By the time Gómez came to power in Venezuela, his original coffee holdings had become a minor contributor to his wealth. He had accumulated land, monopolies on meat and liquor supply, and associated businesses. In power, he continued to accumulate and seemed to regard the state as instrument and guarantor of personal wealth accumulation. When he granted concessions to U.S. and European petroleum companies, he made sure that he and his friends were paid commissions and royalties that represented princely sums in Venezuela but desultory sums for the companies themselves (Roseberry 1983).

But, of course, North American investors and corporations did not necessarily share these national, political, and personal dreams. The investment and accumulation strategies of the corporations might intersect with the ambitions of Latin American powerholders at certain points, but the pursuit of the investment strategies brought with them a series of unforeseen consequences and transformations. Some of the consequences might not be regarded as unfortunate by the powerholders. The railroads in Mexico were built with North American and European capital. Although they were eventually controlled by the Mexican state, they facilitated a much closer connection with North American and European business. Establishing Mexican ownership of the railways increased Mexico's foreign debt, the construction of railways included vast land grants to foreigners, and the railroads became important infrastructural links for North American investments such as American Smelting and Refining in the north and International Harvester in Yucatan. All of these consequences fit well within Díaz's vision of progress for Mexico's future (Bazant 1977; Coatsworth 1981).

Yet these consequences and transformations introduced new social forces, conflicts, and resentments. It should be remembered that increasing U.S. involvement came at a time when the nature of foreign economic activity was changing dramatically. The basic economic model during the late nineteenth and early twentieth centuries was one based on the export of agricultural and mineral raw materials and the import of finished goods for a relatively small domestic market. For most of the nineteenth century, this had not necessarily involved foreign control of export and import trade. Rather, the primary link with European markets was the trading company, owned by British or German families who set up residence in particular countries. Their sons and daughters would be born in Latin America and educated in Europe before continuing and expanding the family business. The trading company would have long-established contractual relations with European firms and with local producers of tropical agricultural products, importing European textiles and tools, exporting coffee, sugar, and cacao. Much of the control of production, and some of the control of marketing, remained in local hands. Railroads built in the late nineteenth century were among the first examples of large-scale foreign capital investment. With the rise of imperialism, the preferred form of investment involved direct control of production or extraction and commerce, often with an enclave character. The new form was especially evident in mining—nitrates, copper, and petroleum—but also in agriculture—bananas and sugar.

The enclaves were more important in some countries than

others. In a significant analysis, Fernando Henrique Cardoso
and Enzo Falleto (1979) distinguish between two forms of outwardly focused development in Latin America during the late
nineteenth and early twentieth centuries. In both, development
was based on exports of raw materials. In the first type, however, control of key aspects of production and exporting remained with a local bourgeoisie, which exported cattle, coffee,
and other goods. Foreign corporations would still be present,
but a local bourgeoisie was not necessarily displaced. Examples
include Brazil, Argentina, Uruguay, and Colombia. In the second, mining and agricultural enclaves were controlled by foreign corporations. Examples include Porfirian Mexico, Venezuela, Chile, and the Central American states.

This distinction is problematic. One might, for example,
question the inclusion of Mexico as an enclave economy. Despite the enormous activity of foreign corporations, Mexico
had a more diversified economy than one would normally
expect in enclave situations. Moreover, the various developments on which Cardoso and Faletto place emphasis (development of a national bourgeoisie, middle classes, political
incorporation of middle classes, development of nationalist
and populist alliances, and so on) occurred early in Mexico,
unlike other enclave situations.

These two types were to develop quite differently in the twentieth century. In addition, as we shall see, the relationship between "enclave" and "national" economic sectors in places like
Costa Rica, Colombia, and Venezuela carried important economic, social, political, and cultural consequences. More importantly, the different class relations within particular countries
cannot easily be subsumed within a national control/foreign
enclave distinction. If we look solely at the coffee economies,
each of which was characterized by local control (though enclaves devoted to other commodities came to dominate some of
these countries), the class structures through which coffee was
produced, processed, and marketed varied enormously—from
the free-labor immigrant *colonato* in São Paulo to small producers in Venezuela, Colombian Antioquia, and Costa Rica, to large
farms with dependent laborers in Colombian Cundinamarca

and El Salvador, to large farms with migrant indigenous labor in Guatemala. The internalization of the external in each of these settings, and the consequent social, political, and cultural processes, were quite distinct.

Moreover, some of the changes that were introduced in so-called enclave economies deserve more extended comment. As enclaves developed, economic activities and elites that had been important at earlier moments were displaced. At times the displacement was direct, as in the replacement of sugar hacendados in Puerto Rico and Cuba by North American firms. Elsewhere it was indirect, as in the temporary displacement of coffee elites by United Fruit in the banana sector of Costa Rica, or the permanent displacement of coffee elites by Standard Oil and Anglo-Dutch Shell in the petroleum sector of Venezuela. In Venezuela and Costa Rica, the new activities did not compete with the old for territory. For Costa Rica, bananas were grown in newly incorporated Atlantic lowlands, while coffee was grown on the Central Mesa toward the Pacific; for Venezuela, petroleum was extracted near Maracaibo, while coffee was grown in the Andes. Yet the establishment of foreign enclaves involved political and economic displacement. That displacement might take a regional form, e.g., the shift of economic power from the Central Mesa to the Atlantic lowlands or from the Andes to the Maracaibo basin and growing commercial cities. The paradoxes of such displacement were especially pronounced when the powerholder came to power with regionalist associations and then oversaw the relative decline of his own regions. Such was the case with Gómez in Venezuela, whose primary identification was Andean and who staffed the government with Andeans but who set in motion forces that undermined Andean economic hegemony.

The social, political, and cultural consequences of this displacement were important. The establishment of enclaves created social groups who felt embittered, resentful, and opposed. We have already encountered one current of opposition among nineteenth-century conservatives. This new current, or set of currents, had its locus among displaced liberal elites, people who did not question many of the basic tenets of free trade and liberal philosophy. They valued progress and felt that progress could best be achieved through foreign trade. But they had not been *vendepatrias,* and they resented both the foreigners and the local elites who associated with them. We get a sense of this feeling in Pablo Neruda's poem, "Los Abogados del Dólar" ("The Dollar's Lawyers"), which assumes a critique of the companies but reserves it harshest judgments for the Latin American agent of the companies, who "dresses like a gringo, spits like a gringo, dances like a gringo, and moves up" (Neruda 1955: 173).[10]

This current of opposition might be quite diffuse. In Mexico, in 1910, it combined with other elite and nonelite segments in the revolution. More commonly, it would take less political forms, or its political forms would concentrate on particular aspects of the transformed complex. It would not necessarily concentrate on the U.S. presence, although a growing U.S. presence may serve to precipitate resentment. Rather, opposition would concentrate on local and national themes and events. It might concentrate on the dictatorial rule of a Díaz or a Gómez, and its demands might be for democracy or no-reelection.

In all of these forms, the liberal elite current of opposition could combine with other currents as they developed and took different shapes in the course of the economic and political changes of the middle and late twentieth century, including social democratic and more radical anti-imperialist forms of opposition. We find a good fictional account of this twentieth-century current across generations in Adriano González León's Venezuelan novel, *País Portátil (Portable Country)* (1967). The novel moves back and forth between the activities of an early-twentieth-century *caudillo* general in the Andes and those of his grandson, an urban *guerrillero,* in Caracas in the 1960s. The example is not that far-fetched and has its analogues in actual Andean families. An illuminating example is that of the Gabaldón family: the father, José Rafael, was an Andean caudillo and an early associate of Gómez who ended up in the opposition and led one of the more notable, and unsuccessful, revolts against him; his son, Joaquín, who was a member of the student "generation of 28" that led a student strike and precipitated

forms of opposition to Gómez that eventually led to the founding of Acción Democrática and other political parties; and his
youngest son, Argimiro, who was killed with the guerrillas in
the early 1960s (Roseberry 1982).

Although American investors encountered powerholders who
seemed to share their general outlook and vision for the future, they also encountered and helped to generate social
groups that did not share that outlook and came to oppose it. It
would be wrong, however, to view the split as one between
"American" or Americanizing elements and anti-American or
anti-Americanizing elements. One of the more interesting paradoxes in these social movements is the connection of several of
them to segments of U.S. life and politics. As U.S. imperialism
generated oppositional currents in Latin America, it also generated them in the United States. This was especially true in relation to the more directly political and military expression of
imperialism, the control of Cuba and Puerto Rico, the manipulation of Panama, or the military occupation of Nicaragua, Haiti,
and the Dominican Republic. These oppositional currents in
the United States were in turn connected with a variety of progressive and socialist movements in the early twentieth century.
Latin American and U.S. oppositional currents could enter into
direct contact, in part because leaders of Latin American oppositions would go into exile. Though exile might take them to
other Latin American countries or Europe, it could also take
them to New York, New Orleans, or Los Angeles, where they
might go to school, form friendships with progressives, actively
participate in and contribute to their movements, and place
their own struggles in international (and sometimes internation-
alist) perspective.

This is crucial for any cultural analysis of Americanization.
Oppositional currents of various sorts might be "anti-American"
and would actively reject and oppose U.S. domination and
intervention. They might also have an affection for certain
aspects of life in the United States based on remembered experiences and continued associations, and sometimes sophisticated understandings of political life and possibilities in the
United States. These oppositional formations would, in turn,

be differentiated and diffuse, some connecting with socialist and progressive groups in the United States, others connecting with liberal representatives of the Democratic party, or foundations and universities. The liberal segment, calling for greater democracy or more autonomous development, might simultaneously reject certain (especially economic) forms of U.S. presence and intervention and admire certain other (especially political and cultural) forms of U.S. life. Thus various political constituencies in the United States might share a general sense that Latin America was important and a general vision of a developed, "democratic" future but would differ on specifics, on practical alliances and allegiances. These different constituencies would, in turn, have connections with representatives of different social, economic, and cultural groups in Latin American countries.

———

With these observations, we move beyond the period of outward expansion and into the variety of economic, political, and cultural experiences of the middle and late twentieth century. Although we can attempt a general sketch of the basic dimensions of those experiences, the limitations of such a sketch must be stressed. A variety of general histories has foundered on the attempt to impose a uniform economic or political model upon the recent history of Latin American nations—from dependent capitalism on the economic side to populism and bureaucratic authoritarianism on the political. Most have in mind the experience of a particular country (say, Argentina or Brazil) and attempt to extend their understanding of that experience to other countries in ways that are inappropriate. But this does not mean that analyses at a general level should be suspended altogether or that we should simply restrict ourselves to the experience of particular states and regions. Those particular states and regions have experienced *similar* moments in the development of North Atlantic capitalism in *different* ways, in part due to the uneven development and expansion of capitalist sectors (here coffee, there bananas, there copper, there petroleum) and in part due to the different responses of particular states, which in turn rest upon different internalizations of the external. As long as our general analysis draws our attention to common experiences, forces, and trends in such a way that we develop a set of basic questions that we can take to particular situations, rather than a restrictive model that is imposed upon them, a discussion carried out at a general level is not only defensible but necessary. My approach to the general characteristics of the present, then, is developed in this spirit. I am sketching a set of economic, political, and cultural forces to which Latin American states and regions have been subject, along with some of the economic, political, and cultural consequences and contradictions of those forces. Throughout, I am outlining a set of questions that can be taken to the analysis of various internalizations. Following Cardoso and Faletto, I stress the collapse of the outwardly focused model and the growth of a domestic market and of the new social groups that participated in that market. If we see each of these terms as a *problem*— "collapse," "growth," "domestic market," "new social groups"— we have begun to outline a series of historical questions that can guide our study of particular situations.

The displacement of elites and regions, and the political and cultural effects of such displacement, were not the only characteristics of the period of outward expansion. Outwardly focused development also involved the emergence of new economic and social groups and forces, both in "national" and "enclave" economies. It involved the emergence of working classes in enclave areas (mines, petroleum camps, plantations) and in growing cities. It involved the growth and ramification of the state. Economic expansion and state formation stimulated the growth of the capital cities, and those near enclaves and ports. In turn, this growth stimulated the emergence of middle classes composed of state employees, merchants, clerks, artisans, and service workers of various kinds, and so on. It also stimulated the growth of "marginal" urban groups who had left the countryside but found no "formal" place in the economy.[11]

All of these processes occurred according to different time frames, in response to different events, and with different effects in particular countries. For the most part, they occurred earlier in the "national" economies than in the "enclave" ones. With the collapse of the outward period and model in the 1930s and 1940s, the national economies were able to enter periods of import substitution and industrialization due to the size of their domestic market. They occurred much later in "enclave" economies (1940s and 1950s in Venezuela; 1960s and 1970s in El Salvador and Nicaragua).

These processes have created new economic, political, and cultural space for the expression of U.S. power and influence, but they have also generated new sets of contradictions, which in turn overlay sets of contradictions inherited from the past. We might consider these by first exploring the dimensions of power and then reviewing the sources of limitation. Cardoso and Faletto place great stress on the economic and political aspects of this period. The growth of cities, working classes, and middle classes created a large domestic market for consumer goods. A major economic and therefore political issue concerned these new groups and the market they presented. With the growth of urban working and middle classes, the outward model was subject to challenge: would the market be supplied by foreign or local industries? For local entrepreneurs anxious to capture that market, their goals involved immediate political questions and issues: exchange rates, tariffs, taxation policies, state investment in transportation and communication infrastructures. Cardoso and Faletto see much of the history of twentieth-century Latin American states in terms of a struggle between two power blocs—the export bloc composed of export merchants, landed oligarchs, and their rural retainers, and a nationalist bloc composed of industrial entrepreneurs, urban middle and working classes, and the like. The political struggles of these new groups took the form of movements toward democracy, populism, and nationalism (Cardoso and Faletto 1979; Laclau 1977; Bergquist 1986; Germani, di Tella, and Ianni 1973).

With the demise of the export-import model and the rise of a domestic market, the nature of foreign economic activity in Latin American states changed dramatically. Again, one would have to take into account the different processes and conjunctures of specific countries, and the move from the export-import model to the domestic-market model was usually accompanied by profound economic and political crises. As nationalist and populist regimes came to power, they attempted to expand and consolidate domestic markets, entering into regional agreements, adopting more restrictive tariffs, and providing various protections and incentives in an attempt to stimulate local industry. Paradoxically, however, this has not resulted in decreased foreign participation in national economies. Rather, the expansion of domestic markets has increased investment opportunities for a wider range of foreign corporations. As the focus of activity shifts from agricultural and mineral export, new industries may be established to produce consumer goods for local and regional markets. Some of these may be formed by local entrepreneurs, some by multinationals, some by mixed or joint ventures. The attempt to develop domestic markets has often intensified dependence on foreign multinationals and increased debt to foreign banks. Industrial development has often been concentrated, at least in its initial stages, in consumer industries—especially light industries producing nondurables. These have been dependent on machinery and raw materials produced and purchased elsewhere. Even as some Latin American states have moved into heavy industry and machine and steel production, they have often been dependent on foreign technology and participation, all of which must be paid for.[12]

More differentiated domestic markets and industrial structures have therefore facilitated a more ramified and entrenched multinational presence, one that has moved from an extractive, enclave character to one that is involved in industrial development and commerce for a growing urban and small-town population, as well as the control of a variety of services.

Politically, the period since the mid-twentieth century has been characterized by the emergence of the state as the principal local actor in dealings with multinationals. At times, as in Brazil, such dealings involve what Peter Evans calls a "triple alliance" of multinational capital, local capital, and the state (1979). More often, however, local capital is relatively weak, and the principal relationship is one between particular states and particular multinational corporations. States may attempt to set limits upon foreign capital or to require various forms of joint participation and mixed enterprise. As a result, states become junior partners to foreign corporations and principal economic actors in local arenas. This involves a remarkable expansion of the state apparatus, but as Cardoso and Faletto note,

> What lends dynamism to this form of state, and what characterizes its movement, is *not* the bureaucratic aspect it may have assumed in some countries . . . but rather its *entrepreneurial* aspect, which leads it to ally itself, in production, with the multinational corporation. Somehow, the state has become a strategic element, functioning as a hinge that permits the opening of the portals through which capitalism passes into industrializing peripheral economies. (1979: 202)

The nature of political activity and struggle has changed during this period as well. Struggles during the nineteenth century often involved attempts by factions led by caudillos to capture relatively small states. Caudillos formed alliances with each other, and they fought for and about ideas—liberal or conservative—as well as fighting in the service of regions and personal ambitions. By welcoming the active presence of foreign corporations, however, the last of the caudillos had set in motion forces that undermined the original bases of their power. In the process, they used expanding state machineries to consolidate their power, but the new types of states that emerged were states in which such caudillo rule no longer had a place.

It is common to refer to leaders of parties and states in mid- and late-twentieth-century Latin America as caudillos, but this represents an illusory continuity. In the first place, the emergence of new social classes and groups—working classes in plantations, mines and oil fields, and cities; middle classes composed of government workers, clerks, small merchants, and professionals in growing towns and cities—has produced a variety of political expressions such as labor unions and political parties that press a range of democratic, progressive, and fascist demands at times through official channels and at times through military struggle. Leaders of these parties may have charisma and act like caudillos, but we need to pay more attention to the movement than the leader. These movements, of a national rather than a regional character and with important international connections, represent something qualitatively different. Moreover, even when states are under the rule of a particular strong man, the nature of that person's power has changed. They now depend on a professional military, trained at home in the United States, and on a professional bureaucracy.[13]

As in the economic realm, the growing complexity of the state and politics has created new and multiform possibilities for the expression of U.S. power. We are familiar enough with the litany of U.S. machinations in its presumed backyard. In many ways, the recent history of military intervention and blatant manipulation in Central America and the Carribean represents a direct continuity with past military occupations, manipulations, plots, threats, and murders. Even as we recognize such continuity, we can see it as evidence of a right-wing extreme within a range of official pressures that have been placed on Latin American states. More subtle and less militaristic pressures are available and have been used, depending on the political conjuncture in the United States and the nature of the political process and presumed crisis in particular Latin American states.

But we need to see a variety of official and unofficial expressions of connection between U.S. and Latin American politics as well. Beginning with state apparatuses and the people who staff them, we need to recognize the role of U.S. officials and educators in advising state officials and training bureaucrats and military officers. Such training may be part of an official program, as in the active role of the U.S. military in forming professionalized officer corps in Latin America and in counterinsurgency training. Likewise, local schools of public administration may be set up with the help of U.S. agencies or private U.S. foundations and may be staffed with U.S. educators (perhaps through special arrangements with particular U.S. universities) or Latin Americans educated in the United States.

If we look beyond the level of the state to the activities of political parties and movements, we see an ever wider range of possibilities. Here too education and the activity of the Area Studies components of private foundations play important roles, as militants in various sorts of movements—including, of course, opposition movements—may have wide experience in the United States. Or foundations may give grants to labor and social action groups, or provide support for local cooperatives. Familiar examples include AFL-CIO sponsorship and support of various Latin American labor unions in recent decades through the American Institute for Free Labor Development (AIFLD), a descendant of Samuel Gompers's earlier efforts in World War I, as well as the support of peasant cooperatives and self-help groups by the U.S. government's Inter-American Foundation. We should also consider the continuous efforts, of which "Project Democracy" is the latest example, of the U.S. government to influence public opinion through sometimes clandestine support of newspapers, magazines, and political organizations. Such influences affect both the substance and style of Latin American politics. One recent example of changing style is the participation of U.S. political consultants like David Garth as media advisers to Latin American politicians in election campaigns.

It would be a mistake, however, to view all of this as a uniform expression of U.S. power, to see these diverse efforts as expressions of an ideological state apparatus. Much of the pressure and influence does come from agencies and departments of the government, but it also comes from private foundations and individuals. And the individuals who come to the United States to study may come with bureacratic aspirations, entrepreneurial ambitions, or longstanding interest and activity in opposition movements. They may connect with, learn from, and, more importantly, contribute to a variety of oppositional movements in United States. When we think of an Americanized politics, then, we should not think solely of the State Department's sycophants.

The growth of a domestic market and the emergence of what Cardoso and Faletto refer to as the "middle classes" have had profound social and cultural effects as well, opening space for new expressions of U.S. power. The growth of a domestic market depended upon the emergence of new social groups living in growing towns and cities. This has meant the growth of a population with a new set of consumption needs and interests. These needs might involve a rejection of anything with the taint of the countryside and backwardness and a celebration of anything considered modern. The urban middle classes might want wheat bread rather than products made from corn meal. They might not want potatoes or other Andean products. Depending on the available technology and the fads of the period, they might want—and need—refrigerators, washing machines, cars, radios, stereos, televisions, VCRs. They want to see films, take trips, shop at supermarkets and malls. In these and other ways, we seem to witness the emergence of a new current that shares certain cultural values that we might regard as "American." The earlier group was a portion of the liberal elite that shared with U.S. investors and promoters an evolutionist, developmentalist vision. The new group is rooted in an urban middle class that is trying to create a "modern," convenient, consumer-oriented way of life. Indeed, when we think about Americanization, it is often this diffuse urban group, their demands, and the proliferation of urban services and businesses designed to serve them that come to mind, as is evident in the stereotypic images with which we began this essay.

We need to beware, however, of caricature and a patronizing tone. First, it should be stressed that many of the new articles and forms of consumption do represent needs and conveniences for an urban working population. The outsider viewing these changes in the context of a presumed rural, traditional, Hispanic past might view them as a form of loss or debasement—a movement from a more genuine to a spurious culture. But this may misread both the past and present and does not take into account the fact that these changes may be felt and experienced as forms of social and economic advancement, increased comfort and leisure. Indeed, these caricaturable styles of consumption depend upon the emergence of less easily caricaturable ways of life. Second, the caricature depends upon a particular group within the new middle classes who have the means to purchase these goods and realize some of their dreams. It would be more enlightening to develop a more differentiated understanding of the goods that make up the new urban middle-class package. Some of the goods, like clothes, convenience foods, refrigerators, radios, and televisions, represent widely diffused consumption goods—in many settings, "necessities," although style and cost will vary widely. Other items will be much less widely diffused. Certain aspects of consumption styles, with wide and obvious variation due to differences in personal resources, may have wide currency within the population—from cities to small towns, from upper middle class to working classes. The consumption styles are therefore rooted in a middle class but are not specific to them.

Even as we approach a less patronizing and more differentiated understanding, however, we need to recognize that the new ways of life and consumption styles open new possibilities for the expression of U.S. power and influence. A few examples will suffice. The demand for modern, elite, or convenience foods creates a dependence on imported foods, which are often provided by U.S. exporters. In urban jobs, many of the opportunities open to the new middle class may be in businesses that are either subsidiaries of U.S. corporations or have extensive commercial dealings with them. Knowledge of English becomes an important job requirement for aspiring managers and secretaries. Television opens many avenues for Americanization in obvious ways, such as the importation of dubbed versions of U.S. dramatic series and comedies or movies, and the broadcast of commercials advertising U.S. products. Here we find a direct linkage between the rise of a social group with urban ways of life and tastes and the proliferation of a domestic market with strong participation by multinationals. The development of new technologies makes this connection even more direct. For example, new cable systems and satellite dishes make it possible to produce a much broader variety of programs, such as sports events and dubbed versions of the programs produced by protestant evangelists in the United States.

———

In all of these ways, Latin America seems to be becoming more and more like an appendage of the United States. But each of the dimensions of the present situation that we have considered—economic, political, and cultural—has generated its own contradictions, some of which are inherent in the dependent form of development that characterizes Latin American states and some of which rest upon formations and movements from the past that are still active in the present. We shall consider the economic, political, and cultural dimensions of these contradictions in turn.

In the first place, although the economic model is one that intensifies connections with multinationals, those mutinationals are not necessarily headquartered in the United States. This has become increasingly important as the United States has entered a prolonged economic crisis. This is why it is important not to glibly identify the new life styles and ways of life as "American." Japanese commerce and capital are becoming increasingly important, especially in automobiles and electronics, as is European, especially German, capital. Indeed, state planners in more nationalistic regimes actively court non-North American capital in an attempt to diversify their contacts with multinationals. The result is not an economy that is less dependent on multinational capital and participation, but it may be (or may become) an economy that is less dependent on the United States.

Second, the process of internationalization implies an internationalization of labor as well, for both political and economic reasons, as increasing numbers of Latin Americans from Mexico, the Caribbean, and Central America are immigrating to the United States. This, too, is "Americanization," of course, but it implies a series of social, political, and cultural processes that are much more interactive and have more dynamic effects on the United States than a linear acculturationist model might foresee. Here the multiple implications of the phrase "Americanization in the Americas" become more apparent.

Third, it should be noted that the model of development sketched above is one that depends upon an expanding domestic market, but one that places inherent limits upon that expansion. Whole sectors of the economy—and this often means whole regions—remain excluded or incorporated in partial and uneven ways. To a certain extent these sectors are generated by the uneven character of the development process itself. Others, however, are the social precipitates of earlier historical periods. As portions of the economy are industrialized, the economic process is centered in space—a few industrial centers, port facilities, and administrative cities. Whole regions, some of which might have been important in earlier periods, are not incorporated. Within these regions live populations of peasants, semi-proletarians, and others. The economist may see them in terms of their functions within a model of disarticulated accumulation (see, e. g., de Janvry 1981), but they may see themselves in other terms. They are trying to get jobs, hold on to their lands, bring in a harvest, get a decent price for their crops, pay a doctor, feed their families, maintain their independence. As they sell their goods and as they purchase clothing, they too enter a domestic market dominated by multinationals. But they do not necessarily do so as functions of an economic model, or they do not fit easily within Cardoso and Faletto's broadly defined middle classes. They come with their own projects, their own sense of their place in a community or region or ethnic group, at times with their own language, their own sense of history.

These groups provide an important link to our discussion of politics. The model outlined above generates its own oppositions. Partly because it depends upon the restricted expansion of the domestic market, it rests upon the emergence of social groups with political and economic aspirations that cannot be satisfied. For particular regimes in particular economic conjunctures, this may mean a deepening contradiction between the maintenance of a model of accumulation and the satisfaction of political and economic demands from large segments of the populace. As a result, as Cardoso and Faletto note, the entrepreneurial state is increasingly an authoritarian state. Authoritarian regimes cover a wide range, from relatively open and formally democratic to extremely repressive. The difference between the two extremes is hardly negligible, and many more possibilities for movement are open at the former extreme than at the second. The regimes that emerge are, of course, products of local, quite specific forces, events, and struggles. I simply want to suggest that the specific regimes share a more generalized model of accumulation and a fundamental political contradiction. They therefore generate a multiform opposition, composed of elements of an old displaced elite, encountered earlier, middle classes whose aspirations cannot be satisfied, workers pressing for less repressive conditions and a greater portion of the products of their labors, and peasants and semiproletarians who are the direct and immediate victims of expanded disarticulated accumulation. Such oppositions coalesce in a variety of movements that range from regional and ethnic associations to multiclass political parties.

Although some of these movements provide space for U.S. influence and control, they may have much wider international connections. The most important state-building parties have been connected with European Social Democratic and Christian Democratic parties. Depending on local histories and conjunctures, both at times have been subject to U.S. pressures and willing to cooperate with U.S. directed initiatives. But they have also been part of wider international movements and interests that cannot be subordinated automatically to the will of the U.S. State Department. The international connections of oppositional groups are even more obvious. Even as the AIFLD establishes connections with nonradical unions, communist groups of various persuasions have long been active, at times clandestinely, in labor and party organization. The recent importance of liberation theology in some countries provides another example. The movement has included individual U.S. priests, but the leadership has been elsewhere—essentially and profoundly Latin American—as recognized by theologians and activists who have attempted to import and reinterpret liberation theology for a North American protestant context.

This brings us to cultural contradictions. It is important to place this discussion in the context of economic and political forces and contradictions lest we repeat the mistakes of an older acculturation literature that took cultural traits at face value and assumed linear cultural change. One can only understand cultural meanings if one can show how goods and symbols are interpreted and used. Particular people in particular circumstances may adopt certain practices or purchase certain goods that appear to outsiders as "American," but the practices and goods appear and are reproduced within uniquely Latin American contexts.

Let us take an example from the anthropological literature. In Andean Ecuador, Blanca Muratorio (1980) has studied the recent conversion to evangelical protestantism of the majority of Colta Indian peasants in the Colta region of Chimborazo Province. On the one hand, we might see this process as another example of cultural imperialism, and we would not be wrong. The protestant missionaries are representatives of the North American Gospel Missionary Union, which had translated the Bible into Quichua. Studies of the activities of this and related groups raise serious and justifiable concern among anthropologists and Latin American *indigenistas*. On the other hand, Muratorio has suggested that the peasants have converted to protestantism, in part, as an attempt to maintain their ethnic identity. The conversions occurred during a period in which the old hacienda structure—including the region's largest estate, owned by a Catholic order—was being reformed, and peasants were facing a reformist state bureaucracy staffed by *mestizos*. In addition, movements within the Catholic Church pushing liberation theology increased the cultural space for religious freedom and experimentation. Finally, the translation of the Bible into Quichua was seen as a way of preserving a threatened language and way of life. A number of aspects of this example are worthy of note. First, the attempt to use protestantism, with its individualistic ethos, in an effort to maintain a group identity is filled with obvious contradictions, as Muratorio notes in detail. It will almost certainly carry social and cultural consequences that could not be foreseen by the peasants. Second, the example underlines the importance of avoiding a simple power model that sees cultural forces coming from the outside and being either accepted or resisted. Here an external cultural force (protestant missionary activity) enters a region divided by class antagonisms that have their own history and have taken their own cultural forms. The North American cultural form is adopted by a particular group for use *within that class context.* It simultaneously represents a form of accommodation (the adoption of a foreign set of forms) and of resistance (to the Ecuadorian state and Catholic Church).

One cannot approach a discussion of culture that abstracts cultural symbols from form and use. And a discussion of form and use directs us to specific economic, political, and social conjunctures. If we return to the caricatured list of consumption goods and aspirations presented earlier, it is insufficient to point to such consumption styles and the social groups that pursue them and contend that they represent a process of Americanization. They may represent a project of Americanization on the part of missionaries, cultural officers of the State Department, and entrepreneurs, but the process itself is much more complex. In the first place, it encounters important limits, some of which are imposed by the accumulation process and political structure themselves, which produce a large social sector with urban and modern aspirations that cannot be met. These aspirations may still be pursued, but under constrained circumstances. Second, the use of specific consumption goods fits within a particular individual life and project in Venezuela or Mexico or Brazil, which is in turn tied to the aspirations and possibilities of particular groups and classes, neither of which can be reduced to an opposition between cultural homogenization or resistance.

———

Unfortunately, such an opposition is implied by most of our "-ization" words. Modernization, Westernization, and Americanization can imply linear processes connecting polar opposites. In his throw-away phrase, then, Darcy Ribeiro pointed us in the right direction. Perhaps the operative label should not be Americanization but Puerto-Ricanization, Mexicanization, Peruvianization, and so on. We are still dealing with "-ization" words, but words that direct us to specific historical processes. There is always a danger that the latter set of words can be placed at a polar extreme from "Americanization" as part of a romantic search for cultural authenticity, an artificial separation of the history of capitalism (or in this case the history of

U.S. expansion) from a society's "own" history. This too would be a mistake. The understanding of any of these processes should direct us to powerful external forces, especially, in this century, the United States. By placing an emphasis on particular national experiences, however, we can see that these forces are inserted in particular contexts of power, each of which represents particular internalizations of the external.

POLITICAL ECONOMY

Thus events of striking similarity, taking place in different historical contexts, led to totally disparate results. By studying each of these developments separately, and then comparing them, one may easily discover the key to this phenomenon. But success will never come with the master-key of a general historico-philosophical theory, whose supreme virtue consists in being supra-historical.

—Karl Marx, letter to *Otechestvennye Zapiski*

European History and the Construction of Anthropological Subjects

In his big and important book, *Europe and the People Without History*, Eric Wolf (1982) begins and ends with the assertion that anthropology must pay more attention to history. The type of history he advocates is one that is written on a global scale, that takes account of the major structural transformations of world history, and that traces connections among discernible communities, regions, peoples, and nations that anthropologists have often separated and reified as discrete entities. He sees this effort, in part, as recapturing the spirit of an older anthropology that attempted to grasp civilizational processes. The principal weakness of such efforts, according to Wolf, was their failure to confront questions of power and domination, their removal of anthropological subjects from the economic and political processes associated with the making of the modern world. Wolf's object is to remedy that failure by producing a historical account that traces the major social, economic, and political transformations that have occurred in the Western world over the past six centuries and that connects these transformations with the histories of the "people without history"—the primitives and peasants encountered, analyzed, and objectified by anthropologists. There is no way to describe such a project without making it seem grand: it is. To assess its theoretical and substantive arguments is a daunting task.

   The book has other antecedents in addition to the ambitious
but politically naive anthropology of earlier generations. For
one thing, there is a more recent tradition in anthropology, to
which Wolf has been a major contributor, that has consistently
placed culture in history. Wolf's earliest work, including his
doctoral fieldwork in Puerto Rico (1956a), represents such an
attempt. In addition, his early typological essay on Latin American peasantries (1955) developed a historical interpretation of
rural peoples in Latin America that suggested a profound reworking of the culturalist tradition of community studies. A
fuller statement of this interpretation, concentrating in this instance on the colonial encounter between Spaniards and Indians during the colonial era, can be found in Chapter 5 of
Europe. One can clearly trace, then, a continuity from Wolf's
early work to his most recent, even as the theoretical and historical material grows in sophistication and elaboration. Theoretically, *Europe* represents Wolf's clearest and most explicit use of
Marxist concepts, although such concepts also influenced his
early work. Substantively, the book represents a remarkable
compilation, condensation, and interpretation of historical and
ethnographic material from around the globe.
   Aside from the anthropological traditions that influence
Wolf's work, a whole body of work has developed over the past
two decades that has taken as its point of departure the connection between apparently traditional societies and the formation
of the modern world. Often associated with dependency theory,
especially the "catastrophist" view of Andre Gunder Frank
(1967; 1969; on catastrophism see below, Chapter 6), the perspective has received its most elaborate scholarly treatment in
the world-system theory of Immanuel Wallerstein (1974). During the 1970s, this point of view became quite popular among
liberal social scientists in the United States, so much so that a
major Latin American sociologist could complain of the "consumption" of dependency theory in the United States (Cardoso
1977a)—a consumption that he felt signified the loss of its critical edge. Whatever we might think of the politics of academic
consumption, the popularity of the literature has meant that
individual historians, anthropologists, and sociologists—many

of whom reject basic aspects of dependency or world-system theory—have been conducting regional case studies that re-interpret earlier work and place particular regions within the history of the modern world. Wolf has been able to use this new scholarship in attempting his own historical synthesis, one that explicitly challenges—both in conception and substance—world-system approaches.

Wolf has read widely and well. He begins the book with an attempt to place the peoples and societies a world traveler might have encountered in 1400, the trade routes that con-nected them, and the civilizational processes that either were or were not successful in incorporating them. This effort, based on a remarkable synthesis of historical, ethnohistorical, and ar-chaeological research, comes closest to realizing Wolf's stated goal of emulating the global vision of an older anthropology. The survey serves as a base line for Wolf's discussion of the emergence of Europe as a global power and the reorientation of world areas toward the production of goods destined for a world market. Unlike Frank and Wallerstein, however, Wolf contends that the sixteenth to the eighteenth centuries in Eu-rope were not characterized by capitalism but that economy and polity continued to be dominated by tributary relationships. Mercantile accumulation in the emerging European powers was unable to transcend a tributary framework even as that frame-work received greater elaboration with the creation of new state structures. The only state that was able to make the transition, and this for special reasons and at a later period, was England.

Wolf then turns his attention to the impact of the period of mercantile accumulation upon four major world areas. A discus-sion of the Iberians in America assesses the emergence of Latin American peoples within a colonial structure designed to create and protect a tributary population. An examination of the fur trade leads to a description of the response by native North American populations as the trade moved westward, the politi-cal alliances formed with English or French powers, the mercan-tile activities of particular groups, and the creation of entirely new "tribes" and ritual complexes. An analysis of the slave trade facilities a discussion of state formation in West and Southern

Africa, and the emergence of new economic and political complexes as African populations were divided into raiders and
raided, civilized and barbarian. And a discussion of the development of trade networks in the Pacific provides the necessary
context for an examination of political and economic transformations in India and China. In each of these areas, Wolf makes
use of anthropology in two ways. First, he is able to utilize a
growing body of ethnohistorical literature that has examined in
some detail the transformations that occurred at local levels
during this period. Here Wolf further develops his well-known
ability to synthesize a voluminous literature and produce a
more global picture of what is happening in, in this instance,
"Latin America" or "North America" or "Africa" without losing
sight of regional and temporal complexity and differentiation.
Second, having traced a history of economic, political, and cultural formation and reformation, Wolf situates famous anthropological examples of North American or African "tribes"
within that history, showing their emergence as part of a configuration of responses to a particular form of incorporation
into circuits of mercantile accumulation.

Wolf then moves to a discussion of the capitalist transformation, which he considers to have occurred with the Industrial
Revolution. Although most authors tend to concentrate on the
Industrial Revolution in England alone, Wolf examines textile
production in England in conjunction with cotton production
in the American South and Egypt and the fate of textile production in India, contending, quite correctly, that they were all
component elements within a single structural transformation.
After a theoretical treatise on the dynamics and contradictions
of uneven development under capitalism, Wolf turns his attention once again to the creation of anthropological subjects.
First, he looks at the commodities that were associated with the
international division of labor that accompanied the industrial
era—the agricultural and mineral raw materials, the foods and
food substitutes—and examines the incorporation of various
world areas into that division of labor. Second, he examines the
mobilization of labor in industrial enterprises and plantations
with special attention to migrations—of contract laborers to

plantations or displaced peasants incorporated into an industrial order. The discussion begins and ends with a treatment of labor-market segmentation, a theoretical statement at the beginning that leads to a historical account of the creation of ethnic segmentation. Again, anthropology and anthropologists are used in two ways—as sources for Wolf's synthetic interpretations and as objects of criticism. In some cases he is able to use one historically minded anthropologist to criticize others, as in his use of Robert Wasserstrom's research in Chiapas (1983).

The book succeeds at just about every level that matters to Wolf. The historical analysis, from the global vision at the beginning through the description of European transformations to the examination of the creation of anthropological subjects at different moments in world history, is masterful. There are, of course, few scholars who can aspire to this sort of writing, which requires close attention to a bewildering mix of local and regional details as well as large-scale syntheses. For those of us who cannot approach such an analysis, the book will remain a valuable reference work for many years. The theoretical analysis is also stimulating. The chapter on modes of production (1982: 77–100), about which I shall offer some critical comments, provides a sophisticated and spirited defense of the concept in a period in which—partly in overreaction to "Althusserian" or "structuralist" writers—mode of production analysis was dropping out of favor. The first three pages of that chapter provide one of the most eloquent statements of Marxist method I have encountered. The chapter on "Crisis and Differentiation in Capitalism" (ibid.: 296–309) goes beyond the ritualistic references to "uneven development" and attempts to define it and analyze the dynamics of uneven development under capitalism. Depending in part on the work of Ernst Mandel (1978), Wolf largely succeeds in this attempt. The afterword (Wolf 1982: 385–391) offers, in a disappointingly short and summary form, some rich observations on culture, politics, and ideology.

More important, the historical analysis has been carefully thought out theoretically. Aside from the explicit criticism of Frank and Wallerstein (ibid.: 21–23; 296–298), the entire book is a demonstration of the importance and possibility of an alternative account. Where world-system theory has relatively little to say about the "periphery," making social and political processes in such areas a function of the dynamics and requirements of capital accumulation at the "core," Wolf turns his attention to the history of those who have been denied history—either by imperialists or by their academic spokesmen and critics. This is especially true in his treatment of social processes in various world areas during the period of commercial expansion, when Wolf pays attention to the active engagement of anthropological subjects in the creation of those new social and cultural forms that were emerging in the context of commercial empires. In this, Wolf has helped restore a crucial balance.

———

Wolf tends to make some of his most important theoretical arguments as part a historical analysis, just as Marx embedded some of his most important arguments regarding the movement from absolute to relative surplus value in historical chapters on the struggle over the length of the working day, the movement from manufacture to industry, and so on (see below, Chapter 6). For Marx, theory and history could not be separated, a lesson subsequent generations of Marxists have not always learned as well as one might hope. As his book demonstrates, Wolf has learned it quite well. In working toward a critical assessment of what Wolf has accomplished, however, I shall concentrate on the more obviously "theoretical" aspects of the book. That this breaks up what Wolf correctly regards as a unity, I readily admit and regret.

One of the book's weaknesses is a consequence of its strengths. Its scope allows Wolf to present a civilizational process in broad outlines, but two kinds of analysis suffer. In the initial world survey, Wolf is very good at presenting the long cycles that have produced, say, a China, but he can pay little attention to what we might call the short cycles, the conjunctures of event and trend that are shaped by and shape the structural changes that seem to take centuries to emerge. This is, of course, a necessary consequence of the author's object in the chapter, but it implies a theoretical understanding of history that can leave history-making out of account. That this is not Wolf's understanding is clear, not only from the whole body of his work but from the other sections of the book. His discussion of the emergence of Europe and the creation of anthropological subjects in the periods of mercantile accumulation and capitalist development shows sensitivity to the conjuncture of event and trend. But even with such care, attention to regional differentiation must suffer. Wolf is at his best in analyzing the main lines of, or most important regions in, a process, e.g., the nuclear areas of Latin America or the westward movement of the North American fur trade from the northeast to the northern plains. As he turns his attention to divergent lines or less central areas, his analysis weakens. At times it seems to be directed to a more complete sense of the variety of types encountered. At other times, as Wolf discusses particular populations, one gets lost in a list of names without the sociological analysis one has come to expect from his other discussions. When one encounters an entire area that seems not to be characterized by any dominant tendencies, this sense of being lost in a list of names is heightened.

But these matters are relatively trivial. Of more importance are theoretical issues suggested by Wolf's analysis of modes of production. The mode of production chapter is a revised version of an earlier paper (Wolf 1981). Like the original version, this chapter offers an impressive account and defense of Marx's materialism and of the importance of a mode of production concept for an analysis of the fundamental relations people enter into with other people and with nature as they transform themselves and nature in production. Also like the original version, this chapter analyzes three modes of production: capitalist, tributary, and kin-ordered. The present version, however, offers a more detailed analysis of the relationships and dynamics of the various modes, and it also places more limitations on the applicability of mode of production analysis. Both versions eschew evolutionism and begin with capitalism, arguing that our understanding of tributary and kin-ordered modes of production is colored by our understanding of capitalism. The chapter in *Europe*, however, develops this argument in more detail. In the passage in which Wolf develops this argument, he contends (and this is one of the book's central theses) that the societies studied by anthropologists are not examples of earlier evolutionary stages but products of the encounter between the West and the Rest, that the apparently primitive or precapitalist are secondary, "indeed often tertiary, quaternary, or centenary" phenomena (1982: 76). He argues further that he is not trying to categorize all societies but to isolate basic relationships characteristic of capitalism and the societies encountered by European expansion. Moreover, the utility of mode of production analysis does not lie in classification but in an understanding of "the strategic relationships involved in the deployment of social labor" (ibid.). Given these important conditions and reservations, I shall discuss problems associated with his analysis of capitalist, tributary, and kin-ordered modes. Although I recognize the importance of Wolf's order of presentation, I shall discuss capitalism last. To avoid any hint of evolutionism, however, I shall consider tributary modes first.

By tributary mode of production (ibid.: 79–88; cf. Amin 1976), Wolf understands a situation in which direct producers, individually or in community, possess means of production, and surplus product is appropriated from them by extra-economic means. Such appropriation implies that labor is "mobilized and committed to the transformation of nature primarily through the exercise of power and domination—through a political process" (1982: 80). The tributary mode therefore includes, as part of the definition, a state, and in Wolf's view the state can be either strong or weak. Power may rest primarily with the state or primarily with particular individuals. The strong extreme corresponds with Marxists' definition of an Asiatic mode, while the weak extreme corresponds with their definition of a feudal mode. Wolf correctly emphasizes that strong and weak states were variable outcomes of similar relationships and that particular states oscillated back and forth between the two extremes. He therefore contends that Asiatic and feudal modes "exhibit a family resemblance to each other" (ibid.: 81) and should be treated as a single mode of production. He argues further: "Reification of 'feudalism' into a separate mode of production merely converts a short period of European history into a type case against which all other 'feudal-like' phenomena must be measured" (ibid.).

Although I have no desire to restore Marxist orthodoxy, I should point out that one of Wolf's central points violates his own rules for argument. He contends that Asiatic and feudal modes "exhibit a family resemblance to each other," which is most certainly a classificatory argument. Differentiation between feudal and Asiatic forms becomes important when we consider the potential of certain "strategic relationships" for the emergence of wholly new relationships. Granted that feudalism characterized a short period of European history (although it can only be considered short by taking a rather long-term view), there were two differentiating aspects of feudalism that proved crucial, a weak state and a weak community of producers. Both allowed more room for individual maneuver that was fundamental in the context of the accumulation of mercantile wealth. Wolf demonstrates that tributary states were not necessarily undermined by mercantile accumulation and could, in fact, consolidate control with mercantile wealth. State consolidation and mercantile accumulation under feudalism, however, could grant more autonomy to merchants. Simultaneously, the weakness of the community of producers was important in the emergence of differentiated petty commodity production, upon which Marxists have laid such stress in their analysis of the development of capitalism (Dobb 1963; Hilton, ed. 1976). In short, certain outcomes became possible with mercantile accumulation under feudalism that were not possible under Asiatic states. A structural trend that may have only represented a variant form within a classificatory family of relationships combined with a series of events from the fourteenth to the eighteenth centuries to produce something wholly new in Western Europe. Feudalism becomes "universal," then, because it is so particular, because of its world-historical significance (cf. Godelier 1978). This is, of course, an argument from the evolution of capitalism, and it sees importance in feudalism not in terms of its characteristic relationships and dynamics but in terms of what came after it. That there are logical problems with this sort of analysis I readily admit. Beyond logic, it might be argued further that the evolutionary significance of feudalism is irrelevant to the historical problem of the incorporation by mercantile empires or a capitalist system of a variety of tributary systems. Given such an interest, however, I contend that more attention to variation within a family of relationships is important. Just as mercantile accumulation was internalized differently in Asiatic and feudal systems, producing different results, different tributary systems respond to capitalist expansion in different structural ways.

The kin-ordered mode (Wolf 1982: 88–99) presents another set of problems. Wolf sees kinship as a set of symbolic constructs concerning filiation, marriage, consanguinity, and affinity that define the relationships into which people are placed. In a kin-ordered mode, social labor is mobilized through these relationships by reference to the symbolic constructs (ibid.: 91). Labor is mobilized under capitalism through the purchase and sale of labor power, under tributary modes through political domination, and under kin-ordered modes through kinship. Reference to kinship as a relation of production has been developed most clearly in recent years by French Marxists and those who follow them (Meillassoux 1972; 1978; 1981; Godelier 1972; 1977; Terray 1971; Siskind 1978). Wolf mentions in particular the work of Meillassoux, and his influence is most evident in the discussion of seniors and juniors and in the classic anthropological distinction between two types of kin-ordered modes depending upon whether nature is transformed. Several aspects of Wolf's discussion are insightful, e.g., the consideration of kinship itself, the analysis of sources of conflict and tension in kin-ordered modes, and the treatment of the emergence of hierarchy.

But Wolf's discussion of kin-ordered modes leaves one confused. It is never clear whether he is trying to reconstruct the structure and dynamics of kin-ordered modes in prestate situations or of kin-ordered modes in a world of tributary states and mercantile accumulation. Wolf's initial discussion of modes of production indicates that one should avoid an evolutionary reading and that he is discussing the basic features of various modes of production in order to assess the impact of European expansion upon them (1982: 76). Further, he begins the section on kin-ordered modes by denying that primitive populations are our contemporary ancestors. He then contends that most discussions of such populations emphasize what they are not rather than what they are (ibid.: 88, 89). His analysis of what they are is an internal analysis of kin-ordered modes with scant reference to tributary states or mercantile empires. Such references generally come as he discusses a set of relationships (e.g., between seniors and juniors) that will become important as the population is incorporated within a system based on the accumulation of mercantile wealth. Further, the mode of production chapter follows the chapter surveying the world as of 1400. The tributary and kin-ordered modes are made to apply to the populations one encountered in that period, and the discussion of tributary modes refers to societies that actually existed in the centuries preceding the emergence of capitalism. It would seem, then, that the kin-ordered modes also have a historical existence and are seen, in this reconstruction, as prestate societies. Yet all of Wolf's sources are based upon ethnographic analyses of kin-ordered societies of the present as if they were indeed our contemporary ancestors. Wolf is, of course, well aware of this problem with classic anthropology, and the whole book is a largely successful attempt to address it. More immediately, his introductory remarks in the mode of production chapter refer to the literature criticizing the concept of tribe as a product of external incorporation (ibid.: 76). But nowhere in the kin-ordered mode section does Wolf engage in a critical dialogue with the sources of his reconstruction. The importance of such a dialogue becomes apparent when one begins to notice how often words like "management" or "managerial command" or "mobilization" are used to refer to the activities of leaders in kin-ordered societies.

Critical discussion would be most appropriate with reference to the French Marxist literature on West Africa. A whole literature on the lineage mode of production developed in the 1960s and 1970s, beginning with Meillassoux's essay on traditional societies based on "auto-subsistence" (Meillassoux 1978; 1981;

Terray 1971; 1975; 1979; Rey 1975; 1979; Dupré and Rey 1978; Kahn 1981a). This essay discussed relationships between seniors and juniors and paid attention to the seniors' monopoly of bride wealth, their ability to appropriate labor and control marriages, and so on. The next generation of French Marxists proceeded to debate whether such a system was exploitative. Terray, considering Meillassoux's work among the Guro and limiting himself to the precolonial material, initially argued that the situation was not exploitative (1971). He later changed his mind under the influence of Pierre-Philippe Rey, who maintained from the beginning that it was exploitative (Rey 1975; 1979; Terray 1979). Meillassoux has been willing to talk of exploitation but not of class in lineage-based societies (1981). Yet none of the authors seriously questioned the basis for their reconstruction of lineage modes of production. Meillassoux has much to say about capitalism, but in his *Maidens, Meal and Money* (1981) he reconstructs a lineage mode without reference to capitalism and then plops capitalism on top of it in the second part of the book. Terray's subsequent work paid more attention to states and state formation (1974; 1975), but he has not made that work engage his earlier discussion of lineage modes. Among the participants, Rey is most willing to discuss colonialism and the relationships between lineage societies and Europe (1975; 1976). But he then imagines that he is saying something about prestate societies, never making basic historical distinctions. Rey's ethnographic sources are inappropriate for a discussion of exploitation among primitives.

Catherine Coquery-Vidrovitch, in an essay that is cited by other French Marxists but that seems not to have had a major impact on their thinking, outlines what she calls an "African mode of production" (1978). We need not accept such a label to recognize the importance of her model of weak states based upon wealth accumulation through long-distance trade and slave labor. Other subject populations, not turned into tribute producers, are able to preserve their basic social relations and communities. They are, however, participants in long-distance trade networks and nontributary subjects of the weak states. These local populations are, in large measure, the ones studied

by French Marxists. A "lineage mode" may therefore be preserved, but it does not take a great imagination to see that their
participation within long-distance trade networks and weak
states will have a profound effect upon relations between seniors
and juniors, instituting an expansionist logic that Meillassoux
sees as inherent in the *internal* logic of the lineage mode. In an
article that develops this point in a rigorous fashion by means of
an examination of Dahomey, Katz and Kemnitzer have explored
the relationship between lineage modes, the state, and an expanding world system (1979). The point is that some of the fundamental tensions and relationships French Marxists have seen
in lineage-based societies can only be understood in the context
of state formation and long-distance trade. This is a point with
which Wolf will be in full agreement. Again, the book as a whole
is a demonstration of this, and specific sections also treat the
point, as in the discussion of the formation of slave-raiding and
slave-providing populations in West Africa (Wolf 1982: 217ff.).
But in his discussion of the kin-ordered mode, he suspends this
critical appraisal and seems to revert to a kind of evolutionism.

Wolf's discussion of capitalism likewise provides numerous
insights and provokes a few questions (ibid.: 77–79; 296–309).
His understanding of capitalism is extraordinarily rich. I have
already indicated that I regard some of his theoretical discussions of capitalism (e.g., the treatment of uneven development) to be rewarding. In addition, I am in fundamental
agreement with his criticism of world-system theory and his
definition of capitalism in terms of the commodity form of
labor power. In his understanding, however, the commodity
form of labor power becomes virtually synonymous with industrial labor, and the development of capitalism is identified with
the Industrial Revolution of the late eighteenth and early nineteenth centuries. A number of questions can be raised, the
first having to do with labels and timing. One of the interesting questions that came out of the "transition debate" between
Maurice Dobb and Paul Sweezy (Hilton, ed. 1976) had to do
with the characterization of the period between the fourteenth
and sixteenth centuries, when feudalism was in decline and
capitalism had not yet emerged. Sweezy saw feudalism ending

in the fourteenth century and postulated a system of precapitalist commodity production that characterized the ensuing two centuries. Dobb preferred to label the period "feudal" up until the sixteenth century. Wolf is clearly willing to see a tributary mode of production and tributary states in force until the Industrial Revolution (1982: 101–125). Yet such an interpretation needs to confront more directly the political events of seventeenth-century England.

Another problem that requires more discussion takes us beyond the question of timing and forces us to confront the identification of industrial labor and the commodity form of labor power. In the first place, such identification does not pay sufficient attention to the transformation of the English economy during the two centuries prior to the Industrial Revolution—the "freeing" of peasants from estates and the growth of domestic manufacturing beyond the major cities. Both signified the growth of a potential factory proletariat, a group of people stripped of control over means of production whose labor power was becoming a commodity. Of course, Wolf does not ignore this development. He discusses it in some detail and produces statistics showing that some 40 percent of the English population had left the land by the end of the *seventeenth* century (ibid.: 269). But he does not make this material confront the theoretical question of the commodity form of labor power. Second, although the Industrial Revolution quickly transformed textile production and, secondarily, metallurgical branches of the economy, other branches maintained their craft character for a much longer period. Dobb notes, for example:

> Not until the last quarter of the [nineteenth] century did the working class begin to assume the homogeneous character of a factory proletariat. Prior to this, the majority of the workers retained the marks of the earlier period of capitalism. . . . As late as 1870 the immediate employer of many workers was not the large capitalist but the intermediate sub-contractor who was both an employee and in turn a small employer of labour. (1963: 265, 266)

Yet few would contend that capitalism did not emerge until sometime after the publication of *Capital*. Third, workers with a connection to threatened craft traditions but who were not yet subjected to factory discipline were the leading figures in the nineteenth-century political definition of the proletariat as a class (see, e.g., Thompson 1963; Sewell 1980). We need to pay more attention, then, to what Marx called the formal subsumption of labor to capital (1977 [1867]: 645, 646, 948–1084), the creation of the commodity form of labor power on farms and in small shops as journeymen found the path to the status of master craftsman blocked. I do not mean to deny the importance of the Industrial Revolution. I simply want to suggest that the capitalist mode of production should not be limited to a particular form of production.

We are now in a position to move beyond modes of production and consider political questions raised by Wolf's book. It is always an unfair request of such a big book, but one wishes that there were yet another chapter that paid more attention to politics. As the book stands, it traces the jumbling up of various regions and peoples with the development of certain kinds of commodity production (e.g., coffee, tea, cocoa, sugar) in the nineteenth and twentieth centuries and the migration of peoples to work in factories and on plantations. But the conclusion to these analyses is often simply an assertion of connection. For example, after a brief look at Wasserstrom's ethnohistorical work in Chiapas, Wolf concludes:

> Zinacantan, Chamula, and other Tzeltal- and Tzotzil-speaking communities in the vicinity of San Cristóbal Las Casas in highland Chiapas have been studied intensively by American anthropologists since the 1940s. Most of these studies have dealt with them either as "tribal" survivors of the ancient Maya, maintained in relative isolation from outside contact, or as parts of a colonial Hispanic society preserved in encapsulated form within a modernizing Mexico. Tzeltal and Tzotzil, along with other Native Americans in Central America, however, were drawn early into the networks of mercantile expansion . . . and they have participated actively since the nineteenth century in

the commercial coffee and corn economy of the area and in the
politics of the Mexican state. These involvements, in turn, have
altered their agricultural adaptation, changed their class structure, and affected their political and ceremonial organization.
Their continuing identity as inhabitants of "Indian" communities is thus not a corpus of unchanged traditions maintained in
unbroken fashion from a distant past. It is, rather, the outcome
of a multitude of interrelated and often antagonistic processes
set in motion by capitalist development. (1982: 338, 339; cf.
Wasserstrom 1983)

Those of us who share this view will appreciate the accumulation of case material from various parts of the world, but we will
want to know more. We will want to see anthropological subjects
not only as products of world history but also as actors in that
history—accommodating themselves to some developments, resisting others, and so on. Yet this passage is offered as a conclusion regarding Chiapas rather than a starting point. Of course,
to say that anthropological subjects have intervened in history
as political actors tells Wolf nothing new. He emphasizes this at
various points in the book. In addition, his *Peasant Wars of the
Twentieth Century* (1969) examined *one* form of that action. Indeed, the present effort can be seen as a fundamental revision
of the discussion of "North Atlantic capitalism" in the Conclusion to *Peasant Wars*. Because *Europe* treats capitalist development in such detail, however, the political questions it raises
take us well beyond the problem of peasant participation in
revolutionary movements.

For example, Wolf's discussion of the "new laborers" (1982):
354–383) traces the creation and reproduction of ethnic divisions within a segmented labor force. As in other sections of the
book, his analysis of historical connections shows that they nonetheless occur in a *dis*connected manner—that is, in this case,
that uneven development creates a differentiated, fractionated
working population. This raises the political questions of how,
or whether, or in what ways, such working populations might
organize themselves as a working class. Lest there be any misun-
derstanding, I am not here making the easy point that Wolf

pays insufficient attention to "agency," defining agency solely and romantically as some form of heroic resistance. As I have argued elsewhere in this book (see Chapters 2, 4 , and 8), the emphasis on resistance is often overstated in the recent litera- ture (Scott 1985; cf. Rebel 1989a; 1989b). My point is simply that the kinds of historical processes that Wolf has outlined do more than establish certain kinds of connections for anthropo- logical reflection and discourse. They also have profound politi- cal and cultural consequences for the actors themselves: they open up possibilities for certain kinds of connections and close off others; they make possible certain kinds of action (resis- tance, accommodation, active support) in this time or place but not in that time or place. One wishes that Wolf had moved more forcefully from an establishment of anthropological connec- tions to a discussion of such political and cultural questions (see below, Chapter 8). Despite an Afterword that contains some important suggestions regarding politics, culture, and ideology, however, this problem is not directly confronted.

━━━

Wolf's book is, nonetheless, politically consequent. State- ments of historical connection must once again be raised as a challenge to conservative orthodoxy. The book was published just as an ascendant political philosophy and its attendant aca- demic sycophants were attempting to banish historical un- derstanding from politics. Oppositions such as tradition and modernity were (and are) once again prominent (see, e.g., Kirk- patrick 1979). This book, which so carefully traces connections that others find convenient to ignore, will serve an important educational function. Like everything Wolf writes, it is quite readable, and the research is impressive. One can see, as one could see with *Peasant Wars* before it, this book being used to good effect in classrooms across the United States, challenging the official version of "our" history and "their" history and insisting upon the unity of the two branches of inquiry. Wolf has therefore once again made his scholarship intervene in an im- portant political conjuncture. In the 1950s, his writing was not addressed to a public audience, but he was a leader in a group that was trying to redirect anthropological inquiry toward radically historical questions during one of the ugliest periods in the recent history of the American academy (see Steward et al. 1956; cf. Mintz 1978; Wolf 1978; Roseberry 1978a). In the 1960s, his *Peasant Wars* grew out of and contributed to the teach-in movement in response to the Vietnam War. The present book challenges dominant understandings in a political moment Wolf could not have foreseen when the book was begun.

But the book is not simply a response to resurgent conservatism. Its historical vision offers a profound challenge to those thinkers in anthropology who develop their critique of the capitalist present by turning to putatively *pre*capitalist societies as counterpoints and alternatives. In doing so, this group of writers seems to be in search of an uncontaminated, "authentic" past (cf. Cohn 1980; 1981; O'Brien and Roseberry forthcoming; see below, Chapter 8). Such a search requires a sharp distinction between "our" history and "their" history—the capitalist ship and the authentic precapitalist shore (Ortner 1984; see above, Chapter 2), a distinction for which Wolf's book serves as an effective challenge.

Let us take an example. Shortly before Wolf began working on *Europe,* Marshall Sahlins published *Stone Age Economics* (1972), turning to primitive societies as a counterpoint to capitalist economies. He argued that, unlike capitalism, primitive economics was inherently underproductive in relation to capacity because primitives did not produce in accordance with norms of maximization and expansion but in accordance with the socially defined needs of the household. One might raise questions regarding Professor Sahlins's understanding of capitalist rationality and use of resources, but the immediate problem is in his approach to anthropological subjects as part of his understanding of primitive societies. To develop his analysis of the structure of underproduction, Sahlins elaborates a domestic mode of production, resting on the household and its response to consumption requirements. Of immediate relevance to the Wolf book is the fact that Sahlins uncritically examines ethnographic material from the twentieth century to support his arguments regarding the underproductive character of primitive economics. His calculations regarding one of the cases, Mazulu village among the Gwembe Tonga, shows that the village *as a whole* is producing less than it requires. His theory told him that some households would be underproductive while others would be overproductive, but he never fully confronts the problem presented by Mazulu village (ibid.: 73, 74, 103–114). Perhaps an observation by its ethnographer will help. For the year during which research was conducted and the statistics used by Sahlins were gathered, Thayer Scudder writes:

> During 1956–57 half (nine) of the adult men of Mazulu village were out of the Valley for periods of three months to over a year, while at least two of the nine who remained within the Valley worked several months for contractors clearing bush along the future lake shore margin. Of the remaining seven, one was an invalid while three others had stopped participating in wage labour because of their age. Out of fifteen of the village men on whom I have data, eleven had already made four or more work trips to the Plateau. While some of these trips had been for over two years, the modal length was under a year with the mean returning to the Valley just prior to the beginning of the rains and the main cultivation season. Then, when the harvests were in, some of these would again leave the neighborhood for outside work. (1962: 156)

One might choose to analyze cultivation in such a village in terms of a domestic mode of production, but one should at least insert that mode within the logic of a capitalist mode that employs most of the adult men of the village. This Sahlins does not do. Indeed, his detailed presentation of Scudder's statistics on village economics does not include the data on migration. In pursuit of an anticapitalist economics, then, one of our most important authors ignores capitalism.

I do not mean to imply, nor does Wolf suggest, that our understanding of anthropological subjects should be reduced to an analysis of the dynamics of the capitalist mode of production. Shanghai did not become Kansas City, however much some capitalists and Congressmen might have desired such an outcome. Noncapitalist relations shaped, and in many cases continue to shape, the lives of most of the peoples anthropologists have studied. One of the paradoxes of the history of capitalism has been its development in noncapitalist milieus. Such situations are not unaffected by the encounter with capitalism, however, and in many cases *non*capitalist relations have been created as a direct or indirect result of capitalist development. Anthropologists turn such situations into images of our past, into *pre*capitalist relations, at the expense of a more profound historical and political understanding. It is with pleasure, then, that one reads a critical analysis that rejects pseudohistorical oppositions and explores with such care the historical processes by which primitive and peasant pasts have become a fundamentally altered primitive, peasant, and proletarian present. Eric Wolf has made possible a deeper understanding of our anthropological and political task.

Anthropology, History, and Modes Production

At this point in the development of the literature, an author with conscience who sets out to write yet another essay on the articulation of modes of production should begin by apologizing to his readers. It is an approach that seems to have caught fire and burned itself out rather quickly. In the process it generated a literature that is so extensive that only the most dedicated bibliophile can keep up with it. Yet a sympathetic or curious reader who looks at only a small portion of the literature will soon discover that there is little agreement among writers on the definition of a mode of production, of different types of modes of production, of the nature of their articulation, or exactly what is being articulated, or whether a situation is characterized by *dis* articulation, and so on. An essay by Pablo Mariñez (1981), which was not based on an extensive bibliography, found twenty-five different precapitalist modes of production being used in analyses of Latin America, including Andean, Asiatic, peasant, communal, simple commodity, feudal, Indo-hispanic, primitive, tributary, and tropical. When one attempts to "articulate" these modes with a capitalist mode about the nature of which there is equal disagreement, one begins to wonder about one's sanity. And when one then encounters a criticism of the Althusserian philosophy that inspired so much of the Latin American literature on modes of production by a sophisticated historian like E. P. Thompson (1978a), one is tempted to wish the literature a speedy demise and to vow never to use the phrase "mode of production" again.

Why, then, this essay? I write because I am convinced that the mode of production literature addressed and offered some resolution to a number of methodological and theoretical issues associated with the history, political economy, and anthropology of Latin America. Further, it was associated with a political debate and struggle that went beyond the limits of the mode of production perspective and that is far from being resolved. The literature, in short, generated some heat, and I am concerned that scholars abandoned the perspective too quickly. This essay represents, then, a settling of accounts, an argument for a particular point of view. It develops this argument by returning to the original context in which the mode of production literature emerged. The essay then examines the problems and prospects generated by the literature and suggests a perspective that carries us beyond articulating modes of production but also makes a discussion of modes of production a necessary historical and political task.[1]

Although the mode of production literature did not originate within and has not been limited to an anthropological discourse, this essay concentrates on anthropological usages and understandings. I shall begin with anthropological approaches to peasants as they developed in that line of peasant studies inspired by Julian Steward and his students (Silverman 1979). We can see in this 1950s literature the recognition of a crisis of anthropological theory and method, a recognition that methods for the study of primitives did not serve those studying peasants in "complex societies." The problem was aptly expressed in a paper by Robert Manners addressing community studies in the Caribbean. After noting that community studies must "take cognizance of the centuries of struggle among Western powers for political and economic dominance of almost every island," he continues:

Every community study in the area . . . will in some measure have to take notice of the past effects and cultural end-results of the vagaries of sugar production, or coffee, or cacao, or cotton, or indigo; of the production and sale of rum; of the shifting periods of mercantilist and capitalist forms of exploitation; of the presence or lack of gold deposits in the earlier contact period; of the activities of missionaries of all kinds; of the West Indies' geographical position with regard to the mainland; of trade, smuggling, barter and the like. . . . (1960: 82)

Peasants were, quite simply, not isolated from wider historical processes. They lived in and paid taxes to states. The products of their labor were bought and sold on the world market. And yet, in their daily lives and community traditions and values, they seemed to be isolated (or to isolate themselves) from that wider world. They were, then (or so Kroeber thought), part societies and part cultures. How were we to understand these anthropological subjects in terms of the world-historical processes through which they emerged or by means of which they maintained themselves without simplistically reducing the dynamics of their communities to the dynamics of world history? What did the anthropological perspective mean when the assumptions of holism were so clearly inadequate?

Perhaps the clearest statement of this problem, in conjunction with an admirably crafted attempt to resolve it, can be found in *The People of Puerto Rico* (Steward et al. 1956; cf. Mintz 1978; Wolf 1978; Roseberry 1978a). The book was based on a series of community studies, but the community studies were directed toward an understanding of Puerto Rico in its historical, political, economic, and cultural complexity. Each community specialized in a specific commodity. Through an introductory economic history and through their individual community studies, the authors attempted to show how the communities fit within the larger historical processes that had shaped them, that had produced particular class configurations, and so on. Finally, the authors attempted to view their community studies in the context of "the fundamental similarities in the processes of proletarianization as these have developed throughout the world" (Steward et al. 1956: 505). The authors thereby laid the foundation for an anthropology that would take proletarianization as a focal point. They developed this further in a series of typological essays that can be seen as attempts to capture the unity and diversity involved in the creation of anthropological subjects at the conjunction of local histories and world history (see Wolf 1955; 1957; 1959b; Wolf and Mintz 1957; but see as well Rubin, ed. 1960; Service 1955; Wagley and Harris 1955; Harris 1964).

Nonetheless, the innovative literature of the 1950s remained a minority tradition, as peasant studies in North America were dominated by the Redfield tradition, with its emphasis on the local community, culture, and values (see Silverman 1979). The dominance of this perspective was only threatened with the radical critique, both within and without anthropology, generated in response to the Vietnam War. Within anthropology, we could point to the work of one of the contributors to the 1950s ferment—Eric Wolf. The obvious example is his *Peasants* (1966), which continues to set the terms for debate in peasant studies. Perhaps more important as a criticism of the prevailing orthodoxy was his *Peasant Wars on the Twentieth Century* (1969). Peasants, principally through their own action and in part because of academics' changing perceptions of their action, were once again placed in world history. The theoretical and methodological crisis, which had never disappeared, once again loomed large. The literature addressing the problem in the past two decades has been extensive (e.g., Adams 1970; Forman 1975; Cook and Diskin, eds. 1976; C. Smith, ed. 1976; Stavenhagen 1975; Orlove 1977; Halperin and Dow, eds. 1977; Wasserstrom 1983; Roseberry 1983; Mintz 1973; 1974a; 1974b; Warman 1981). Two of the contributors to the Puerto Rico project, Wolf and Mintz, have gone beyond their original concentration on rural cultivators and made major contributions to a reconceptualization of anthropological subjects in terms of world history (Wolf 1982; Mintz 1985). Because some of the recent anthropological literature overlaps with or enters into dialogue with the dependency and mode of production literature, we may set anthropology aside for a moment and examine the movement outside anthropology.

Here we may point to the popularization of dependency theories through the writings of Andre Gunder Frank and others (Frank 1967; 1969; cf. Baran 1957; Amin 1976; Wallerstein 1974; 1979). The literature has a long and rich history (see F. H. Cardoso 1977b). Nonetheless, its proliferation is a phenomenon of the 1960s in Latin America during a period of apparently unalterable U.S. hegemony. The literature developed an elaboration and critique of the ideas of Raul Prebisch and his followers in the Economic Commission on Latin America as well as a critique of Latin American communist understandings of rural regions. Despite numerous disagreements among contributors to the dependency literature, there was general agreement in emphasizing a systematic *connection* between the development of some countries and the underdevelopment of the majority, on the historical creation of a situation of dependence that served as a limiting condition in the development of underdeveloped countries, and on the extraction of surplus from the underdeveloped by the developed. It was their approach to rural regions, however, that most clearly connected with an anthropological problematic, and it was the development of that connection that made the literature attractive to many anthropologists interested in peasants. Briefly, in opposition to dual economy theorists who talked of discrete urban modern sectors and rural, traditional sectors and defined development as the diffusion of modernity, and in opposition to orthodox Marxist treatments of the countryside as feudal, dependency theorists such as Frank emphasized the *capitalist* character of the countryside, the historical creation of backwardness as a product of capitalist evolution. Despite differences in interpretation and tone, the connection between this view and the minority tradition in anthropological peasant studies emerging from *The People of Puerto Rico* should be apparent. Much of the anthropological peasant literature of the 1970s and 1980s has been written in dialogue with dependency perspectives, either "consuming" them (F. H. Cardoso 1977a) or criticizing them. We must, then, pay more detailed attention to some of the problems associated with the dependency literature before moving to the mode of production literature.

While dependency perspectives can be classified according to numerous criteria, two broadly divergent approaches may be discerned. The first emphasizes the *persistence* of dependence despite changes in political, economic, and social relations between developed and underdeveloped nations. The second emphasizes *movement:* the transition from one form of dependence to another or from one situation of underdevelopment to another. The first approach is exemplified by Frank's analysis of the "development of underdevelopment" (1967; 1969), and the second is exemplified by F. H. Cardoso's analysis of "dependent development" and "structural movement" (1972; 1973a; 1977a; Cardoso and Faletto 1979). Both approaches emphasize the historical creation of underdevelopment in the context of capitalist evolution, and both see dependence as a conditioning or limiting situation. Beyond a broad historical framework, however, the first approach is inherently static while the second is dynamic. They differ in their approach to periods of political or economic transition. The first, in its extreme forms, tends to view such changes as "epiphenomenal." The conditioning situation of dependence is thought to have been forged in the sixteenth century when Latin America was incorporated within the expanding capitalist system. From that point, whatever changes may occur (e.g., political independence) are not thought to alter the situation of dependence. Rather, they represent variations on a theme. History happened (in the sixteenth century); it no longer happens. The other set of approaches tends to stress the fact that capitalism is a constantly developing and transforming system. While Latin America has long existed within a capitalist system, that system has experienced (and continues to experience) multiple transformations that change both the form and content of relations between developed and underdeveloped societies. Rather than viewing changes in the nature of dependence as epiphenomenal, then, this set of approaches would view them as central, affecting the nature of class relations within countries as well as relations between developed and underdeveloped countries.

Despite differences among individual writers, there are two basic elements to the first approach. One is the insistence on the capitalist system or the world system as the essential unit of analysis with the corollary principle that the dynamics of the system are determined by the needs of the core or metropolis. The other is the contention that, short of a socialist revolution, the basic situation will not change. Capitalism will grow, develop, transform itself technologically, and suffer occasional crises of more or less importance. Peripheral countries may become semiperipheral (and vice versa), and occasional semiperipheral countries may enter the core. But the system as a system is remarkably stable and has remained so for four centuries. There is much in this last point, however pessimistic its import, with which those who do not share the theoretical approach might agree. The system has been remarkably stable and, despite the deepening crisis, does not seem on the verge of collapse. We must disagree with the dismissal of movement *within* that situation of systematic stability, however. This gets us to the importance of our first point. The purely systemic understanding, with all that is dynamic coming from the core, or from the maintenance requirements of the system, leads to a disparagement of dynamics from below and results in an impoverished understanding of the contradictions, possibilities, and potential instability of the system itself.

Much of the criticism of this version of dependency and world-system theory is based on dissatisfaction with its systemic understanding. The criticism may look to particular countries and examine the possibilities for *movement* within them, examine the particular class configuarions that emerge, their relations with each other, and their connections with or opposition to multinational firms or the superpowers. This is the essential characteristic of the second version of dependency theory mentioned earlier (see Cardoso and Faletto 1979; cf. Henfrey 1981: 27–32). A second line of criticism, which may or may not have a concern for movement, addresses more specifically the sources and nature of *differentiation* within the system. This line has close connections with the anthropological problematic discussed earlier and is the one that has paid attention to the concept of "mode of production." To address this connection and the significance of mode of production perspectives, let us return to the anthropological study of peasants. As a result of the methodological and theoretical ferment of the 1970s and 1980s, anthropologists did fewer and fewer "community studies." Rather, many began to turn to some form of "regional study." It is not always clear, however, that the move to regional studies is accompanied by any radical rethinking of theory and method. There is no obvious sense in which the region resolves any of the problems associated with the articulation of local history and world history. Indeed, it may actually make for more impoverished analyses in that we may still be stuck with a worm's eye view (Smith, ed. 1976, 2: 3), yet we will be more removed from the daily lives, hopes, and feelings of the people we study, which will rob our accounts of a distinctive anthropological focus. Clearly, we must be careful in defining regions, but even with careful definitions, theoretical innovation is still essential. For that innovation to occur, we must move beyond spatial understandings of the communities and regions in which peasants live. Of course, such regions have economically, ecologically, or politically defined boundaries. But our analyses will remain at a low level as long as the concepts we use to analyze regions are bound by similar criteria. In order to truly articulate local history and world history, we need to move beyond community/region/nation/world conceptions and move toward concepts that point to relationships that are less easily reified. The search for such concepts makes the mode of production literature relevant for anthropologists. The mode of production concept, in conjunction with other concepts such as social formation, offered the *possibility* of an analysis of differentiation within a capitalist totality that would take sufficient account of anthropological subjects and avoid the reduction of that differentiation to its spatial expression. The dilemma for mode of production theorists, as presented thus far, was not altogether unlike the dilemma for anthropologists trying to understand "their" valley. For anthropologists, the problem was how to articulate local history and world history. For mode of production theorists (including some who happen to be anthropologists), the problem was how to understand differentiation within a totality. The second problem, while related, is not reducible to the first. But further discussion of their connection requires that we pay more detailed attention to modes of production.

———

I have thus far referred to the mode of production literature only in the context of an attempt to understand differentiation within a capitalist totality. But the mode of production critique of dependency theory (to the extent that it is possible to talk of "the" critique) is directed to the very definition of capitalism. Frank, with apparent support from Marx (1977 [1867]: 247; 1967b [1894]: 332–333), saw the capitalist system arising with the development of the world market—on which it depended and which it in turn helped to create. Wallerstein, who accepted this conceptualization (1974: 38, 77), argued further that the development of a capitalist world economy "involved a division of productive labor that can only be properly appreciated by taking into account the world-economy as a whole" (ibid.: 126). This, of course, was simply another way of saying that capitalism implied the development of a world market, but it allowed him to argue further that the distinguishing characteristic was not the existence of "free labor" throughout the system but the worldwide division of labor itself (ibid.: 127).

If the "modern history of *capital*" begins in the sixteenth century (Marx 1977 [1867]: 247; emphasis added), however, it is not altogether certain that we can talk of *capitalism* on a world scale from such an early date. More orthodox Marxists have criticized the Frank and Wallerstein perspective as "circulationist." By circulationism, they refer to a definition of capitalism in terms of *exchange*, or the development of a world market, in contrast to a definition stated in terms of a mode of *production*. Ernesto Laclau, who wrote the central criticism of Frank's early essays, noted that long-distance commerce and the development of world markets had long preceded capitalism and had been characteristic of early modes of production (1971). He preferred a definition of capitalism as a mode of production based on the existence of free wage labor, a conceptualization that finds support in numerous passages in Marx's work. Maurice Dobb, in criticizing earlier circulationist views, had provided a most influential Marxist definition of capitalism as:

> a system under which labour-power had "itself become a commodity" and was bought and sold on the market like any other object of exchange. Its historical prerequisite was the concentration of ownership of the means of production in the hands of a class, consisting of only a minor section of society, and the consequential emergence of a propertyless class for whom the sale of their labour-power was their only source of livelihood. Productive activity was furnished, accordingly, by the latter, not by virtue of a legal compulsion, but on the basis of a wage contract. (1963: 7)

This condition did not obtain in much of Latin America for most of its colonial and postcolonial history. If it accurately characterized more of Latin American reality by the mid-twentieth century, there were still significant sectors of the various national economies that were not based on free wage labor (e.g., the peasantry, petty commodity producers and traders, latifundia, etc.). They were therefore, according to the definition as it was applied, not capitalist. Yet those sectors, in the past as well as the present, were caught up in the world-historical processes associated with the making of the modern world. How was this relationship to be understood?

Laclau was interested in preserving the value of Frank's criticism of the dual economy notions of both Latin American Marxism and modernization theory while maintaining the more orthodox definition of capitalism as a mode of production based on free wage labor. He did this by making a distinction between an "economic system" and a "mode of production" (1971: 33). This allowed him to conceive of a worldwide system of exchange dominated by a capitalist mode of production (an economic system that might correspond with Frank's capitalism or Wallerstein's modern world system) that incorporated a series of capitalist and noncapitalist modes of production.

This conceptualization had an enormous influence on Marxists and became the principal point of attack against Frank and other circulationists (cf. Assadourian et al. 1973). Within Latin America, the literature was directed primarily toward an analysis of colonial and nineteenth-century history (e.g., Assadourian et al. 1973; Cueva 1977; C.F.S. Cardoso 1975a; 1975b; Quintero Rivera 1973; Palerm 1976a; Sanoja and Vargas 1974) and the twentieth-century presence of apparently noncapitalist elements in Latin America (e.g., Stavenhagen 1978; Montoya 1978; Archetti 1981; Cook 1982; C.D. Scott 1976; Smith 1979; Llambí 1981; Palerm 1976b; 1980; Bartra 1974). The literature was by no means homogeneous. Some attempted a synthesis with dependency literature, providing a richer analysis of structural differentiation in underdeveloped social formations. Some produced concepts of modes of production not mentioned by Marx that seemed to be of particular relevance to Latin America and other underdeveloped regions (e.g., a colonial mode of production). Others were content to limit themselves to the more or less "official" modes of production and found Asiatic or feudal modes of production in Latin America. For example, although Laclau insisted on a narrow definition of capitalism, he provided a broad definition of feudalism, which he applied to most of Latin American history. Before these trends, and the academic and political issues that inform them, are discussed, however, we might retreat a few paces and examine the concept of mode of production.

CONCEPTS AND DEFINITIONS

Any discussion of Marx and modes of production must begin by noting that Marx was never as rigorous in conceptualizing modes of production as have been subsequent generations of Marxists. As C.F.S. Cardoso notes (1975a), there are at least three uses of the phrase in Marx's writings: (1) a descriptive usage, "without a real theoretical dimension," as in "an agricultural mode of production"; (2) an epochal usage, designed to refer to modes of production that dominate entire periods of history; and (3) a usage that refers to secondary modes of production, which never dominate historical periods but may characterize certain aspects of those periods (e.g., "petty commodity mode").[2] Cutting across these usages can be found a synthesis of two of the central tenets of the Marxist tradition: (1) the emphasis on production as a basic and determining social activity; and (2) the emphasis on historical specificity, the notion that "laws of motion" in society are socially constructed and, rather than being valid for all types of society, are only relevant for particular epochs. Neither aspect by itself is startling. It is the unity of the two emphases in a concept of mode of production that gives the concept its power. The socially constructed laws of motion are to be understood in terms of the mode of production that characterizes a particular epoch. We are able to analyze these laws because the mode of production concept draws our attention to two types of relationships: (1) forces of production (methods and means of appropriating and transforming nature, including technology, work organization, and so on) and (2) relations of production (methods and means of appropriating and transforming labor). The concept therefore articulates and treats as a unity human/nature relations and human/human relations (see Cook 1973; Wolf 1982; Roseberry 1978a; 1983). Each mode of production specifies a particular type of sociality and a particular relationship with nature, the combination of which forms the basis for a determinate class structure. The dynamic relations between classes, in turn, define the laws of motion of a particular epoch. They do not do so, however, in the simple or formulaic manner implied by this brief outline. The complex relationship between mode of production, social classes, and laws of motion receives fuller treatment in the final section of this essay.

To further develop the mode of production concept, we must place it in opposition to two popular usages with which many anthropologists will be familiar: (1) cultural materialism and (2) structural Marxism. For the cultural materialists, the mode of production is given an extremely limited definition. In his clearest statement of his method, Marvin Harris (1979) divides the world into infrastructure, structure, and superstructure. "Infrastructure" is divided into a mode of (subsistence) production and a mode of reproduction (demography, mating patterns, etc.). "Structure" refers to "domestic economy" (family structure, domestic organization, etc.) and "political economy" (political organization, division of labor, class or caste structure, etc.). "Superstructure," finally, refers to art, music, ritual, sports, games, etc. (1979: 52–53). This rigid separation of structures is the basis for a deterministic problematic in which the infrastructure "probabilistically" determines the structure and superstructure (ibid.: 55–56; see above, Chapter 1).

Of the many areas in which a Marxist understanding of mode of production would differ from Harris's understanding, we shall concentrate on two. The first concerns the definition of mode of production itself. A Marxist concept combines much of what Harris divides into infrastructure and structure. What Harris calls a mode of production would incorporate only a part of what Marxists call productive forces. Second, the attitude toward productive forces is somewhat different. While some Marxists, particularly those influenced by Althusser, have little to say about productive forces, placing their emphasis on the dominance of the relations of production, Marx himself stressed that the interaction between humans and nature in the production process *transformed* nature. The whole understanding of the human/nature relationship to which the concept of productive forces refers is more active, with humans as the subject of a process by which they transform nature and, in the process, transform themselves (Marx and Engels 1970 [1846]: 62–63 et passim; Marx 1964a [1844]: 177–193).[3]

The second literature that has appropriated the mode of production concept is structural Marxism, that is, the work of Althusser and his followers.[4] The Althusserians were by no means of one mind and differed on such crucial issues as the very definition of mode of production, social formation, social class, and so on. An adequate treatment of what is too often loosely termed "Althusserianism" would have to differentiate among the various authors *and* trace the writings of individual authors through their careers of critiques and autocritiques. I do not enter into such a discussion here. Despite diversity, there is a set of shared assumptions that allows us to tie the various structuralist approaches together. The first is that one of Marx's central contributions was the distinction between a level of phenomenal appearances and a basic underlying reality. While one may question whether this is a "central epistemological premise" of Marxism (Wright 1978: 11), it is clearly an important aspect of Marx's (and Hegel's) method. The common example is the analysis of exploitation in capitalism, which begins with the level of appearances—the circulation of commodities, the exchange of equivalents—and penetrates that level to examine the extraction of surplus value through the sale of the commodity *labor power* and its use as *labor*. The surface relationship of commodity exchange at equal values facilitates and obscures an actual relationship of exploitation.

This distinction between a level of appearances and an underlying structural reality is important for an understanding of three of the basic concepts of the Althusserian tradition: mode of production, articulation, and social formation. Again the definitions vary, and the usages are in many cases contradictory. Mode of production may be narrowly defined as a concept of a precise combination of forces and relations of production (or labor processes and dominant relations of appropriation), or more broadly as a concept of a combination of several structures or levels or instances (economic, juridico-political, ideological, theoretical) determined "in the last instance" by the economic. Already in these definitions the term "articulation" may creep in, as articulation may refer to the precise combination of forces and relations of production, or to the connections among structural levels. But articulation may also refer to the connection of a mode of production to a social formation, or to the connections among modes of production within a social formation (see Foster-Carter 1978: 52–54). Social formation is most commonly defined as a concept of the social whole, composed of the same structural levels that appear in broader definitions of the mode of production. But the precise definition depends upon one's understanding of mode of production and articulation. The same language is being used to discuss three different problems, depending on one's definition of terms: (1)

the relationship between an abstract model (mode of production) and a concrete case (social formation); (2) the distinction between an economic base (mode of production) and a social whole including base and superstructure (social formation); and (3) a social whole (social formation) composed of various modes of production, one of which will be seen as dominant (Roseberry 1978b). In the second usage, the mode of production concept is given its more restricted, "economic," meaning. In the first and third usages, the mode of production concept may be given either a restricted or more expansive meaning since the distinction between mode of production and social formation is located elsewhere.

In all these usages, mode of production is regarded as an abstract concept that allows one to grasp structures that lie behind the level of appearances. In an early work that adopts the first and third articulation problematics, Poulantzas clearly expressed the distinction. After he defined the mode of production expansively as an articulated combination of economic, political, ideological, and theoretical levels, he claimed:

> The mode of production constitutes an abstract-formal object which does not exist in the strong sense in reality. . . . The only thing which really exists is a historically determined *social formation*, i.e., a social whole, in the widest sense, at a given moment in its historical existence: e.g., France under Louis Bonaparte, England during the Industrial Revolution. But a social formation, which is a real-concrete object and so always original because singular, presents a particular combination, a specific overlapping of several "pure" modes of production (as Lenin demonstrated in *The Development of Capitalism in Russia* [*sic*]). Bismarck's Germany is characterized by a specific combination of capitalists, feudal and patriarchal modes of production whose combination alone exists in a strong sense of the term; all that exists in this sense is a social formation historically determined as a particular object. (1975: 15)

As Foster-Carter noted (1978: 54), the term "articulation" was here reserved for the relationship among levels in a mode of production. The combination of modes of production was described as a combination, an overlapping, or a domination. It was Pierre-Philippe Rey (to be discussed below) who adapted the language of articulation to the combination of modes. But the point I want to stress here is the stated relation of mode of production as abstract to social formation as concrete. This is to be related to the distinction between surface appearances and underlying structural reality, knowledge of which is to be gained through a privileged form of theoretical practice (Althusser 1971).

But further discussion of structuralism requires that we consider the second assumption: that any reference to an active, constituting human subject is an example of voluntarism, historicism, humanism, anthropologism, or other dark sins. To the extent that reference to a subject *is* historicist (in the Hegelian sense of history as unfolding Spirit) or voluntarist (with an emphasis on an individual or class subject *choosing* or willing a particular historical outcome), the structuralist rejection of "the subject" is valid. But, as numerous critics have pointed out, there is no necessary reason for reference to human subjects to take this turn. By lumping completely different approaches under the label "historicism," the structuralists constricted themselves in a number of ways.

First, they placed themselves in an essentially pre-Marxian antimony between idealism and materialism, history and structure, ideology and science. The very texts of the early Marx that they rejected as humanist were the ones in which the antinomies were shattered. Second, when linked to the structuralists' first assumption (the distinction between appearances and underlying structural reality), the second assumption led them into a rationalism from which there was no escape. The level of reality was, by their definition, structurally, rather than socially, determined. Humans were seen as "bearers" of structural relations, and the structures themselves were conceived as logically prior to human action. They were abstract-formal modes of production arrived at through theoretical practice. Therefore, classes and other social phenomena were seen as structural effects (cf. Poulantzas 1975: 58–70; F. H. Cardoso 1973b). The rationalism of this scheme is evident when we attempt to analyze change and transformation. Despite a variety of approaches, all of the structuralists shared this attitude toward change: fundamental contradictions were seen as contradictions between structures (see Godelier 1972: 77–82). These problems should be kept in mind when reading structuralist exegeses on modes of production and social formations, economic, political, and ideological instances, relative autonomy, and so on. They were elaborate theoretical exercises for the production of the basic structures from which classes and other "effects" could be deduced.

As the mode of production literature developed in Latin America, it borrowed much of the language of the Althusserians, in part because many of the contributors to the literature studied in Paris. "Social formation," for example, referred to a social whole, usually a nation-state. "Articulation" generally referred to a combination of capitalist and noncapitalist modes of production within a social formation. Despite the language, however, much of the literature was far removed from its Althusserian origins, in part because the literature was not conceived as a scholastic exercise but as an attempt to understand the political and economic formation of Peru or Mexico or Venezuela and the position and role of the peasantry or other groups in political processes and struggles. This led to no small amount of empiricism, but it also allowed many authors to escape the rationalism of an Althusser and recapture the Marxian focus on class formation and class struggle. In the worst of the literature, mode of production analysis became an end in itself, a labeling exercise. In the best, it became a means to another end—class analysis. As indicated earlier the mode of production literature in Latin America addressed two central and related problems: (1) colonial and nineteenth-century history, and (2) the presence of apparently noncapitalist sectors in the twentieth century. I shall address the second issue, especially as it concerns the literature on peasantries, in Chapter 7. Here I concentrate on approaches to and understandings of history.

ARTICULATION AS HISTORICAL PROCESS

Beyond all of the debates about labels between mode of production and world-system theorists, the historical problem to which
those debates allude is indeed significant. If we follow Marx's
definition of capital in the strict sense not as a thing but as a
social relation between capital and labor power as a commodity,
we are confronted by the most vexing difficulties in the analysis
of the expansion of capitalism. We may talk about the investment of capital in a noncapitalist region, but our language then
implies a concept of capital as a thing. As a social relation,
"capital" exists within a capitalist mode of production, but "it"
does not exist, by definition, in a mode of production in which
the basic presuppositions for capitalism (that is, the social relation defined by the separation of labor from means of labor) do
not yet exist. Those presuppositions must be created through a
social process that involves an interaction between "capital"
(that is, the social relation of separation of labor from means of
labor and all of the institutions through which that relation is
expressed) and "noncapital" (that is, some type of union of
labor with means of labor and all of the institutions through
which that union is expressed). The historical problem is this:
how are we to analyze this process without reducing it to what it
may become (capitalism) or to what it once was and no longer is
(not-capitalism)?

For the world-system theorists, there is little problem. For
them, capital is not defined as a social relation (or at least not
the same social relation to which most Marxists refer). Once
noncapitalist regions have been incorporated within the capitalist division of labor defined by the world market, they are capitalist because the relations of production that define the core
define the system (Wallerstein 1974: 127). Despite the numerous traps that some mode of production theorists have set for
themselves, their literature is the only one that has been willing
to confront the *historical* problem directly. This confrontation
with historical process has been the mode of production literature's greatest strength, even if that strength sometimes remains an unrealized promise. The *questions* authors within this

tradition have asked are important, even if the answers have been elusive.

The problem was most clearly addressed outside the Latin American context by Pierre-Philippe Rey, who saw three stages in the articulation of capitalist and noncapitalist modes of production when "capital" intervenes in noncapitalist formations (Rey 1976: 81–109; Bradby 1975; Foster-Carter 1978).

1. In the first stage, capitalist and noncapitalist modes of production articulate solely through circulation. Commodities produced through noncapitalist relations enter into capitalist circuits of exchange, but the basic unity of labor with means of labor in the noncapitalist mode is not necessarily threatened. Commodity production and circulation long precede capitalism and are in no way incompatible with noncapitalist production relations. Capitalism may therefore be reproduced by selling and purchasing commodities with noncapitalist sectors without necessarily breaking up those relations.

2. Stage two comes, for Rey, when the requirements of capitalist accumulation and reproduction can no longer be met by this form of articulation. Capitalists may need additional labor power or new means of production, and the former unity of labor with means of labor in the noncapitalist mode must be broken to provide either or both of these newly defined commodities. Because, according to Rey, this separation cannot be accomplished at the economic level alone, violence is necessary. "Articulation," as a process of expanded reproduction of capitalism and destruction of noncapitalist relations, is in this stage a predominantly political process. Even though the former unity is broken, the old forms through which that unity was expressed continue to exist. Capital is therefore accumulated through noncapitalist forms that are now dominated (politically) by capitalist relations of production and reproduction. Rey characterized this period as one in which capitalism is "taking root."

3. In the third stage, capitalism no longer "needs" noncapitalist relations, and its relations of production are established without the necessity of political intervention. According to Rey, this stage has arrived in the United States alone.

Rey applied his scheme to West African history. Leaving aside the question of its applicability to that region, we can note that its relevance for Latin America is problematic. This must be kept in mind when one reads the debates that emerged on the necessity of violence. Whether we consider Africa or Latin America, however, the violent nature of "articulation" in the first stage (essentially, the historical period that preceded imperialism) is underemphasized. This is clear with the African slave trade and the colonization of Latin America. As a result, the relative violence of the second stage (and the tortured discussion of political vs. economic domination throughout) may be overemphasized.

But I shall not discuss the stages as stages, the necessity of violence, or the dominance of the political or economic. More importantly, Rey has illuminated the historical problem in such a way that we can approach an understanding of the relevance of the mode of production literature and its most important pitfalls. Although his language is less evocative than Ortner's discussion of the capitalist ship and the noncapitalist shore (1984; see above, Chapter 2), he has raised a series of questions that makes possible a more serious and careful consideration of the issues. He has outlined three broadly conceived historical *possibilities*, in each of which mode of production analysis must take a different form. In discussing these possibilities, I stress that they are not conceived as stages. Roughly, the first and second possibilities could characterize parts of Latin America in the colonial and immediate postcolonial period, with the second possibility becoming more important in the late nineteenth century. The second and third possibilities could characterize parts of Latin America in the middle and late twentieth century. However, I stress that these possibilities are simultaneously present in an unevenly developing capitalism. Too often we think of capitalism as an undifferentiated, expanding whole. "It" *is* a totality, but it is characterized by the *unevenness* of its development. That unevenness results in the distinct possibilities (which are nonetheless not separate or discrete) to which I refer.

In the *first* possibility, capitalism does not dominate noncapitalist modes of production, although they may "articulate" through the circulation of commodities. The phrase "does not dominate" implies that the unity of labor with means of labor is intact and the laws of motion of the noncapitalist mode have not been interrupted. In such situations, it is extremely important that we have concepts with which we can characterize the type of unity and the laws of motion without reducing them to the terms or logic of capitalism (see Harbsmeier 1978; Kahn 1981b; Clarke 1981). Despite articulation through circulation, those laws of motion must not be analyzed in terms of the logic and needs of capitalist production and reproduction. In such situations, mode of production analysis offers more possibilities for historical understanding than does world-system analysis, *as long as* the very terms in which modes of production are discussed can be freed from capitalist categories (an outcome that is by no means guaranteed and for which there are few successful examples).

In the *third* possibility, the unity of labor with means of labor has been broken, and capitalist relations are dominant. This situation may exist even where apparently noncapitalist social groups (e.g., peasants, artisans, and so on) are actively present in the social formation. The simple existence of social group that does not correspond to "pure" capitalist classes does not indicate the existence of another mode of production unless the apparently problematic groups exist within relations of production and reproduction that can genuinely be considered noncapitalist. They may exist as part of the total reproduction process of capital; indeed, the very logic of capital reproduction may create such ambiguous class positions (Wright 1978: 61–87). In such a situation (and it surely applies to many aspects of contemporary Latin America that have been analyzed within the articulation literature), reference to the articulation of modes of production is at once too much and too little. It is too much because it implies a dynamic, or law of motion, that does not exist. It is too little because it locates that dynamic in terms of an abstractly conceived mode of production rather than the concrete action of the problematic groups themselves (see below, Chapter 7, for a consideration of one such problematic group).[5]

The most important historical problems concern the intermediate, *second* possibility, the one Rey refers to as capitalism "taking root." Rey expresses the problem fairly well:

> In the case of the transition from the feudal to the capitalist
> mode of production, it seems obvious that one begins the
> study of the necessity [*sic*] of that evolution with feudalism,
> since capitalism is born there. On the other hand, in all the
> other known historical examples of capitalist development
> from within a noncapitalist social formation, capitalism was
> imported from elsewhere, already grown and strong. One
> therefore has the temptation to analyze the necessity [*sic*] of
> its development only from the point of view of its own laws.
> Nevertheless, we will see that it is not possible to follow this
> unilateral vision and that the phase of transition cannot be
> understood except in terms of the internal characteristics of
> the mode of production dominant before the intrusion of
> capital. The social formation should take its own form of
> transition to capitalism. The social formation of transition
> therefore finds itself submitted to a double history, where
> the contradiction between two orders of necessity is made
> manifest: on the one side the history of capital itself, which is
> essentially written outside of these social formations; on the
> other side, the history of the specific transition of the modes
> of production articulated with it. (1976: 82–83)

Even within this passage we can see where the very real historical problem is diverted. Our labels, and the ideas they express, prejudge the issue. It is apparent in the reference to capitalism "taking root." However much Rey wants to see transition conceived in terms of the modes of production into which capital is inserted, there is no doubt about the end result of that process. It is seen as a *transition* to capitalism. The double history has a single, teleological end. But if the historical process during this period is one that cannot be reduced to the situation that existed before capitalism entered the picture or to the situation that might exist if capitalism becomes dominant, then our current ideas about history and our current concepts of modes of production do not serve us well.

In a well-known passage, Marx describes three outcomes of conquest: "In all cases of conquest, three things are possible. The conquering people subjugates the conquered under its own mode of production . . . ; or it leaves the old mode intact and contents itself with tribute . . . ; or a reciprocal interaction takes place whereby something new, a synthesis, arises . . . " (1973 [1857–58]: 97; cf. C.F.S. Cardoso 1975a). We have numerous examples of subjugation and tribute, and our concepts and ideas serve us well enough in their analysis. We also have examples of historical syntheses, and our concepts have thus far not proved adequate for the task. We have not yet shown ourselves capable of grasping, *theoretically*, something new. In this case, reference to modes of production that do not relate to or address this problem, however numerous we make them or however convoluted our discussions of their articulation, cannot obscure (although the language is certainly obscurantist) our failure.

If we are really talking about something new, and we take the assumptions behind the mode of production concept seriously, then new sets of class relations emerge, and new laws of motion—based upon the class relations—result. These laws of motion (and the interests of the newly dominant classes) cannot be reduced to the needs of capital or the interests of the capitalist class as a whole. We therefore do indeed have a double history, a transition without an easily definable end point. Of course, I do not mean to suggest that later periods of history might not find the new modes and classes and dynamics subjected to more powerful pressures from the centers of capitalist development. Indeed, just as noncapitalist modes may be subjugated by the laws of motion of capitalism, so may these synthetic modes. But such an outcome is not immanent within the synthetic mode itself.

For example, I have examined a situation in the nineteenth-century Venezuelan Andes in which merchant capital was being invested in coffee production. The investment of capital was associated with the transformation of forms of landed property, the creation of a property-owning, commodity-producing peasantry, and the rise of a merchant class that was able to force ties of dependence upon the peasantry. Entirely new class relations emerged, and the resulting dynamic could only be understood in terms of the imposition of a form of capital in the region. Models of precapitalist modes of production that treated capital as an external feature would be inadequate. Yet neither was the region subjected to a capitalist dynamic. The merchants were not agents of industrial capital or of a capitalist mode of production. They were pursuing their own interests, which could not be reduced to and were often in conflict with the interests of larger capitalists. That the merchants and the coffee economy they dominated were later displaced during Venezuela's petroleum era should not obscure the alternative trajectory of the nineteenth century (Roseberry 1983).

The point is that we are dealing with determinate *and* contingent historical processes. We must understand the interaction between noncapitalist and capitalist modes in Latin American history across five centuries in terms of what existed before contact, the nature of the contact and the transformation of social relations that resulted, the new relations and dynamics that were instituted, the contradictions engendered by those relations, and the manner in which those contradictions were resolved and, in turn, set in motion new contradictory relations and dynamics. This analysis must take into account Latin America as a whole and its position within a developing world system. Yet it must simultaneously grasp the regional diversity of Latin America in terms of ecology, prehistory, historical incorporation, etc. We must, in short, analyze regional processes of class formation. Such analyses make room for, indeed require, anthropological understanding.

For example, if one were trying to analyze the impact of coffee production on agrarian class formation in nineteenth-century Latin America, one would first have to come to grips with coffee production and consumption as world-historical facts, analyzing developing international marketing and distributional networks and changing consumption patterns as coffee moved from coffee houses into the home. But one would also have to explain the remarkable diversity of production arrangements and class relations that resulted from the production of this world-historical product—from capital-intensive plantations in Brazil to haciendas and dependent (as well as independent) small farmers in Venezuela, Colombia, and Costa Rica, to large estates with resident and nonresident laborers in El Salvador, to large estates with migratory indigenous laborers in Guatemala. Such an investigation would need to pay close attention to the markedly different societies into which coffee production was introduced (Roseberry 1986a; see C.F.S. Cardoso 1975b for a preliminary comparison of Central American coffee-producing countries along these lines).[6] One must, then, examine several quite distinct expressions of the "internalization of the external" (see Chapter 4).

——

Much of the best anthropological and historical work that has paid attention to regional processes of class formation has avoided the mode of production literature entirely, even as it has contributed to a resolution of the issues raised by that literature. It would seem, then, that the theoretical problems associated with mode of production analysis point toward historical and anthropological solutions. We cannot leave our discussion at that level, however. "History" does not present itself as a master key. As Godelier suggests, history does not explain anything but must itself be explained (1977: 49) It will be remembered that this essay began with a problem in anthropological and historical writing that pointed toward the necessity of a theoretical discourse. Clearly some sort of synthesis of theory and history is necessary, but most of our popular models drive wedges between them.

The most important wedges concern the problem of "law." I have referred at various points in this essay to the "laws of motion of particular modes of production," and this phrase must now receive critical attention. Throughout Marx's writing, one will find references to basic, fundamental laws—of accumulation, of population, and so on. Of course, Marx did not see them as natural laws that applied to all historical epochs. Rather, each mode of production had its own laws of motion. Nonetheless, he did see what he was doing as scientific, and his reference to law is fundamental to any under-standing of him. For many readers, such an emphasis—even when laws only apply to particular modes of production—raises the problem of human agency, choice, and contingency. While this problem has been elaborated by a number of West-ern Marxists whose distinct analyses have been lumped by more orthodox writers as Hegelian or "voluntarist" (e.g., Lu-kács 1971 [1922]; Gramsci 1971 [1929–35]; Korsch 1971 [1923]), the question of human agency has been most often raised outside the Marxist tradition as part of an emphasis on individual choice. More recently, human agency and history have been treated as central problems in the Marxist tradition by E. P. Thompson and his followers.

More theoretical readings of Marx may emphasize the "scien-tific" Marx, the Marx of fundamental laws of motion. These can be found, for example, in the Second and Third Internationals, and in such recent movements as the Kapitallogik formation in Germany (see Harbsmeier 1978) or the Althusserians. While the Althusserians would reject the more economistic versions of Marxian scientism, they continually stressed the importance of science as opposed to ideology. And we have already encoun-tered their rejection of history. Some scholars who reject this sort of scientism but also seek to avoid voluntarist emphases refer to the laws of motion as "tendencies" (see, e.g., Chinchilla and Dietz 1981). But this avoids the problem altogether and does not take us beyond a contemplative approach (see Lukács 1971 [1922]) to social processes shared by both scientism and voluntarism.

Full discussion of the philosophical and political problems associated with law in theory and history would require a sepa-rate volume. For the purposes of this essay, I concentrate on Althusser and Thompson and examine their readings of *Capi-tal*. For the Althusserians, *Capital* was Marx's most developed scientific work, in terms of which all his other writing was to be evaluated. The book was seen as a theoretical work—the theory of the capitalist mode of production. It was not seen as a histori-cal work. The classic and oft-repeated formulation of this point of view stressed that Marx's *Capital* was an analysis of the *capital-ist mode of production* while Lenin's *Development of Capitalism in*

Russia (1964 [1899]) was an analysis of a *capitalist social formation*. This interpretation must, of course, confront the attention Marx devoted to the history and conditions of capitalism in England (e.g., in Chapters 10, 13–15, 27–32 of Volume 1 of *Capital*). For the Althusserians, these materials were simply intended as examples and rendered the work more accessible to a reading public. No organic relationship was seen, then, between the theory and the lengthy historical discussions.

Thompson denied an organic relationship between theory and history in *Capital* as well, but he preferred the historical parts of the book. For Thompson, Marx's "obsessive" (1978a: 59) encounter with political economy led him into a trap. However much he undermined and transcended the assumptions and categories of classical political economy, in his concern for laws of motion in capitalism he was caught in the same "static, anti-historical structure" (ibid.: 61) that he was criticizing. This was most evident, according to Thompson, in the *Grundrisse* (1973 [1857–58]). The addition of the historical material in *Capital* was the springing of the trap, the beginning of a move beyond political economy (Thompson 1978a: 55–66). *Capital* remained, however, a "mountainous inconsistency" (ibid.: 65).

Perhaps. But it seems to me that both Althusser and Thompson separated what in *Capital* was an indissoluble unity and produced a profound misreading of Marx. If we look at one set of historical chapters, we find that they come at a particularly important place in Marx's book. Marx has just set out his analysis of value and surplus value, the basis for an understanding of capitalist exploitation. In its first theoretical expression, surplus value appears as absolute surplus value. Under this form, the number of hours necessary to reproduce the value of labor power is taken as given. Surplus labor, and by extension surplus value, can only be expanded through an expansion of the working day. Marx then enters into a long historical chapter (Chapter 10) on the struggle in England over the length of the working day. The account of the struggle concentrates on legislation. In the early stages of capitalist development, laws were passed to lengthen the working day, to require apprentices and semiindependent or formerly independent workers to work full days and weeks for emerging masters. With the industrial transformation of the late eighteenth and early nineteenth centuries, however, legislation began to turn in the opposite direction, shortening the working day, restricting the labor of women and children, and so on. This apparent victory for the working class meant that the capitalist was confronted with a reduction of absolute surplus value. In the face of this development, Marx then introduces the concept of relative surplus value. With it, he no longer assumes the number of hours necessary to reproduce the value of labor power as given. Rather, the necessary labor component could be reduced either by reducing the value of labor power or by increasing the productivity of labor. Marx then entered into another series of historical chapters (13–15) describing the process by which capital transformed the work process and the worker, increasing productivity and extracting ever greater masses of surplus value from the laborer.

Let us look at these chapters in terms of the laws of motion of capitalism. It should be clear that these laws are not viewed in terms of the abstract logic of capital or any other ahistorical formulation. Rather, they are set in motion through a struggle between two fundamental classes. The working class struggled to reduce the working day, earned victories in that fight, but was simultaneously confronted by another initiative from capital— the transformation of work. I do not mean to imply that the move from absolute to relative surplus value was represented in historical time. It is, rather, a theoretical movement. Historically, both types of surplus value were present simultaneously. For example, the apparent victory for workers in the shortening of the working day occurred in the context of the Industrial Revolution, or the growth of relative surplus value with the transformation of work. Nor do I mean to imply that a struggle between classes is the only means by which we can understand the movement toward relative surplus value. Marx quite clearly showed that the impulse toward relative surplus value was provided by competition among capitals. Nonetheless, Marx did make the action of humans central to the laws of motion of capitalism. The result of that action was not what the working class envisioned. Indeed, they were further proletarianized in the process. There is, then, no hint of voluntarism in Marx's approach, no suggestion that workers were choosing historical outcomes. Their action, however, and the opposing action of capital are the means through which history is made. It is through struggle that we may write of structure, through struggle that we may envision laws of motion.

Let us return, then, to the problem of theory and history. The historical sections of *Capital* only make sense because they are placed within a theoretical analysis that has sketched the basic relationships of capitalism: the division between capital and labor, the commoditization of labor power, the labor theory of value. On the basis of these relationships, a certain imperative is adduced for the capitalist: the constant expansion of surplus value. These relationships and that imperative are analyzed through a process of abstraction. But there is no sense in which the imperative can be abstractly realized. It can only be realized through the basic relationships, which now take concrete forms and fight historical battles. Through these battles, the relationships themselves are transformed.[7]

This is the sort of understanding that we should take to the analysis of modes of production and regional processes of class formation in Latin America. If indeed "something new, a synthesis" emerged in some periods and in some regions in Latin America, our analyses must be theoretically sophisticated enough to outline the basic relationships that characterized those regions and periods. For this study, a concept of mode of production is essential. It must be seen, however, as a starting point for analyses of class formation and struggle. That is, we must avoid the rationalism of Althusser, which takes the separation of theory and history as a point of honor, and we must avoid the empiricism and formalism of much of the Latin American literature. In both cases, mode of production analysis becomes an end in itself. In the first, one adopts a condescending attitude toward the human subjects of history; in the second, one simply applies labels to history. The labels then imply certain unproblematic relationships and certain laws of motion; the grouping of labels in some form of articulation becomes a way of categorizing structural heterogeneity and calling it contradiction. In contrast, the approach I am calling for is one that uses the mode of production concept as a theoretical tool in outlining certain class relationships. The central focus of study, however, is the formation of the classes themselves, their relations with other classes in space and time, their forms of organization, and their struggles—over the price of corn or coffee, for land, for the state. In this type of study, the mode of production perspective reaches its limits. The limits cannot be transcended within mode of production analysis itself but only with the recognition that the subjects of history, the makers of laws of motion, are neither the concepts nor the conceptualizers.

Agrarian Questions and Functionalist Economism in Latin America

Our discussion of modes of production began with a brief discussion of anthropological work among Latin American peasantries and turned toward approaches to history. In returning to twentieth-century peasantries, I do not attempt to survey the various approaches to peasants within the mode of production literature. Simply at the level of basic categories, the range of opinion is wide—from those who see peasants as part of a noncapitalist mode of production (called "peasant," "simple commodity," or "tributary"), through those who try to understand peasant production and exchange in terms of the dynamics of a capitalist mode of production, to those who abandon the more abstract posturings of the mode of production literature and concentrate on discrete "forms" of production.[1]

Cross-cutting the various divisions among writers concerning labels is a more serious disagreement concerning the positions, roles, and fates of peasantries within the dynamics of contemporary Latin American capitalism. One group of writers projects the eventual or actual disappearance of peasants within capitalist society; another stresses the persistence of peasants in severely disadvantaged positions within circuits of capital and state accumulation. The most sophisticated discussion has occurred in Mexico and has included such authors as Roger Bartra (who places his analytical attention upon and political faith in a proletariat) and Arturo Warman (who stresses the persistence and political creativity of peasants).[2]

To a certain extent, the literature repeats and draws upon themes played out in the Russian literature of the early twentieth century. Of particular interest has been the writing of the Russian Marxists—especially V. I. Lenin's *Development of Capitalism in Russia* (1964 [1899]) and later works—and of the populists ("Narodniks") and neopopulists—especially A. V. Chayanov (1966 [1925]), who offered a profound if often obliquely stated critique of the Marxist understanding.

The reasons for the popularity of this literature are not hard to locate. Russia was a primarily agricultural country in the initial stages of a capitalist transformation that was most evident in industrial pockets in urban areas. Marxists and populists were concerned about the roles and fates of recently emancipated peasants in Russia's capitalist development, and they were especially concerned about their position within revolutionary movements. Nineteenth-century populists wanted to preserve the peasant commune from capitalist intrusion from outside, seeing in the commune the cell form of a future communist society (cf. Shanin 1983). Lenin, whose *Development of Capitalism in Russia* was written as a critique of populist ideas (to which Marx had offered support late in his life), contended that capitalism was already entrenched in the countryside, that peasant communities were differentiated into rich, middle, and poor strata, and that the differentiation was part of an ongoing process of class formation as the peasantry separated into a small petty bourgeoisie and a large proletariat. Chayanov, writing some years later, did not enter this debate. His "neopopulist" school, however, arose in light of the failure of Russian peasants to differentiate into classes as one might have expected, especially after the 1905 Stolypin Reforms, and the fact that peasants in the revolution acted as peasants rather than rural proletarians. Given the circumstances, Leninist theory could not be directly confronted, but Chayanov developed an approach that concentrated on the organizational features and domestic cycles of peasant households. He understood differentiation among households not as a social process leading to class

formation but as a demographic process whereby peasant holdings increased as the number of dependents increased and
decreased thereafter. Chayanov claimed to see his work as complementary to Marxist theory, developing a noncapitalist economics. Whether it was complementary or not, it depended
more on marginalist assumptions than he could ever admit (for
summaries and critiques, see Shanin 1972; Harrison 1975;
1977; 1979; Durrenberger, ed. 1984; Lehman 1982; Donham
1981). Moreover, the different interpretations of the process of
differentiation (social or demographic) implied profoundly different understandings of the positions, roles, and fates of peasants in Russian development.

The formal similarities between Russia in the late nineteenth
century and some Third World societies in the middle to late
twentieth century have often been noted (Shanin 1972), as
have the differences (Shanin 1979). More important, our understandings of peasants within contemporary Latin American
capitalist societies are still framed in much the same terms that
were used in late-nineteenth- and early-twentieth-century Russia. One need only immerse oneself in the differentiation
debates in Mexico and elsewhere to be convinced of the contemporary relevance of the literature. That important questions are at stake is clear from the frequent misrepresentations
and caricatures, both of the Russian literature and of recent
contributions. For example, it is often claimed that Lenin saw
differentiation and disappearance as inevitable, virtually automatic, thus falling into a kind of determinism that makes peasants mechanically disappear and denying to peasants any kind
of agency. The analysis is thus seen to fit within a typical Marxist dismissal of peasants as part of a univocal celebration of the
proletariat. There is some truth here, especially in the later
literature, but it should be remembered that Lenin framed his
analysis as an argument against state policies that were designed to block differentiation; there was little in his analysis
that suggested inevitability.

On the other hand, Chayanov and Chayanovians are dismissed as populists and romantics who, in their celebration of a
disappearing peasantry, served reactionary goals. Here, too,

there is some truth: agrarianist policies that ignore proletarianization may freeze agriculturalists on the land in a semi-
peasant, semiproletarian status that assures continued poverty.
But the truth is hardly uncomplicated. That a populist apprecia-
tion of the peasantry need be neither romantic nor reactionary
should be clear from a careful reading of Arturo Warman's
analysis of the Morelos peasantry in the context of Mexican
capitalism and state formation (1981). An attempt to pay attention to the activities of peasants as they endeavor to hold onto
land and livelihood in the face of such powerful pressures is not
necessarily, though in extreme versions it certainly is, a denial
of those pressures and a romantic search for authenticity. Likewise, a Marxist attempt to analyze the dynamics of capitalist
development that impinge upon a peasantry and subject it to
powerful pressures toward proletarianization is not necessarily,
though in extreme versions it certainly is, an attempt to impose
mechanically determinist laws upon supposedly passive anthropological subjects. As Marx commented regarding the Russian
peasantry: "What threatens the life of the Russian commune is
neither a historical inevitability nor a theory; it is state oppres-
sion, and exploitation by capitalist intruders whom the state has
made powerful at the peasants' expense" (in Shanin 1983: 104–
105). One should not blame the messenger for bringing us bad
news.

We can appreciate the literature and its importance for anthropologists if we eschew a broad survey or review and concentrate on one recent contribution. We can then examine what
that work has to say to anthropologists and what (some) anthropologists might say in response. I turn, then, to the work of a
political economist, Alain de Janvry. In his own essays and in
essays coauthored with some of his former students (see de
Janvry and Garramon 1977; Deere and de Janvry 1979; 1981),
he has been developing a model that fits firmly within a slightly
modified Leninist approach to peasants. This has received its
most thorough statement in his book, *The Agrarian Question and
Reformism in Latin America* (1981). This essay makes no attempt
to evaluate all aspects of his analysis but concentrates on his
basic model of articulated versus disarticulated accumulation

and assesses his understanding of peasants within a mode of accumulation characterized by "functional dualism." After a brief presentation of the model, I offer a critical assessment.

———

De Janvry's model[3] begins with a basic distinction between articulated and disarticulated accumulation (cf. Amin 1976). Articulated accumulation (de Janvry 1981: 26–23), characteristic of "central" economies, depends upon an economy that can be divided along the classic lines of Marx's distinction between a capital goods sector (Department I) and a consumption goods sector (Department II). Sectoral articulation simply refers to the fact that the two sectors supply the goods necessary to satisfy the demand presented by each of the two sectors. The capital goods sector provides the machines and raw materials necessary for further production in both the capital goods and consumption goods sectors. The consumption goods sector produces wage and luxury goods (de Janvry emphasizes wage goods) for workers in both the capital goods and consumption goods sectors. Marx made the basic distinction to demonstrate that all of the value produced in one cycle of production *could* be realized in exchange and that, given the right set of circumstances, capitalism could reproduce itself on a simple or expanded basis without crisis or recourse to external outlets (Marx 1967a [1888]). Of course, capitalism being unplanned, the right set of circumstances is hard to come by, and crises of various degrees of severity are endemic in capitalism. Marx's model was intended to criticize the more simplistic nineteenth-century socialist theories of crisis, emphasizing structurally dictated overproduction and underconsumption.

De Janvry explores some of the literature on crisis, contradiction, and accumulation in central economies, but the discussion is not crucial to our current consideration. More important for what follows are two of de Janvry's conclusions (1981: 31). (1) Under articulated accumulation, labor is both a "gain" and a "loss" for capital. That is, to increase or maintain profits, labor costs must be reduced as much as possible. On the other hand, labor is a market as well as a production cost, and laborers must be paid well enough to purchase the products of the consumer goods sector. (2) The drive to reduce labor costs and increase the market capacity of labor implies the complete proletarianization of the labor force, meaning that "there is a rapid tendency toward *unimodality* and ultimately only two classes" (ibid.).

On the other hand, disarticulated accumulation (ibid.: 32–40) in "peripheral" economies cannot be characterized in terms of a relationship between capital and consumption goods sectors. De Janvry sees two types of disarticulated economy: one in which a modern enclave produces agricultural, mineral, or industrial goods for export; another in which the export enclave is combined with an industrial sector created by import substitution policies. The industrial sector, however, will be devoted to luxury goods. The market for the "modern" sector, then, will be in the exterior (enclave exports) and among the "local bourgeoisie" and "landed elites" (import substitution industrialization). Note that in neither case do workers provide a market for the output of the "modern" sector. This provides the basis for one of de Janvry's basic distinctions. Labor is both a gain and a loss for capital in articulated economies but only a loss (that is, a cost) in peripheral economies (ibid.: 34). Therefore, there is no countervailing pressure against a model of accumulation that decreases real wages as low as possible. Also, as a result, there is no tendency toward full proletarianization. Instead, a "traditional" sector is maintained to provide for the workers part of the consumption needs that are not satisfied in the "modern" sector. Here de Janvry introduces the concept of "functional dualism." In its first approximation, it is worth quoting in full.

> Of the two motives for proletarianization of labor that exist in articulated economies, the first (reducing labor costs) but not the second (creating a home market out of rising wages), applies to disarticulated economies. As a result, labor costs can be further reduced by perpetuating the subsistence economy that partially assumes the cost of maintaining and reproducing the labor force. *Functional dualism* between modern and traditional sectors thus makes it possible to sustain a level of

wage below the cost of maintenance and reproduction of the labor force—a cost that would determine the minimum wage for a fully proletarianized labor force. Here, wage is only a complement between the subsistence needs of the worker and his family and net production in the traditional sector. From the standpoint of the employer, labor is "free" and fully proletarianized; labor is a variable cost paid in cash. But from the standpoint of the labor force, labor is only *semiproletarianized,* since part of the laborers' subsistence needs are derived from production for home consumption. Functional dualism thus provides the structural possibility of meeting the necessity for cheap labor that derives from the laws of accumulation under social disarticulation. (Ibid.: 36, 37)

This first approximation implies that workers in the modern sector have direct connections with the traditional sector, where they provide for a portion of their own subsistence. A second approximation implicitly takes into account urban/rural and proletarian/semiproletarian or proletarian/peasant differences that are not contained in the first statement of functional dualism. In the second approximation, de Janvry considers the problem of providing cheap food for a proletariat whose real wages have been depressed as low as possible. This proletariat, especially in urban areas, may not provide for its own subsistence but must find cheap food in the marketplace. De Janvry considers three mechanisms that can provide cheap food: (1) suppression of prices, mandating food production for sale by traditional sectors, e.g., peasants; (2) imports; and (3) capitalist development in agriculture. The third option, however, given low prices, can only be maintained with cheap labor. It is here that semiproletarian labor is most characteristic. The laborer who works for wages and engages in subsistence agriculture is now placed in agriculture rather than throughout the disarticulated economy (ibid.: 39).

With this basic distinction, then, de Janvry has created the possibility of an analysis that goes beyond the simple oppositions between Chayanov and Lenin. Following Lenin (and Marxist approaches generally), he approaches peasants in terms of their position within a process of capital accumulation. Unlike those theorists who expect a replication in the Third World of the English experience described by Marx, de Janvry sees an incomplete proletarianization, the creation of a class of producers that is neither fully peasant nor fully proletarian: the semi-proletariat. The creation of this class is a result of the logic of functional dualism, which de Janvry sees arising in Latin America in the second and third decades of the twentieth century, although the exact timing differs from country to country. The watershed is the abolition of coercive forms of labor control on haciendas and plantations, the expulsion of internal peasantries, and the creation of smallholder peasants and capitalist farms. The capitalist farms depend on the labor of rural proletarians and "free semiproletarians"—smallholders (minifundistas) who cannot fully provide for their own subsistence and work on capitalist farms as well (ibid.: 81–85).

Although de Janvry's model seems to stake out a middle ground between Leninist and populist approaches to peasants by positing a special kind of peripheral capitalism ("disarticulated accumulation"), he does not leave his analysis at this level. Following Amin this far, he then denies that the economic and class structure he has outlined can be considered stable. His conclusion places him fully within a modified Leninist perspective:

> Growth of the modern sector does not create a tendency to eliminate peasants in response to the need for market creation. However, over the long run, peasants are outcompeted [sic] for access to land by capitalist agriculture and are increasingly proletarianized: *unimodality eventually occurs* by the back door, and with dramatic social costs. Functional dualism is thus only a phase of the development of capitalism in the periphery; it is being destroyed over time by being used today. It does not have its own stable laws of reproduction as Amin and Bartra suggested. Hence, peripheral capitalism is not a distinct mode of production with its own laws of motion, but is only a historically specific stage in the development of capitalism in the periphery. It is this extended period of primitive accumulation, in which a surplus is extracted from the traditional sector via the labor and wage-foods markets and in

which the traditional sector gradually decomposes while sustaining rapid accumulation in the modern sector, that can be properly labeled the development of underdevelopment. (Ibid.: 37, emphasis added; cf. Deere and de Janvry 1979)

Support for this dramatically pessimistic conclusion regarding the future of the peasantry comes as de Janvry elaborates upon his model. It depends upon a characterization of peasants not as a "mode of production" or as a "special economic category" but as a "class or a fraction of a class within different modes of production—a class that is essential in modes like feudalism and transitory (and hence only a fraction of a class) in others, like capitalism" 1981: 106). He then examines the fate of this transitory class within the logic of functional dualism. Given the necessity of cheap food to support the "modern" sector, peasants may serve this necessity in two ways: as commodity producers within the traditional sector and as semiproletarians within the modern agricultural sector. Although de Janvry sees both functions being served historically, he argues that peasants are increasingly removed from commodity producer status and increasingly reduced to semiproletarian status (ibid.: 39, et passim). This contention allows him to account for one of the pieces of evidence often cited by agrarian populists—the growing number, despite pressures, of peasants in many Latin American countries. For de Janvry, such growth should not be confused with resiliency. Rather, it signifies the growth of a minifundista class as part of the logic of capital accumulation:

What the census data evidence, consequently, is a process whereby the peasantry grows in size but simultaneously loses its status as commodity producer. It is forced onto more and more minute and eroded land plots, where it is of necessity increasingly semiproletarianized. And lack of employment opportunities blocks sufficient outmigration and perpetuates rural misery. Thus, while the number of peasants increases, the social relations that characterize these peasants are increasingly those of a labor reserve with erratic and low-paying employment opportunities. (Ibid.: 121, 122)

The peasantry, so reduced even as it grows, eventually will disappear, in part and in some sectors through differentiation (ibid.: 106–118; Deere and de Janvry 1979) and in part due to the impact of the contradictions of functional dualism upon the poorest segment of the peasantry: increasing poverty and ecological degradation that eventually push the peasant into an urban area, perhaps with continued functional dualism in the "informal" sector (de Janvry: 39,40, 85–93).

———

Because I shall have some rather critical things to say about de Janvry's model, we need first to recognize the magnitude of his achievement. Using a rigorous and consistent approach, he has accounted for most of the facts alluded to by agrarian populists by offering a different interpretation. He has offered support for some classic Marxist positions that does not depend upon slavish attention to sacred texts; rather, he places his emphasis on an analysis of the dynamics of capital accumulation in the twentieth century. The model therefore captures one aspect of the powerful forces undermining peasant livelihoods in Latin America today. His understanding of semiproletarians offers an alternative to endless anthropological discussions of peasant, proletarian, and other role sets.[4] Nonetheless, problems remain, and I turn now to a consideration of them.

The first problem concerns the distinction between articulated and disarticulated accumulation. Some contrast between central and peripheral (or among central, semiperipheral, and peripheral) economies is an important first step in understanding the dynamics of uneven development. Thus far, however, most attempts to formalize the distinction, by creating different models of accumulation for center and periphery or by postulating hypothetical relationships and processes, have proven unsatisfactory. Noting that failure, Fernando Henrique Cardoso (1977a) likens it to the failures of positivist science in general, enclosing indeterminate human processes within determinate and rigid structures. For Cardoso, one of the negative implications of such formalism is the denial of movement to the so-called periphery. De Janvry also criticizes those dependency models that see everything as externally imposed. Nonetheless, some aspects of de Janvry's formalism suffer the consequences alluded to by Cardoso.

For one thing, it assumes too much "articulation" at the center, excluding a sense of contradiction. Granted, he writes of "sectoral disproportionality" between the two sectors. And granted, he does point to contradictions in "articulated" economies (the classic ones of the "tendency for the rate of profit to fall or the financial surplus to rise"; de Janvry 1981: 31). The resolution of these contradictions points to individual adjustments, state intervention, and the necessity of "external" relations. He also notes that no economy is ever "perfectly articulated" (ibid.: 44). Nonetheless, the very distinction between articulation and disarticulation creates a false image of economics and politics at the center. Marx postulated the distinction between capital and consumption goods departments to show that capitalism could be reproduced from one cycle of production to another and that the structural underconsumptionist understanding of capitalist crisis had no *necessary* basis. The division into departments was not designed to be limited to or to characterize a single "economy," and one suspects that Marx would be horrified at such formalization. Furthermore, the "external" resolution of contradiction in the center breaks apart the presumed internal articulation of the sectors, shunting production into cheap labor areas. This breaks apart the unity of labor as both loss and gain at the center, creating an increasingly superfluous and unemployed working population constantly engaged in "retraining," and throwing into question the "full proletarianization" aspect of the model and its consequent emphasis on the unimodality of the class structure.[5]

Likewise, the model of disarticulated accumulation is flawed. I shall leave aside, for the moment, the use of ideas and labels such as "traditional" and "modern." It is most interesting that wage-good production is excluded from the modern sector in disarticulated economies at the level of definition, just as luxury goods are not mentioned in de Janvry's characterization of the consumption goods sector of articulated economies. Yet if we consider import substitution industrialization as it has developed in

Latin America, it is clear that some products have been destined for a "local bourgeoisie" and "landed elites" while others can more properly be understood as "wage goods," e.g., in food processing, textiles, and the like. This is not to deny that import substitution is fraught with contradictions, many of which (e.g., exacerbated balance of payments problems) are discussed by de Janvry (see as well Chapter 4, above). But the exclusion of wage-good production is not necessarily one of them, and de Janvry's postulation of such exclusion is a bit curious. It is also the basis for one of his central arguments concerning the creation of functional dualism. Wage-good production was to be relegated to the traditional sector or to a capitalist sector that nonetheless depended upon a semiproletariat with connections to a traditional sector. This has certainly happened, and in agriculture the disjunction between export production and food production is especially marked in many countries. But I would argue against inclusion of this development as a *necessary* aspect of an economic model. The disjunction is the result of political decisions by particular classes and class fractions and is therefore contingent. Consideration of such questions takes us beyond the possibilities of a bipolar model.[6] For now, we may simply note that the postulation of full proletarianization at the center and semiproletarianization at the periphery depends upon assumptions and definitions that are seriously open to question.

───

But I began this essay with the general question of the positions, roles, and fates of peasants in the development of Latin American capitalism. We turned to de Janvry, who has provided one rigorous, clear, and pessimistic answer. Our critique must now consider that answer. It cannot have escaped notice that peasants, as *actors,* are not present in de Janvry's model. They function within a particular model of accumulation, are called up in the twentieth century as part of a functional dualism between traditional and modern sectors, provide cheap food and cheap labor to the modern sector, and eventually disappear. Likewise, the traditional sector (composed in part of peasants) is devoid of content. It too serves as a function of the modern sector, filling gaps that the modern sector, because of disarticulated accumulation, cannot fill. How would attention to the presence of peasants alter our understanding of their positions, roles, and fates in Latin American capitalism? A consideration of the areas in which they are not present in de Janvry's account will help us address this question.

To begin with, peasants are not present *historically* in de Janvry's model. We should remember that de Janvry sees the logic of functional dualism arising in the twentieth century with the abolition of coercive forms of labor mobilization and the creation of minifundistas with the expulsion of small producers from haciendas. One positive aspect of de Janvry's account here is that he does not reduce peasants to an undifferentiated precapitalist past. Indeed, the peasants that most interest him are the products of a particular form of capital accumulation and have no deep historical experience as smallholders or as part of a community of producers. Anthropologists, however, can point to peasants who do have such experience. In an often misunderstood article, Eric Wolf (1955) pointed to two "types" of peasants in Latin America: the closed corporate community in nuclear areas, corresponding to indigenous communities that were preserved and reshaped to serve the twin colonial ends of labor and tribute; and open communities, beyond the nuclear zones, that arose in the nineteenth century in response to widening commodity markets in Europe and North America. The types, as types, and the characteristics Wolf attached to them, are less important than the exercise in anthropological and historical understanding. Wolf saw the emergence of particular types of producer in part as a result of particular local relations and processes and in part as a specific form of incorporation within global processes of accumulation. Of immediate interest is the fact that neither type fits de Janvry's model very well. Certainly, the history of many corporate communities is inseparable from hacienda or plantation histories. But in most cases community history is not reducible to hacienda history or a particular model of accumulation, and even where the result of that intertwined history has been a class of minifundistas, one should not simply write out of account community traditions of landholding, reciprocal labor, and the like.

It may be more useful to see a variety of intertwined histories, of regional processes of class formation in which a local peasantry emerges in a particular constellation of forces, or a particular field of power. For example, if we were to compare the emergence of peasantries in Morelos, Oaxaca, and Yucatan in Mexico, we would have to examine each peasantry in the context of colonial and postcolonial relations with haciendas, merchants, state administrators, and the Church. But each of these contexts offered fundamentally different features; the peasantry that emerged in each region showed remarkably different tendencies as well. In colonial Morelos, sugar haciendas developed in the lowlands. Indigenous communities in the lowlands suffered at the hands of the haciendas, losing lands and seeing their towns occupied by Spaniards and mestizos. The haciendas entered into symbiotic relations with highland indigenous communities, however, drawing off seasonal labor and purchasing maize and wood. Community structures were weakened in the lowlands, strengthened in the highlands, in relationship to the same sugar haciendas. In Oaxaca, haciendas were relatively undeveloped as the city of Oaxaca became a center of colonial administration and mercantile accumulation that depended upon indigenous control of agricultural resources. In the relatively marginal Yucatan, colonial cattle and maize haciendas existed alongside indigenous communities in the northwestern portion of the peninsula, presenting little demand for Indian land or labor. It was only toward the end of the colonial period that haciendas began to expand, drawing peasants onto the haciendas or pushing them onto open lands to the east and south.

Nineteenth- and twentieth-century processes affected these regions unevenly as well. The expansion of agricultural estates in late-nineteenth-century Porfiriato had profound effects in Morelos and Yucatan, with sugar estates expanding further in lowland Morelos, even extending into the highlands, as estates attempted to secure their own supplies of maize, pasture, and fuel. It was here that the agrarian revolution exploded in the early twentieth century, as peasants fought to defend land and community against an encroaching agrarian capitalism. In the Yucatan, northwestern estates turned toward henequen in the late nineteenth century, creating a large plantation zone in which indigenous peasants became rural proletarians. The southern and eastern parts of the peninsula remained outside of this process, however, partly for ecological reasons and partly because the Caste War of the mid-nineteenth century had created an escape zone in which small-scale maize production could flourish. The Mexican Revolution came to the Yucatan from the outside, bringing with it an agrarian socialism that took firmer root than elsewhere. In Oaxaca, the liberal laws of the nineteenth century resulted in an increase in private property and the dissolution of some community lands, but the land remained in (individual) indigenous hands. Power continued to rest with Oaxaca City merchants who entered into relations with small producers and marketers, but these powerholders did not encroach upon peasant landholding. Oaxacan peasants were not active participants in the revolution. Given the different histories and structures of class relations of each region, the twentieth-century *ejido* has taken a different form in Morelos, Oaxaca, and Yucatan. Ejidos were set up rather quickly in Morelos, where household production within the ejido structure has predominated, establishing a basic division between those who have access to ejido land and those who do not and, within ejidos, those who control land distribution and those who do not. In Yucatan, henequen plantations were appropriated and turned into collective ejidos, in which ejido workers entered into direct relations with the state through ejidal credit institutions. Despite nominal control through the ejido, they remain rural proletarians. Ejidos have been less important in Oaxaca, where community and individual landholding within indigenous communities was less threatened and therefore less dependent on the intervention of the Mexican state.[7]

The nature of capitalist development and state formation in each of these regions is different, even as they fit within the same general framework of Mexican capitalism. The class structure of each region is different, as are the behavior, consciousness, and

politics of the peasantry. A model of disarticulated capitalism
that attempted to flatten out these differences in the context of a
model of functional dualism would leave us in a poor position to
understand the actual behavior of peasants. De Janvry does offer
a typology of farm enterprises that includes many of the rural
types encountered by anthropologists, providing a fuller description than one would expect from his model (1981: 109–
114). But he leads from that directly into a characterization of
class structure that obliterates the differentiation that he has just
recognized and therefore strips the peasantry of historical (and
therefore social) context.

Second, peasants are not present *economically* in his model. For
example, the model of functional dualism calls for peasants to
produce wage goods as part of a general cheap labor policy and
then to be gradually pushed out of commodity production altogether. But many small producers follow a different economic
logic. For example, in the Venezuelan Andes a group of
commodity-producing small farmers emerged in the nineteenth
century as part of the formation of a coffee economy. Although
these peasants were commodity producers, coffee was not a wage
good in Venezuela in the late nineteenth and early twentieth
centuries. In this century, coffee has declined in importance as
an export crop, but many farmers continue to grow coffee. They
do not provide cheap food; they do provide cheap labor; but that
is not everything one needs to know about them. Continued
production of coffee may fit within the reproduction strategy of
the peasant or semiproletarian household even when it makes no
sense as part of a larger model of development.[8]

Here we encounter a common tension between the dynamics
and reproduction logic of an economy as a whole and the dynamics and reproduction logic of peasant and semiproletarian
households. Unfortunately, bourgeois economists and government planners are not alone in ignoring the latter. For example,
in a classic comment on proletarians with land in Russia, V. I.
Lenin observed:

> It should be added that our literature frequently contains too
> stereotyped an understanding of the theoretical proposition

that capitalism requires the free, landless worker. This propo-
sition is correct as indicating the main trend, but capitalism
penetrates into agriculture particularly slowly and in extremely varied forms. The allotment of land to the rural
worker is very often to the interests of the rural employers
themselves, and that is why the allotment-holding rural worker
is a type found in all capitalist countries. (1964 [1899]: 178)

If we expand our frame of reference to include smallholders as
well as allotment-holding rural workers, it is clear that Lenin
offers an observation with which de Janvry can agree. Both
view the peasant (or rural worker) primarily in terms of "the
interests of the rural employers themselves," or in terms of the
interests of other employers within the modern sector. Neither
questions or pays any attention to the interests of the peasants
or rural workers. Postulating one set of interests and one logic
(however contradictory that logic might be), they are therefore
able to envision a process by which the peasant disappears and
"unimodality" results. But we find increasing evidence that
peasant households may engage in wage labor as part of a diversified strategy of household reproduction. Of course, this strategy is often forced on households that cannot reproduce themselves with their own resources, and many of them may be in
the process of proletarianization or stabilization at a semiproletarian level. Others, however, may be engaging in wage
labor in order to recreate or stabilize a peasant livelihood. For
example, Douglas Holmes (1983) has examined the peasant-
worker phenomenon in Europe, and especially in Italy, showing
how the peasants engage in wage labor on a temporary basis in
order to put their farms on a firmer footing. Henri Favre (1977)
has written an account of indigenous communities in northern
Huancavelica, Peru that used wage labor on the coast as part of
a strategy to liberate themselves from white-dominated communities in the highlands, move to higher elevations, and establish
newly independent communities. Also in Peru, Gavin Smith
(1989) has explored the multiple strategies used by residents in
and migrants from Huasicancha to reproduce pastoral households in the highlands. Residents and migrants form complex

"confederations of households" that pool and shift resources among wage labor in cities and mines, fruit selling in Lima, and pastoralism in Huasicancha. As they do so, they enter the national economy and become subject to its dynamics and contradictions. But they also establish a series of enterprises and pursue projects that cannot be understood solely in terms of that larger economy.

Third, peasants are not present *politically*. My summary of de Janvry's model concentrated on its more strictly economic aspects at the expense of his discussion of politics. Although he does discuss politics, a number of critical comments must be made. To begin with, he makes too narrow a distinction between what he calls "objective" and "subjective" factors, in which the "objective" refers to economic processes, strictly conceived, and the "subjective" refers to class relations and conflict, politics, culture, and so on (1981: 2, 3, et passim). In this view, one has primary objective laws of development, elucidated in the economic model, and secondary subjective forces with which one can account for variation within the model. But this denies class relations and conflict—in short, politics—their presence and consequence as material forces, as constitutive aspects of the "laws of motion" of any social formation (see Chapter 6). A good example of de Janvry's approach can be found in his discussion of class, state, and politics under disarticulated accumulation (ibid.: 40–45). Here he sees two types of class alliance as possible: (1) a "disarticulated" alliance—dominated by international capital, a dependent (*comprador*) bourgeoisie, and landed elites—that will pursue the expansion and consolidation of the outwardly focused aspects of the economy; and (2) an "articulated" alliance—composed of a national bourgeoisie, agrarian bourgeoisie, peasantry, and proletariat—that will pursue national development and attempt to articulate the various sectors through import substitution and the like. The contradictions de Janvry sees in each form are interesting but will be passed over here. Of more relevance is the fact that the class alliances are deduced from an economic model that simultaneously creates the classes and sets limits upon their "subjective" action. Of course, there must be a profound interrelation between class politics and economic process, but de Janvry has perceived that relationship in a one-directional fashion. In addition, subaltern classes (peasants, proletarians, semiproletarians) are present only as allies or followers of dominant class fractions pursuing their own class projects. That this is a common phenomenon is clear from experience, but it should be rendered more problematic. How does a dominant fraction exercise hegemony? What images of a common past or present might a dominant fraction use to present its particular projects as a universal project? What are the inherent weaknesses and limitations of such as a presentation?

The model also leaves out of account the possibility of resistance. De Janvry does point out that a semiproletariat or proletarianizing peasantry does not necessarily see itself as a proletariat and may continue to demonstrate a peasant consciousness (ibid.: 267). This, however, is seen simply as another subjective factor that does not alter the objective logic that defines the peasantry as a "transitory" class in capitalism. Of course, peasants are threatened by powerful world-historical forces, some of which de Janvry has elucidated. But unless we consider class consciousness and action as a *material force*, rather than as a "subjective factor," our understanding of the historic fate of peasants will be impoverished. We might return to Huasicancha, Peru, as described by Gavin Smith (1989), for an example. Huasicancha is known for its longstanding militance, from the War of the Pacific in the late nineteenth century through a series of struggles in the twentieth century. That militance has taken the form of resisting hacienda attempts to expand onto community lands, invading hacienda lands in an attempt to expand community pastures, rustling hacienda sheep, engaging in protracted guerrilla struggles against the military forces of the state, and so on. The decades-long struggle has produced defeats and victories, the most significant victory being the award, in the 1970s to the community of a large tract of land from the old hacienda. Significantly, although the award came in the context of a general land reform and hacienda expropriation, Huasicanchinos refused to associate their particular struggle with state programs and did not form a state-sponsored agricultural cooperative. Smith explores the idiom of community in the pursuit of these struggles in Huasicancha, but that community is not romantically invoked. One of the most interesting aspects of Smith's account is his explicit linking of Huasicanchinos' strategies of livelihood with their forms of resistance. This allows him to explore a variety of internal tensions, provoked in part by the different types of household confederations (e.g., those tied to pastoral and those tied to agricultural strategies in the highlands), that are partially expressed and partially hidden through community struggles.

An even more dramatic example comes from El Salvador. Carlos R. Cabarrús (1983), an anthropologist and Jesuit priest, has written a splendid study based upon his evangelical and political work from 1974 to 1977 in El Salvador, especially but not exclusively in Aguilares. He starts with an analysis that traces the intense economic and political pressures that undermined an already impoverished peasantry over the past two decades, arguing that the process was one that was leading toward proletarianization with unemployment. He contends that the process provoked a choice between proletarianization or rebellion, but he does not leave the analysis at such a mechanistic opposition. He shows how a segment of the threatened peasantry turned to the paramilitary organization, ORDEN, which, in classic clientelist fashion, offered employment and security to a proletarianizing peasantry. He also shows how another group took the more difficult step of challenging the process that was undermining their livelihoods. In painstaking detail, he discusses the evangelical mission of the Jesuit fathers, the establishment of Christian base communities, the creation of the Federation of Christian Peasants (FECCAS), and the opening up of political consciousness with evangelization. He describes the growth of a militant movement, first on a local level and later on a national level, through a series of tentative actions met by repression, provoking more militant actions, which in turn attract stiffer repression, and so on. In addition to the ethnography of a revolution in formation, one of the strengths of this study is its village-level analysis of ORDEN and of the relationships and antagonisms—of kinship, local politics, and national politics—between members of ORDEN and FECCAS, both of which draw upon the same class of threatened peasants and semi-proletarians. The outcome of the struggle in El Salvador cannot be predicted; the Christian peasants of Aguilares have encountered economic, political, and military forces of extraordinary, international scope. (In a tragic aside, Cabarrús notes that all of his informants have been killed.) His account demonstrates the importance of an understanding of peasants that does not reduce their actions to a secondary, "subjective" level.

The Salvadoran example suggests the lack of a *cultural* presence in de Janvry's model as well. Unfortunately and paradoxically, many cultural anthropologists and political economists can agree upon a culture concept that is far removed from social action. Culture is then seen to be primarily about "meaning," or subjective experience. The political economist may therefore feel justified, in the context of a model that sharply distinguishes between objective and subjective factors, relegating the subjective—and by extension the cultural—to a secondary level. When the anthropologist complains that the political economic model "ignores culture," but can only hold up a model of culture as subjective experience removed from activity, the political economist may legitimately wonder why culture should be considered at all.

The culture concept called for in this book, however, is one that includes activity and is itself a material force. In alluding to the historical, economic, and political presence of peasants, then, we have also suggested their cultural presence. Three decades ago, when Mintz and Wolf showed how coffee-producing peasants and sugar-cutting proletarians used common cultural forms (ritual coparenthood or *compadrazgo*) in profoundly different ways (forging vertical alliances in the coffee zone and horizontal, class-specific alliances in the sugar zone), they were making an argument about the uses of cultural form in social action (Mintz and Wolf 1950; cf. Mintz 1982). Likewise, when Venezuelan peasants resort to forms of reciprocal labor they had earlier abandoned as an attempt to solve labor problems caused by a drain of labor to work for wages on larger coffee farms, they are solving an economic problem and are using cultural forms in new ways

(Roseberry 1983). When Huasicanchino pastoralists use the language of community as part of a struggle for land, their struggle is simultaneously political and cultural. When Salvadoran peasants find in the Gospels a message of liberation and create political organizations that forge a synthesis of socialism and Christianity, their creation is as much cultural as it is political.

I do not pretend to have provided adequate statements regarding peasant economics, politics, or culture, but I do hope to have provided enough examples to illustrate one of the principal weaknesses of de Janvry's model—and all other models that leave no room for the action of peasants. His "functional dualism" might more properly be labelled "functionalist economism." It is economistic because it elevates to a central position a conception of economics devoid of class relations and struggle. The laws of motion are mechanically conceived in terms of the needs of capital. Although classes are mentioned, they are not central to the model and do not involve a relational sense. That is, the interests and actions of subaltern classes are not taken into account and are simply subsumed within the interests and actions of elites (who, in turn, are responding to the requirements of different capitals). A call for the "presence" of subaltern classes—in this case, peasants—in a model need not imply a romantic picture of peasant independence and equality. Nor does it require a model of a peasant mode of production. It does imply a sense of peasants as a class (or classes, or a fraction of a class), and it recognizes that peasants enter into relationships with capitalists at a disadvantaged position but in pursuit of particular interests. A model that does not take those interests and projects into account necessarily leads to erroneous conclusions about the fate of the peasants.

CHAPTER EIGHT

The Construction of Natural Economy

In order to make modern life intelligible I have made a construct which is called the Middle Ages. What may have been the actual conditions of that era is a matter of complete indifference to me, and it is ridiculous to claim to refute my theories with objections drawn from historical essays.

—Werner Sombart, Comments at 1903 Heidelberg Conference

Between the simple backward look and the simple progressive thrust there is room for long argument but none for enlightenment. We must begin differently: not in the idealisations of one order or another, but in the history to which they are only partial and misleading responses.

—Raymond Williams, *The Country and the City*

We need now to engage the terms "culture," "history," and "political economy" in light of the various discussions in this book. The culture concept sketched at the beginning of our considerations was one that was closely connected with politics. Our stated concern was an attempt to understand the political shaping of culture and the cultural shaping of politics, an effort to view culture as "socially constituted and socially constituting." Such a project required a concern for history—a consideration of the political creation of images of Venezuelan history in Chapter 3 and a more wide-ranging exploration of economics, politics, and culture in Latin American history in Chapter 4. In the second part of the book, we have considered some of the implications of a historical political economy of the sort outlined by Wolf. Throughout, our discussions have stressed the unevenness of capitalist development and the inadequacy of our models for capturing that unevenness—especially in relation to the historical development of capitalism (Chapter 6) and the positions, roles, and fates of peasants within capitalist societies (Chapter 7). We have not yet fully engaged our consideration of culture and politics (Part One) with our discussion of political economy (Part Two). This is the task of the concluding essay. Here I consider the implications of a historical understanding of uneven development for our approaches to culture and politics, especially among peasants and proletarians in a developing capitalist world. Although I refer to particular historical examples encountered earlier in the book, the present essay is less concerned with specific cases than with a discussion of how we might think about particular cases. Throughout, the discussion is grounded in a consideration of particular texts.

———

We might begin with the work of E. P. Thompson. In his classic book, *The Making of the English Working Class* (1963) and in a series of essays (most especially his 1967; 1971; 1974; 1978b), Thompson has stressed the active presence of precapitalist traditions, values, and communities in the experience and consciousness of early proletarians. In his reexamination of the Luddites, for example, Thompson restores to them an active consciousness, defending a way of life, using religious imagery and other symbols from the past in the present, and attacking the instruments of a future at a moment when the shape of that future was by no means certain. Likewise, "Time, Work-Discipline, and Industrial Capitalism" (1967) traces the transformation of notions of time with the creation of an industrial order, the loss of artisan independence and rhythms of work and leisure, and the growth of a proletariat subjected to factory work-discipline. "The Moral Economy of the English Crowd" (1971) dissects the food riots of eighteenth-century England and examines the structure of

crowd behavior in terms of its connections with "some legitimiz-
ing notion. By the notion of legitimation, I mean that the men
and women in the crowd were informed by the belief that they
were defending traditional rights or customs; and, in general,
that they were supported by the wider consensus of the community. . . . " Furthermore, Thompson continues, "these grievances
operated within a popular consensus as to what were illegitimate
practices in marketing, milling, baking, etc. This in turn was
grounded upon a consistent traditional view of social norms and
obligations, of the proper economic functions of several parties
within the community, which taken together, can be said to constitute the moral economy of the poor" (ibid.: 78, 79).

Thompson's understanding represents an advance in at least
three senses. First, as noted in Chapter 3, it serves as a corrective to both those Marxist and non-Marxist versions of economic history that have written the history of capitalism as the
history of capital. Thompson pays attention to the social relations and cultural forms associated with and created by working
people in the capitalist transformation. Second, unlike some
other social historians who have turned to a discussion of cultural theory and of mentalités as part of a concerted effort to
avoid political questions, Thompson always places his understanding of culture within a discussion of class relationships and
politics. Most important, however, is the third advance—the
understanding of culture as consciousness. Thompson has been
heavily criticized for *reducing* class to consciousness, and despite
his own protestations (e.g., 1978b: 149–150), there is some
truth to the criticism. Reductions aside, however, Thompson
correctly insists upon the inseparability of the two questions for
any writer who takes class-based politics seriously. The question
of whether of not, and under what conditions, people act in
class ways depends not simply upon "objective" determinations
but also upon "subjective" evaluations. And the subjective evaluations in turn depend upon their own lived experiences,
where the supposed distinctions between objective and subjective disappear. Thus Thompson's emphasis on values and
traditions—upon *culture* —as constitutive elements of class consciousness represents an important advance. These values and

traditions are seen to rest upon the experience of *community,* and it is toward an analysis and understanding of community that my critical remarks are addressed.

As noted in Chapter 3, in Thompson's early work, a cultural feeling of community was seen to rest in the actual experience of community-based social relations. In *The Making of the English Working Class* and some of his subsequent essays (especially 1967 and 1971), he tends to treat the precapitalist community in unambiguous, uncritical terms. The "traditional rights and customs" and the "wider consensus of community" that inform the "moral economy of the poor" are treated in an unproblematic manner. The experiences of artisans over the centuries preceding the eighteenth century, especially their relationship to merchant capital, are not considered. They become instead part of a community-based precapitalist past. What one misses in these works is a historical understanding of tradition itself, an understanding that would draw our attention to the social and political processes through which ideas and images of community are constructed.

It should be noted that in his more recent work in social history (e.g., 1974 and especially 1978b), Thompson moves toward such an understanding. He now pays much more attention to the historicity of popular culture and places his understanding of popular culture less in a traditional community with traditional values and more within a dialectical relationship between emerging classes.

For the moment, however, I want to concentrate on the surprising connection between his earlier work and some of the assumptions of modernization theory—not in order to pillory Thompson (who has, after all, gone beyond these views) but in order to explore some wider issues in social history and politics. Simply put, Thompson was not alone, even among critical thinkers. Modernization theories made an opposition between traditional and modern societies, defined modern society in terms of a few key characteristics, and defined traditional society in terms of the absence of those characteristics or the presence of quite different ones. In creating such models, these writers could place themselves within a line of thought that included virtually every major social thinker of the nineteenth century, Marx included. There was a convergence between celebratory and critical versions of history in terms of the way they understood some aspects of the historical process. This is most clear when we concentrate on what they had (and have) to say about working people in the making of the modern world. In both the dominant versions of Marxism and in modernization theory, the historical process (whether it was called modernization or industrialization or the development of capitalism) might be seen as a passage from the peasant (or the artisan) to the proletarian. Valuations might differ: the process might be celebrated as freedom from bondage or criticized as enslavement to capital. But in both the celebratory and the critical perspectives, peasants and artisans might be taken as unambiguous, ahistorical starting points. We need, then, to begin our exploration of the culture and politics of working people with another excursion into history. To discuss the problems with the sort of oppositional history outlined above, I concentrate on one set of ideas that had wide currency in the late nineteenth and early twentieth centuries—the idea of natural economy and its opposite (money economy or market economy or commodity economy).

Why bother? Surely, after the development of a series of ethnographic studies in economic anthropology, few people could take seriously the idea of a natural economy. Nonetheless, it is the contention of this essay that the concept continues to influence our thought, even among those who could only use the phrase while grimacing and placing it within quotation marks. This continuing influence can be seen in three related areas. First, our concepts of peasantries owe much to the ideas associated with natural economy. This is most obvious among those who are influenced by Chayanovian assumptions, but it also plays an important if residual role in the identification of our ideas of peasantry with our ideas of household economy (Roseberry 1986b). Second, as indicated in the discussion of Thompson, our conceptions of the historical process, especially those directed toward the emergence of capitalism and the process of proletarianization, depend upon definitions of peasants that may in turn be rooted in natural economy assumptions.

Finally, many of our ideas about the politics of peasants and first-generation proletarians are rooted in the above noted definitions of peasants and conceptions of the historical process. By subjecting the concept of natural economy to a historical critique, I hope to call into question many of our latter-day assumptions about peasants and proletarians, their experience of and their reactions to the modern world. I do this, first, by examining discussions of natural economy from the late nineteenth and early twentieth centuries, second by examining some key texts from Marx, and finally by turning toward more recent literature.

———

A full account of the history of the concept of natural economy is beyond the scope of this essay. Such an account would have to take us at least as far back as Aristotle's *Politics*, through Enlightenment ideas concerning natural law and the state of nature, eighteenth-century Physiocratic understandings of nature and economics and their contribution to classical political economy, to nineteenth-century discussions of social and cultural evolution. Although connections can easily be traced to classical literature, the concept of natural economy that emerged in the late nineteenth and early twentieth centuries was so influenced by contemporary intellectual, political, and social movements that it differed from earlier conceptions of nature and natural law in important ways.

One of the currents that deserves mention is the dominance of evolutionary thought in the nineteenth century. Although evolutionists might produce elaborate schema of stages from primitive origins to a civilized present, the stages were often embraced by an overarching opposition, as in Maine's (1970 [1861]) movement from family to individual and from status to contract and Morgan's evolution from societas to civitas (1974 [1877]). This opposition, in which one's understanding of the present was contrasted with a postulated primordial condition in which the defining characteristics of the present were absent or were reversed, affected the work of others who were not, strictly speaking, evolutionists. Perhaps the classic example here would be the work of Ferdinand Toennies, who was not primarily interested in evolution but in the postulation of different types of "will"—natural and rational—that could be simultaneously present in various sorts of society. Yet his opposition between *Gemeinschaft* and *Gesellschaft* was tied to an understanding of the historical process—from isolated homesteads ("The study of the home is the study of Gemeinschaft, as the study of the organic cell is the study of life itself" [Toennies 1957 [1887]: 53]) through peasant villages, in which the spirit of Gemeinschaft was most truly represented, to towns and finally urban Gesellschaft (ibid.: 231–234, et passim).[1]

A second influence, especially in Germany, was the growth of agrarian history, itself not unrelated to the rise of nationalism. Writers such as Georg von Maurer, Otto von Gierke, and August Meitzen, in attempting to reconstruct the primordial German character, were most interested in the lives and conditions of peasants. Debates concerning the relative freedom or unfreedom of the peasant, the relative weight of individual households and community or Mark associations, and so on, took a primordial past as their ostensible subject; but what was really in contention was the present—in this case, the construction of Germany.

A third influence was the rise and increasing dominance of capitalism. If Anthony Giddens is correct in arguing that the three great social thinkers of the nineteenth and early twentieth centuries (Marx, Weber, and Durkheim) had an "overwhelming interest . . . in the delineation of the characteristic structure of modern 'capitalism' as contrasted with prior forms of society" (1971: xvi), it should not be surprising that other figures shared that concern and project. Among economists, this was especially important for the German historicists. In contrast to increasingly dominant neoclassical assumptions regarding the universality of bourgeois rationality, the historicists limited that form of rationality to capitalism and sought out other forms that would be characteristic of precapitalist epochs.

As the historicists attempted to reconstruct a noncapitalist past, they turned to the literature of the agrarian historians.

The past that was to become the object of a model opposing capitalism (or commodity economy or money economy) with precapitalism (or natural economy) was therefore rural and European. Tribal and feudal society and, within both, the peasant became the starting points for a historical process and the counterpoints to the capitalist present. Let us explore this movement in the work of two characteristic and influential thinkers: Werner Sombart and Karl Bucher.

Sombart explicitly invoked the feudal past and painted an idyllic portrait of relations between lords and peasants in an era in which "man was the measure of all things." His primary interest was in the elucidation of the spirit of particular economic epochs. In contrast to the capitalist spirit, seen as the union of the spirit of enterprise ("the greed of gold, the desire for adventure, the love of exploration") and the bourgeois spirit ("calculation, careful policy, reasonableness, and economy"), Sombart postulated a precapitalist spirit (1967 [1915]): 22). He distinguished between two precapitalist types, the peasant and the craftsman, both of which were dominated by the same economic outlook. "In a word, economic activities in the pre-capitalist period were regulated solely in accordance with the principle of a sufficiency for existence; and peasant and craftsman looked to their economic activities to provide them with their livelihood and nothing more" (ibid.: 17). He continues:

> As for work itself, for the peasant and the craftsman alike it was lonely, patient effort. Man lost himself in his work. He lived in it, as the artist does, he loved it so, that he would much rather not have parted with his handiwork. When the dappled cow was led from the stables to the shambles, the old peasant woman's eyes were wet; the potter strove hard not to be tempted by the trader's offers for his pipe. But if it had to be sold, then the commodity was to be worthy of its maker. The peasant, like the craftsman, had put something of himself into his product; and in its making the rules of art were obeyed. Can we not understand, therefore, that the craft ideal looked with scorn on scamped work, and on the substitution of bad for good materials? (Ibid.: 18–19)

Karl Bucher was also interested in limiting economizing behavior to the capitalist epoch. Unlike Sombart, however, he did not automatically begin with European feudalism. Rather, he devoted two extensive chapters to a consideration of primitive societies, surveying the work of ethnologists and concluding that primitives had an essentially "pre-economic" outlook (Bucher 1967 [1900]: Chapters 1, 2). Nonetheless, when he turned to his discussion of a progression from what he called independent domestic economy through town economy to national economy, he set aside primitive conditions and began with the "civilized peoples of Europe" (ibid.: 84).[2] Although Bucher did not use phrases like "natural economy" and "money economy," we can see in his stages the basis for such a historical vision. His starting point was characterized by a lack of exchange, and his end point was marked by the dominance of exchange. The middle stage was simply a logically intermediate form of direct exchange. We can also see quite clearly an exercise in which the feudal past is made to represent an opposite of the capitalist present (or, in Bucher's usage, "national economy"). And, in the process, the peasant comes to represent a model starting point. In Bucher's case, the individual household is stressed. In other treatments, emphasis is placed on a peasant community—a significant difference, but one that will not be explored here. For now, the postulation of the peasant ("[production solely for one's needs, absence of exchange] . . . goods are consumed where they are produced" [ibid.: 89]) as historical counterpoint and starting point is what needs to be stressed.

Early Marxist theorists of natural economy, then, were using an idea that was very much in the air. When Rosa Luxemburg postulated a natural economy in which "economic organization is essentially in response to the internal demand; and therefore there is no demand, or very little, for foreign goods, and also, as a rule, no surplus production" (1968 [1913]: 368), her ideas fit within a wider current of social thought. V. I. Lenin, for his part, began his classic *Development of Capitalism in Russia* with a distinction that was to prove crucial for his whole analysis of the creation of a home market for capitalism:

The basis for commodity economy is the social division of labour. . . . Thus, the development of commodity economy leads to an increase in the number of separate and independent branches of industry; the tendency of this development is to transform into a special branch of industry the making not only of each separate product, but even of each separate part of a product—and not only the making of a product, but even the separate operations of preparing the product for consumption. Under natural economy society consisted of a mass of homogeneous economic units (patriarchal peasant families, primitive village communities, feudal manors), and each such unit engaged in all forms of economic activity, from the acquisition of various kinds of raw material to their final preparation for consumption. Under commodity economy heterogeneous economic units come into being, the number of separate branches of economy increases, and the number of economic units performing one and the same economic function diminishes. It is this progressive growth in the social division of labour that is the chief factor in the process of creating a home market for capitalism. (1964 [1899]: 37–38)

Lenin set the opposition up in such a way that much of the argument regarding differentiation and class formation among peasants seemed to follow logically from the development of commodity economy. This, in turn, was related to common misreadings of the presumed automaticity of Lenin's scheme. Although these misreadings ignore Lenin's political argument, they had an accurate basis—Lenin's basic opposition suggests a necessary process from natural economy to commodity economy to capitalism.[3]

———

But Lenin and Luxemburg were elaborating a set of Marxist ideas. We need now to examine more carefully certain relevant passages in Marx's work. We might begin by noting that Marx and Engels were themselves subject to the same influences outlined earlier. From the very beginning, they placed their understanding of the present in terms of an evolutionary process. Their celebration of Morgan's *Ancient Society* is well known.

And, although their evolutionary schemes (presented, e.g., in their *Communist Manifesto* and *German Ideology,* Marx's "Preface" and the *Grundrisse*) included several stages, they sometines contained an overarching oppositional model. Moreover, as they turned their attention to the past, especially the European past, they used the same sources used by the historicists. Both Marx and Engels welcomed Maurer's work and saw in his emphasis on the original importance of the Mark association (as opposed to isolated households) confirmation of their own ideas (see Engels 1972 [1882]; cf. Marx's letter to Engels, 14 March 1868, in Marx 1964b: [1868]: 139). And, of course, all of their work was animated by an attempt to understand and transform capitalism. It was in their use of the past to illuminate certain characteristics of the present that they most often resorted to oppositional models, as we shall see.[4]

In discussing Marx's own use of oppositional models of the past to illuminate the present, I pass over the more obviously evolutionary statements and concentrate on his discussions of capitalism and its immediate antecedents. Marx began his analysis of capitalism with a discussion of commodities and commodity exchange, commodities being the "economic cell-form" of bourgeois society. As he examined exchange value and use value or outlined his version of the labor theory of value, he liked to step back and contrast the relations he was outlining with those that would characterize societies in which commodities would not constitute the economic "cell-form." In these contrasts, as he turned to descriptions of medieval Europe, to the peasant family, to Indian communities, and the like, he would outline largely self-sufficient, natural economies (see, e.g., several passages in Chapter 1 of *Capital,* Volume 1 and Chapters 20 and 36 of *Capital,* Volume 3).

But capitalism, according to Marx, was not simply a society of commodity producers. It was also, and more fundamentally, a society in which labor power had become a commodity, that is, a society in which laborers must work for a wage in order to survive. For that condition to obtain, the laborer must be free in two senses: he or she must not be subject to compulsory labor, that is, must not be a slave or serf; and he or she must be free of ownership or control of means of production and the production process itself (Marx 1977 [1867]: 271, 272). Yet, "nature does not produce on the one hand owners of money or commodities, and on the other hand men possessing nothing but their own labour-power. This relation has no basis in natural history, nor does it have a social basis common to all periods of human history" (ibid.: 273). With this basic condition for capitalism, then, Marx laid the foundation for some of his most important historical contrasts, the ones that are of the most interest given the argument of this essay. I concentrate on two of them: the one contained in his analysis of primitive accumulation and the one contained in the "Formen" (1973 [1857–58]: 471 –515).

In the final section of Volume 1 of *Capital*, after outlining the basic relationships and laws of the capitalist mode of production, Marx turned toward a historical account of the process by which the conditions for capitalist production were created. He concentrated on England and analyzed the emergence of capitalism out of the ruins of feudalism. No exercise in speculative oppositions or search for human origins, Marx's analysis concentrated on the historical situation immediately prior to the emergence of a capitalist mode of production. Because one of the basic conditions for capitalism was the freeing of the laborer from means of production and from bondage, Marx claimed that, "The expropriation of the agricultural producer, of the peasant, from the soil is the basis of the whole process" (ibid.: 876).

The subsequent analysis is well known and requires no summary here. However, I wish to draw attention to one consequence of Marx's exercise. Marx immediately moved to a consideration of the "free peasant," contending that serfdom had virtually disappeared in England by the fourteenth century. His analysis of the separation of the agricultural producer from the soil therefore began in the fifteenth century with a free peasantry and examined the process of its expropriation. There is nothing necessarily wrong about this procedure. Marx situated the peasant historically, and he was in no way seen as a primordial, natural creature. Nonetheless, of the two conditions Marx considered necessary for labor power to be a commodity—freedom from bondage and freedom from control over means of production—only one, the second, receives any attention here. The first occurred prior to the period that interested Marx. Thus the free peasant, in effect if not in fact, became a counterpoint to the proletarian and a starting point in a movement from peasant to proletarian. Not considered was the possibility that the free peasantry, so recently formed, was itself a product of the same historical movements that created the conditions for capitalism and the emergence of the proletariat.[5]

With this point, we anticipate much of the argument that is to follow. Before it can be pursued, however, we need to turn to another text in which Marx considered social forms prior to capitalism and the emergence of the conditions necessary for a capitalist mode of production. Although the "Formen" is often read as an evolutionary account, I think it can be more profitably read as an oppositional exercise and placed firmly within the tradition of oppositional historical models. Marx began the "Formen" with the observation that:

> A presupposition of wage labour, and one of the historic preconditions for capital, is free labour and the exchange of this free labour for money, in order to reproduce and to realize money, to consume the use value of labour not for individual consumption, but as use value for money. Another presupposition is the separation of free labour from the objective conditions of its realization—from the means of labour and the material for labour. Thus, above all, release of the worker from the soil as his natural workshop—hence dissolution of small, free landed property as well as of communal landownership resting on the oriental commune. . . .
>
> In both forms, the individuals relate not as workers but as proprietors—and members of a community, who at the same time work. The aim of this work is not the *creation of value* . . . rather, its aim is sustenance of the individual proprietor and of his family, as well as of the total community. The positing of the individual as a *worker*, in this nakedness, is itself a product of *history*. (1973 [1857–58]: 471, 472)

Capitalism, based on the separation of producers from control over the production process, was contrasted with a prior situation of connection or union in two senses: union with the means of production, and union with a community of producers. The analysis that followed is less closely tied to an actual historical process than was the section on primitive accumulation in *Capital*. Rather, Marx immediately turns to a first form of landed property: "an initial, naturally arisen spontaneous community appears as first presupposition. Family, and the family extended as a clan, or through intermarriage between families, or combination of clans" (ibid.: 472). But this "natural" community receives relatively little attention; it is simply postulated. Instead, Marx moves quickly into a consideration of three historical forms of community, which seems to be a logical exercise in forms of relationship between individual, community, and land (see Godelier 1978; cf. Tokei 1966), with each logical type given a geographical or historical label. Thus we go from one extreme in which individuals are subsumed within a community that defines and determines individual access to land (the Asiatic) to the other extreme in which the community is simply a collectivity of individual families with access to land (the Germanic). The Ancient is a logically, but not necessarily historically, intermediate type.

Several points require attention here. First, Marx's starting point is markedly different from that in the section on primitive accumulation. Whereas in *Capital* he started with free peasant *households* (which he saw as a historical product, although the historical process remained outside the analysis), here he starts with a *community* of producers. The process by which individual property-owning households emerged is seen as part of the same process that created capital as a social relation. The union of producer with means of production is mediated by the union of producers with each other, and the process of dissolution necessary for the emergence of labor power as a commodity is a dissolution of the community as well as a separation of producer from means of production (1973 [1857–58]: 495–498). Although he is engaged in an oppositional exercise that contrasts his conception of capitalism with his conception of a primordial condition, his understanding of the past (and therefore his understanding of the present) could not be more different from that of, say, Karl Bucher. Nonetheless, and this is the second point, he once again has much more to say about the creation of free labor in terms of the separation of laborer from means of production than in terms of the dissolution of ties of bondage. Indeed, in concentrating on the forms of community existing among producers, he has little to tell us about forms of exploitation. The past, then, while based in communities rather than households, is nonetheless based on a free, rather than an unfree, peasantry.

At the beginning of his discussion of primitive accumulation, Marx observes:

> Hence the historical movement which changes the producers into wage-labourers appears, on the one hand, as their emancipation from serfdom and from the fetters of the guilds, and it is this aspect of the movement which alone exists for our bourgeois historians. But, on the other hand, these newly freed men became sellers of themselves only after they had been robbed of all of their own means of production, and all the guarantees of existence afforded by the old feudal arrangements. And this history, the history of their expropriation, is written in the annals of mankind in letters of blood and fire. (1977 [1867]: 875)

Freedom, then, has a dual meaning, as we have seen. But it is not enough to have one historiography (a bourgeois one) that emphasizes one meaning, seeing a movement from unfreedom to freedom, and another historiography (a Marxist or critical one) that emphasizes another meaning, seeing a movement from freedom to unfreedom. The *dual* meaning suggests a *contradictory* process, and the contradictions become concentrated in the peasantry—simultaneously free and unfree, historical starting point and historical product.

I do not mean to single out Marx for special criticism. Any of the non-Marxist conceptions of natural economy would be subject to even more forceful criticisms. By concentrating on Marx,

I mean to draw attention to a complex of problems associated with the concept of natural economy. There is nothing wrong with the oppositional exercise itself. Historical fictions are necessary to draw in sharp relief certain characteristics of the present. Most theorists of natural economy clearly recognized its fictional character, although some thought they were outlining an actual historical process and would simply concede that it was more complex than the list of stages would suggest (see, e.g., Bucher 1967 [1900]: 85). Whatever its connection or lack of connection with an actual historical process, the "Formen" is an especially brilliant formulation to which one can continually return for fresh insight. But any opposition simultaneously illuminates and obscures. This particular opposition, especially as it posits the peasant as starting point and counterpoint, has important implications for our understanding of the historical process and of our present condition that must be subjected to critical scrutiny. If, as Marx indicated in the passage cited earlier, the development of capitalism meant a simultaneous movement toward freedom *and* toward alienation for working people, any oppositional exercise, including Marx's, that emphasizes one side of that movement will leave us with a flat understanding of history and politics.

In discussing Marx's passages in *Capital* and the *Grundrisse*, I suggested two problems that now require more detailed attention. With regard to the section on primitive accumulation, I contended that Marx's taking the free peasantry as a starting point ignored the question of whether the free peasantry was itself a product of the same historical movement that created the proletariat. With regard to the "Formen," I claimed that one must examine elements of freedom and unfreedom in the peasant past and present. Although such a division is false, and although the two points are interrelated, I take the first point as the basis for a discussion of history and the second point as the basis for an examination of culture and politics.

———

In considering historical problems, we can turn from a consideration of nineteenth-century texts toward more recent authors. Here I begin with an anthropologist who was deeply influenced by the oppositional models of the late nineteenth century, Robert Redfield. The development of an anthropological critique of and alternative to Redfield laid the foundation for the approach to history, culture, and politics suggested here.[6]

The basic aspects of Redfield's characterization of folk society, or the opposition between urban and folk, are so well known that I shall not go into them here. I want simply to look at his work in terms of three points. First, although Redfield's work was adopted by modernization theorists, he saw his opposition as part of a critical approach. This is most clear in *The Primitive World and its Transformations* (1953), with the opposition between a technical order and a moral order.[7]

Nonetheless, the critical impact of Redfield's view of civilization was marred by the fundamentally antihistorical nature of the folk/urban opposition. This leads us to the two other points, which suggest a criticism of the understanding of social relations and history that served as a basis for Redfield's critique. The second has to do with the "continuum" aspect of Redfield's work; the third concerns Redfield's own attempt to move beyond it. Although a folk/urban opposition, differently stated, served as a constant in Redfield's work from the beginning, the notion of a continuum from folk to urban held a more restricted place in Redfield's thought—essentially during the late 1930s and 1940s in relation to his work in Yucatan. In *The Folk Culture of Yucatan* (1940), Redfield takes four communities as examples of different points on the continuum (from the folk end to the urban: Tusik, Chan Kom, Dzitas, and Mérida). The most important aspect of the continuum to be emphasized here is that it was made to represent an "as if"—or pseudo—history. Although Redfield knew that there was not, in actual fact, a historical progression from Tusik to Mérida, he thought that the differences found among the communities at the time they were studied in the late 1930s could be taken to represent the kinds of changes that had occurred in an irrecoverable historical process in the move from folk to urban society.

A rather different and instructive perspective emerges in

Redfield's writing in the 1950s, perhaps in response to a growing critical literature. In *The Primitive World and its Transformations,* for example, there is a clearer distinction between primitive and peasant. More important, the peasant is not seen as a midpoint in a historical progression from folk to urban but as the product of an interaction between the folk and the urban. The peasant is a product of civilization and its remaking of the "folk." Indeed, peasants become "remade folk"—folk in their internal relations, which remain kin-bound, solidary, homogeneous, but urban in their external relations through the commercial nexus. While Redfield had earlier suggested, in the example of the Yucatan, a historical movement from Tusik through Chan Kom and Dzitas to Mérida, he now was suggesting an interaction between Mérida and Tusik that produced a Chan Kom. Nonetheless, the possibility of a historical critique of the folk/urban opposition, opened in *The Primitive World,* was not realized by Redfield himself but was taken up by his critics.

Among the most instructive criticisms were those that re-examined the Yucatecan material. Sidney Mintz, for example, pointed out that the communities selected by Redfield were located within the maize belt and that Redfield had ignored the henequen plantations and the rural proletarians who worked on them (1953). Nonetheless, Mintz did not consider the actual historical processes that had characterized the Yucatan or examine the communities studied by Redfield in detail. That task was taken up by Arnold Strickon (1965), who, by means of an examination of the transformation of ecology and economy in the area as a result of the development of estate agriculture and ranching, shows that *all* of the communities can only be understood in terms of that history. The people of Tusik and Chan Kom came from common roots—hacienda and free Maya—but lived different histories. Tusik was formed in Quintana Roo, an escape zone during the Caste War and thereafter, while Chan Kom was established in a frontier band between the henequen zone and the free Maya, producing maize for the henequen plantations. Thus, a pseudohistory that sees a passage from a folk Tusik to an urban Mérida, or an interaction between a folk Tusik and an urban Mérida that produces a peasant Chan Kom, is replaced by a historical sketch that shows that each of the different communities is a product of a unified social process. Because that process affects particular regions differentially— due to geographical placement of core and peripheral zones, cyclical movements, different sets of social relations and historical movements within each region, and so on—a *variety* of "folk" and "urban" communities emerges (see Joseph 1986).

This implies a profoundly different way of looking at anthropological subjects than that suggested by oppositional models, one that has been most interestingly developed by anthropologists such as Wolf and Mintz. From their initial field research in Puerto Rico (Steward et al. 1956) through their typological essays of the 1950s (Wolf 1955; 1956; 1957; Wolf and Mintz 1957) to more recent work (Wolf 1982; Mintz 1973; 1974; 1979; 1985), they have attempted to view a variety of types of rural folk as the differential products of a unified but unevenly developing world-historical process.

Their work points toward an understanding of peasants, their histories, and their connection with *our* history that differs from that of oppositional models. As in Strickon's essay, the position of various types of communities in a historical process is practically reversed. Aside from attention to local and global processes, a central feature of the understanding of peasants in the context of world history is a concept of uneven development. Uneven development has one of its most important effects within the capitalist mode of production in a process that can be called *uneven proletarianization*. This takes its most obvious form in labor-market segmentation (see Gordon 1972; Edwards et al., eds. 1975; Gordon et al. 1982; cf. Meillassoux 1981; Wolf 1982: 354–383), which means the development of a labor force segmented into skilled and unskilled branches with sexual, ethnic, racial, and national characteristics serving as provisional and convenient markers for recruitment into particular segments. Such segmentation can be seen as part of the process of capital accumulation itself. For example, Marx provides a penetrating analysis of the creation of skilled and unskilled with the development of capitalism (1977: Chapters 10–15). His treatment of population and surplus population as part of his model of capital accumulation is also helpful in approaching an understanding of such segmentation (ibid.: 781–802). But uneven development also implicates the history of nonproletarian populations. If Strickon's analysis of Yucatan is correct, it means that we can examine the creation of a variety ot types of toiler (proletarian, peasant, tenant, and so on), at least in part, in terms of a unified and unevenly developing capitalist system (Roseberry 1983: Chapter 7). Thus, instead of an oppositional model that sees a movement from folk to urban, natural economy to commodity economy, or peasant to proletarian, both poles would be seen as the contradictory products of the creation of the modern world.

Such assertions must be made with care. In any consideration of specific situations, one must attempt to grasp the uneven nature of capitalist development, the ebb and flow of commodity markets, the boom and bust cycles of expansion and retraction, and their differential impact on particular regions and social strata. We need to investigate the extent to which the history of specific working populations is directly connected with capital investment (e.g., slaves or wage laborers on plantations, peasants who move into frontier areas in direct response to expanding commodity markets), and the extent to which such peoples have a social existence that precedes capital investment (e.g., peasant and artisan communities in nuclear areas of Latin America). Proper understanding of the latter group requires that we analyze those aspects of their social relations that can be traced to a genuinely precapitalist past and cannot be subsumed within a capitalist dynamic. It also requires that we consider those aspects that can be viewed as a "remade past" (e.g., corporate communities in Mesoamerica that built upon and preserved an indigenous past through the imposition of institutions for colonial administration and labor mobilization). In each case, rural toilers are to be seen, at least in part, as the precipitates of historical processes that involve the intersection of regional and global dynamics.

Clearly, emphasis on uneven proletarianization does not close discussion but opens a complex set of questions. If we return to the problem of class formation, community, and consciousness with which we began our consideration of Thompson, we see that certain kinds of association and consciousness that were taken for granted are now rendered problematic. The very nature and constitution of the "community," tied to precapitalist social relations and experiences and seen as the basis for values and traditions that informed an evaluative consciousness, are thrown into question. At the same time, however, certain new kinds of association and consciousness become possible that could not have been conceived given oppositional theories (e.g., associations of peasants, proletarians, and other types of workers, seen now as differentiated but linked products of uneven proletarianization rather than actors within fundamentally distinct modes of production).

These two problems suggest two areas for discussion in our consideration of culture and politics among working people. The first problem implies a critique of those models that treat precapitalist experience and the existence of a political or cultural community as unproblematic. The second requires a discussion of the politics of cultural creation and community formation in the context of uneven proletarianization.

———

Most of our theories, Marxist and non-Marxist, of the politics of peasant populations, or of proletarians with recent ties to such populations, continue to ignore the sort of complex history sketched above. However much individual theorists might disagree with Lukács, most would share two of his basic assumptions about peasant consciousness and politics: they are tied to a *pre*capitalist past and are backward looking.

> Bourgeoisie and proletariat are the only pure classes in bourgeois society. They are the only classes whose existence and development are entirely dependent on the course taken by the modern evolution of production and only from the vantage point of these classes can a plan for the total organization of society *even be imagined.* The outlook of the other classes (petty bourgeois or peasants) is ambiguous or sterile because their existence is not based exclusively on their role in the

capitalist system of production but is indissolubly linked with the vestiges of feudal society. Their aim, therefore, is not to advance capitalism or to transcend it, but to reverse its action or at least to prevent it from developing fully. Their class interest concentrates on *symptoms of development* and not on development itself, and on elements of society rather than on the construction of society as a whole. (1971 [1922]: 59)

But if the peasant is a historical product and is, in significant respects, a product of the *present,* then this basic assumption must be reexamined.

We have already encountered one prominent model of backward-looking politics in the moral economy literature, especially in James Scott's application of moral economy ideas to the politics of peasants in colonial settings (see Chapter 3). This is but one example of a range of theoretical expressions that share a common, oppositional, historical vision. We might consider another expression in the work of Michael Taussig.

Taussig's well-received book, *The Devil and Commodity Fetishism in South America* (1980), offers a sophisticated Marxist analysis of ideology and consciousness among populations recently incorporated within a capitalist political economy. A basis for his analysis is an opposition between use-value and exchange-value economies, the former characterized by reciprocal transactions and relationships and the latter characterized by nonreciprocal transactions· and relationships. In use-value economies, these relationships are represented, and fetishized, as personal and superpersonal, or natural and supernatural. In exchange-value economies, social relations are represented, or fetishized, as relations between things, or commodities. Taussig's advance is to place commodity fetishism in relation to the natural and supernatural fetishism of use-value economies and consider the manner in which capitalism is understood and represented by people with roots in precapitalist social relations. He applies this analysis to devil imagery and beliefs among rural proletarians in Colombia and tin miners in Bolivia, concluding his introduction to the case studies with the clearest statement of his interpretation:

Thus, the devil-beliefs that concern us in this book can be interpreted as the indigenous reaction to the supplanting of this traditional fetishism by the new. As understood within the old use-value system, the devil is the mediator of the clash between these two very different systems of production and exchange. This is so not only because the devil is an apt symbol of the pain and havoc that the plantations and mines are causing, but also because the victims of this expansion of the market economy view that economy in personal and not in commodity terms and see in it the most horrendous distortion of the principle of reciprocity, a principle that in all precapitalist societies is supported by mystical sanctions and enforced by supernatural penalties. The devil in the mines and cane fields reflects an adherence by the workers' culture to the principles that underlie the peasant mode of production, even as these principles are being progressively undermined by the everyday experience of wage labor under capitalist conditions. But until the capitalist institutions have permeated all aspects of economic life and the revolution in the mode of production is complete, the lower classes will persist in viewing the bonds between persons in their modern economic activities for what they really are—asymmetrical, non-reciprocal, exploitative, and destructive of relationships between persons—and not as natural relations between forces supposedly inherent in potent things. (Ibid.: 37, 38)

Taussig's demonstration of this point is impressive, especially in his discussion of the emergence of devil imagery in the context of colonial Catholicism and the condemnation and transformation of indigenous and slave beliefs. Nonetheless, we might briefly consider the two cases discussed by Taussig in light of his opposition between use-value and exchange-value economies. Of the use-value end, Taussig tells us, "In the precapitalist mode of production there is no market and no commodity definition of the value and function of a good" (ibid.: 36) and, "In precapitalist societies, commodity exchange and the market are absent" (ibid.: 127). Yet what is most interesting about this book is that both of Taussig's case studies contradict such assertions and the opposition upon which they

rest. In the case of rural proletarians in the Cauca Valley of
Colombia, by far the better documented and realized of his
two studies, the peasantry is, as Taussig observes, of recent vin-
tage. This is hardly a deeply rooted precapitalist economy for
which capitalism and a "market economy" are newly introduced
from outside. Peasant villages were begun by runaway and
freed slaves in the nineteenth century, and the people who
founded them already had an intimate and painful experience
of one part of the world economy. No doubt they valued and
defended their *independence,* as Taussig shows, and no doubt the
valuation of independence has especially critical things to say
about proletarian labor in the cane fields. The devil imagery
and the notion of devil contracts strike the reader as an understandable set of beliefs for such a population. But the peasant
villages, independent as they were, were never so removed from
commodity markets—from a "market economy"—as Taussig
suggests in his more rhetorical pronouncements. Instead, they
moved quite quickly to commodity production—especially cocoa and coffee (ibid.: 78, 79)—within a framework of peasant independence but outside the framework of a use-value economy
in which "commodity exchange and the market are absent."
Clearly, we need a more careful consideration of reciprocity
and nonreciprocity, commodity production and exchange, and
ideology within precapitalist modes of production, or among
workers in capitalist modes, than the opposition allows. Indeed,
it may be that we can understand devil imagery of the sort
Taussig is talking about without recourse to a concept of use-
value economy or to remembered reciprocities. We might be
able to understand such imagery and practices in terms of various experiences of wage labor. For example, ideas about devil
contracts might not be unrelated to the experience of piece
wages in the fields (cf. Trouillot 1986).[8]

The Bolivian tin miner case presents a different problem.
Using the Buechlers's (1971) work and that of Bastien (1978),
Taussig traces the conceptualizations of nature and reciprocity
among Andean villagers. As he considers the contrast with miners' ideology, he claims:

> Peasant rites of production mediate the interplay of individuality with community, and in so doing they reflect the principle of inalienability in the constitution of rural life. Miners either come directly from this life or have a background in its dictates and sentiments. Yet the situation they encounter in the mines is one predicated on alienation and the denial of reciprocity. Their rites of labor and of production reflect the contrast. (1980: 214)

The statement that "miners either come directly from this life or have a background in its dictates and sentiments" is simply asserted. It is untrue.[9] Tin miners in Bolivia are not a first-generation proletariat; rather they constitute a multigenerational proletariat. Serious splits between peasants and miners have been successfully exploited by the Bolivian state in repressing strikes. And a most important ethnographer of Bolivian tin miners found that they lacked basic knowledge of simple gardening (Nash 1979). Indeed, as Nash's ethnography (not to speak of the miners' own well-known actions) substantiates, this proletariat is one of the most conscious and militant in all of Latin America, with a union movement of long standing and a history of participation in revolutionary movements. That this multigenerational proletariat can combine militant left-wing politics with devil imagery, indeed, that the unions themselves can encourage devil propitiation rites along with more practical political programs, offers an interesting problem that cannot be reduced to the mediation of peasant/proletarian, reciprocity/nonreciprocity, or use-value/exchange-value oppositions. We need to look more carefully at a proletariat that has severed its connections with a *peasant* past but attempted to maintain its connections with an *indigenous* past and present. And we need to look more carefully at the culture and political economy of organization and repression. Use of devil imagery as an ethnic marker within a class politics suggests the importance of examining such practices within the politics of the present rather than the invocation of an epochal history.

We see that the social relations at both the use-value and the exhange-value end of Taussig's opposition are more complex than he implies and that, as a consequence, the problem of cultural creation and politics is more multifaceted. The complexity is *historical;* the attempt to collapse an uneven historical process into an unproblematic set of oppositions removes our understanding of culture and politics from social being, where it belongs, and places it in an imposed set of theoretical oppositions, where it is misplaced. Contradictions are removed from experience and placed in the circumlocutions of an author's model.

There are two basic problems with models of backward-looking politics, models that place their emphasis on an unproblematic precapitalist experience. First, they consider peasants or first-generation proletarians and the social orders in which they live as historically prior to capitalism. If, however, peasants, in a wide variety of settings, are the products of the past and the present—the products, perhaps not of "capitalism" but of the same historical movement that created a capitalist mode of production in one sector and region and noncapitalist modes in other sectors and regions, that created, in short, the modern world in all its unevenly developed complexity—then this simple view of past experience determining present consciousness must be discarded. The past is constitutive of consciousness, but it is not as unambiguous as the models suggest.

Second, although attention to precapitalist values and traditions serves as a corrective to certain crude formulations expressed in the name of Marx, it tends to romanticize class relations in precapitalist settings. Surely the peasant's or proletarian's experience of those relations, in contrast with new relations introduced by the advent of capitalist development of a strictly conceived sort, will emphasize certain aspects of those relations that compare favorably with the new forms of class domination. But is it unreasonable to assume that peasants will also be aware of certain aspects of the new relations that compare favorably with the past? It is quite probable that peasants' and proletarians' experience of past and present is contradictory and that contradictory being determines a contradictory consciousness. The past, as a storehouse of experiences that inform consciousness, would therefore provide raw material for both protest and accommodation. Unfortunately, the politics of natural economy sees only the negative contrasts and therefore leads us to make unreasonable and, ultimately, demeaning assumptions about the consciousness of working people.[10]

We come, then, to a conclusion that has already been suggested. If natural economy is a historical product, it is also an ideological product of the present. As the moral economists have shown us, it can serve as the basis for a powerful critique of the present. It is a common element in socialist critiques, especially as the capitalist present is contrasted with the image and possibility of a socialist future with important roots in the human past. It can also serve as the basis for a critical response to the first emergence or introduction of capitalist social relations. But that critique can be a constitutive aspect of the consciousness of working people or (or more accurately, *and*) an element in an aristocratic critique of bourgeois society (Williams 1960; 1973). A reflection on the rural past may also be included in bourgeois consciousness, as in the move from unfreedom to freedom, from serf to citizen, and so on. Finally, a simultaneous romanticization and critique of a rural past is present in many statist ideologies, from a fascist extreme (cf. Moore 1966: 490– 508) to less virulent forms, such as the Venezuelan example presented in Chapter 3. In all of these forms, the peasant, or a set of images of the peasant, is an object of contention in the ideological construction of the present.

But we cannot conclude our examination of the culture and politics of working people at this negative level. If we cannot simply call up preexisting communities, values, and traditions, we need to consider the problems and processes associated with community formation. Reference to a process of uneven proletarianization implies the creation of a heterogeneous, fractionated working people that experience enormous difficulty in forming themselves as a working class. This raises a series of problems, discussion of which can contribute to a more careful consideration of culture and politics. We need to examine, first, a number of empirical questions: into what kinds of political communities have such heterogeneous working people been inserted? Around what images of community have they coalesced? This would necessarily lead to a discussion of hegemony, of the connection between proletarianization and state formation, and of a variety of ethnic, religious, and regional movements. A second set of questions is both empirical and normative: what are the weaknesses of such hegemonic political communities? How and under what circumstances are alternative, counterhegemonic political communities formed? Within the range of such counterhegemonic communities, what are the prospects for horizontal, or class-based forms of action? Stated in more cultural terms, Thompson correctly emphasized the importance of a feeling of community in the formation of class consciousness. But how is the feeling of community or homogeneity generated within social relations that are neither communal nor homogeneous? These questions depend upon the historical understanding outlined in this essay. Oppositional historical models lead to epochal treatments of culture and politics, which in turn lead to the expectation of forms of cultural and political resistance based upon the experience of a natural or moral economy, of use value and reciprocity. A historical model that rejects such oppositions and stresses uneven development and uneven proletarianization leads to an understanding of the culture and politics of hegemony as well as the culture and politics of resistance.

We might begin with the problem of hegemony. We need to remember that proletarianization occurs in the context of processes of state formation and consolidation. Theorists of both proletarianization and the bourgeois state stress the importance of an emergent individualization in both processes. For proletarianization, Marx emphasized the separation of the producer from a producing community as well as his or her separation from means of production. This was, of course, a starting point for many oppositional histories, Marx's included. We may have a more complex model and still see the importance of this aspect of proletarian experience. Indeed, the emphasis on uneven proletarianization extends it to other groups of working people such as peasants and tenants.[11] Our emphasis on a heterogeneous and fractionated working people carries with it an expanded understanding of the lack of primordial community experience and sentiments and stresses the fractionated character of working lives.

Likewise, theorists of the capitalist state stress the dissolution of political communities and orders and the creation of a direct relationship (or the *ideology* of a direct relationship) between state and citizen, in which all citizens face the state as equal individuals, without the mediation of estates, orders, or the like. But the state also creates the institutional space for organization, for the creation of new types of political community. In a series of notes on Italian history, Antonio Gramsci (1971 [1929–35]) looked at the bourgeoisie in terms similar to those I have used to analyze the proletariat. He saw a fractionated bourgeoisie that could not form itself as a homogeneous force, could not develop a political and cultural hegemony, and therefore was late in following the French and English examples in the creation of a nation-state. It was nonetheless the state through which a fractionated bourgeoisie could form itself and act as a class.

The capitalist state, Poulantzas reminds us (1973), serves to organize the bourgeoisie and disorganize the proletariat. But this functionalist insight, while telling, is insufficient. Poulantzas does not render the organization of the bourgeoisie sufficiently problematic and thus misses Gramsci's important point; nor does he explore the extent to which the state organizes working people in a certain way (but see his 1978: 63–76). We have already seen some aspects of that organization in Venezuela through the activities of Acción Democrática (see Chapter 3). In that discussion, I stressed the role of a state-building, multiclass political party in bringing together disparate sections of an industrializing bourgeoisie and a fractionated working people composed of industrial laborers, agricultural laborers, and peasants. That organizational activity was tied to a process of cultural creation, a process in which a particular kind of community feeling, based on key images of Venezuela's past, was generated. Here it is useful to recall Benedict Anderson's definition of nationalism as an "imagined community"—the state as nation and the nation as community—"*imagined* because the members of even the smallest nation will never know most of their fellow-members, meet them, or even hear of them, yet in the minds of each lives the image of their communion" (1983: 15). Anderson continues: "all communities larger that primordial villages of face-to-face contact (and perhaps even these) are imagined. Communities are to be distinguished, not by their falsity/genuineness, but by the style in which they are imagined" (ibid.).

The state, then, may serve to organize both bourgeoisie and proletariat, both through its own structure and the structure of the parties that contend for power, and through the creation of images and traditions of a national community. It is important to grasp the power of these structures and images, which requires us to examine particular times and places, particular conjunctures of economic development, class formation, and political domination. One place to begin is with typologies of the sort that Anderson suggests. Thus we may look at the new nations in nineteenth-century Latin America, or the nationalisms that emerged in east and central Europe in the nineteenth century, as particular types of imagined community. This takes us beyond epochal markers like proletarianization and "the" bourgeois state and forces us to examine more limited and suggestive sets of common experiences and structures. But we must, of course, go further and explore the history of specific states. The oppositions of country and city or backwardness and development through which I examined Venezuelan politics in Chapter 3 cannot be understood as generalized oppositions. They acquire their particular significance, their cultural meaning and power, in specific experiences and projections.

As we look at specific histories, we see that political communities are not formed around images of "the state" itself but around particular social and cultural oppositions that create a group or community feeling among heterogeneous folk. They involve movements *for* our people, our culture, our region, the true faith, progress, or democracy; *against* the intruders, the English, the infidels, the agro-exporting bourgeoisie, the dictators. The images, and the movements they inspire, are products of and responses to particular forces, structures, and events—colonialism and its demise, the imposition of a state religion, the autocratic rule of a dictator, the rise or demise of a region—and they derive their community-forming power from their apparent relationship to those forces and events. They involve, in their classic form, vertical or multiclass coalitions.

But full understanding of the hegemonic power of such images of community requires an examination of their institutional elaboration and expression. This is where the state acquires its central role. Movements for a region or the faith or democracy become movements for the state; it is through control of the state that imagined communities can be given material form. If, as Raymond Williams contends, a basic component of any culture is a selected tradition, one of the most important means for selecting and disseminating that tradition is through the institutions of the state itself—schools, print and other media, and the like. Through these forms, the forces and events that gave rise to the imagined community can be constantly recreated even after the actual events have passed or the forces are no longer active. The political community that begins as a regionalist, religious, populist, or anticolonial project, turns to a struggle for the state, and maintains itself through control of the state.

Nonetheless, as has been stressed throughout this book, our understanding of structures of power should be sensitive to sources of weakness and contradiction, to the presence or possibility of resistance, of emergent and perhaps alternative political communities. But we must also resist two powerful temptations. One would be to place our understanding of resistance within an oppositional historical model, to counterpose a genuine popular culture to the spurious hegemonic culture. We have already encountered such attempts in this essay. A second would be to move too quickly to a discussion of working-class culture and politics. We shall engage in such a discussion, but most forms of counterhegemony or alternative culture do not take a class-specific form. Our understanding of both hegemonic and counterhegemonic cultural movements should be placed in the context of class divisions but should not be reduced to specific class positions. Indeed, given the perspective on uneven proletarianization outlined in this essay, we should be surprised when such movements *do* take such a form. We have important historical examples of such movements, and a growing literature in social history is expanding our understanding of the experience and culture of working people even in "unheroic decades" (Williams 1979:135). But we need to place these experiences and movements in a larger context of those forms of hegemonic and counterhegemonic culture and politics that are not class specific.[12]

Given the nature of hegemonic political communities and the political and economic structures in which they are inserted, most alternative movements and images take a form (and may involve contents) similar to the dominant culture. The dominant imagined community may invoke the equality of regions, religions, and persons, but state policies will favor certain regions, classes, or projects. Feelings of disquiet or discontent may take religious or regionalist forms, perhaps eventuating in political movements. These feelings and movements will also involve images of community that can serve as alternatives to the hegemonic.

The new communities emerge in political contexts but need not have political aims. The protestant conversion of Colta Indians in Ecuador (Muratorio 1980; see above, Chapter 4), for example, needs to be understood in terms of the Indians' response to the experience of exploitation, the state, and the dominant Catholic faith. It involved a rejection of certain aspects of the dominant culture and an attempt to maintain ethnic identity through the paradoxical (and fundamentally contradictory) medium of an individualistic religious faith. In certain contexts, however, these alternative communities may take a political form, organizing along religious, ethnic, regionalist, or class lines. Central to our analysis of counterhegemonic communities, then, should be an examination of the cultural forms and symbols around which alternative images of community can be built, and an exploration of the organizational or institutional forms through which such images can be given political expression.

As should be clear from our discussion so far, alternative political communities will often be vertical, multiclass coalitions similar in form to hegemonic communities. They need not necessarily take this form, however. We might close our discussion with a brief consideration of examples of horizontal communities that link various segments of a heterogeneous working people. Let us consider, first, the Huasicanchinos of Peru (Smith 1989; see above, Chapter 7). There the idiom of community served as a powerful material force in Huasicanchinos's struggle for land and livelihood. Rooted in genuinely precapitalist experiences and extended into a present in such a way that it could embrace migrants to Lima and Huancayo, the image of community served to mobilize the Huasicanchinos in a sophisticated and successful struggle against hacienda and state. Although the language of community united a heterogeneous population of pastoralists and fruit vendors, it was an image that was rooted in a specific place and set of conflicts. It could not be extended to embrace pastoralists or migrants from other places.

Yet such extension is often possible. Thompson's *Making of the English Working Class* is a consideration of the economic, political, and cultural processes by which a working class was formed and formed itself. The book ends just as the politics of working people is beginning to take a class form. Likewise, William Sewell, in *Work and Revolution in France* (1980), examines the changing "language of labor" from the Old Regime to 1848, detailing the economic transformations and political and cultural processes by which various types of tradesmen went beyond trade boundaries and divisions and began to see themselves, and to act, as a class. Other examples from the social-historical literature on working-class experience in Europe and North America could be offered at considerable length.[13]

We might consider more recent examples from Latin American experience. Here it would be useful to explore the use of devil imagery and the practice of propitiation rites among tin miners in Bolivia in light of this essay's preoccupations. First, let us note that the tin miners are but one (highly militant) fraction of the Bolivian working population. The union serves as an

effective organizational locus for that fraction and can reach
out toward other groups through oppositional political parties.
But such connections require cultural images as well as political
organization. If our earlier suggestion that propitiation rites
had less to do with remembered reciprocities than with a conscious attempt to connect with and maintain an indigenous identity, then the union's demand may represent an attempt to link
working-class politics with ethnic politics, an attempt to create
an alternative, horizontal political community.

Other examples may involve the creation of new traditions.
The union of liberation theology, base communities, and mass
organizations in Nicaragua, El Salvador, and other parts of Latin America offers an especially interesting example. Here it is
important to recall Carlos Cabarrús's (1983) study of the formation of the Christian Peasants Union (FECCAS) out of Christian
base communities in Aguilares, El Salvador (see above, Chapter
7). The economic process in Aguilares created a highly fractionated semiproletariat, some members of which turned to the
paramilitary ORDEN and some members of which joined FECCAS.
The transformation of FECCAS from a local to a national organization, and its increasing militance in the face of political repression, are in many ways a classic story of political mobilization
and organization. What makes this story unique, and what gives
organizations like FECCAS such promise, is their basis in a process of community formation. These organizations present an
important and innovative resolution of the dialectic of cultural
creation and political organization, one that might transcend, if
given the opportunity their opponents are determined to deny
them, earlier forms of socialist organization derived from European experience.

Such organizations carry their own contradictions, however.
One of the most powerful elements of liberation theology is its
identification with "the people" and their liberation from a
group of earthly oppressors. In a heterogeneous working population of peasants, tenants, semiproletarians, industrial workers,
and the like, the message of liberation theology is one that creates
an oppositional imagined community. In an actual political movement, however, "the people" can include a wide variety of groups

and projects. In Nicaragua, for example, the struggle against Somoza had been carried out by the relatively small group of Sandinista guerrillas for almost two decades. As governmental repression became more extensive and violent in the mid-1970s, however, they were joined by new mass organizations that were tied to Christian base communities, often formed independently of the Sandinistas but entering into strategic alliances with them. In the final months of the revolution, the decisive events consisted of a series of large-scale popular insurrections involving large numbers of people who had no connection with Sandinista and other organizations. The fall of Somoza represented a victory for a "people" that included Sandinistas, other organized groups, and unorganized masses in towns and cities, united by their opposition to Somoza. At the time of the triumph, then, the revolution included, in contrast to some of the other examples discussed in this essay, a large, relatively unorganized vertical, multiclass imagined community, and a much smaller, impressively organized, horizontal, class-specific imagined community. The contradiction between these two was carried over to the revolutionary state.

———

We have begun with culture, turned to history, and ended with politics. This progression should not surprise. Even at their most esoteric, anthropological ideas about culture involve a series of (often unstated) ideas about history, capitalism, the state, political action. By moving in this essay from ideas about natural economy to a consideration of political movements in El Salvador and Nicaragua, I have attempted to make those connections explicit. Werner Sombart was not alone in using the Middle Ages, or the past, or cultural others, in order to make points about the present. He was simply more explicit than others have been. This does not mean, of course, that we cannot make a statement about culture until we have reached a position on the Sandinista government or their U.S.-backed opponents. It does mean that cultural texts are commentaries. They have authors and audiences, and the actions they inscribe have consequences.

When we link the symbolism of La Santísima with the symbolism of the loudspeakers, we begin to engage a world of politics and privilege, power and positioning. Most of us would reject as too vulgar Frederick Jameson's claim that, "The underside of culture is blood, torture, death and horror" (1984: 57). But perhaps we should reconsider. Geertz was aware of the connection when he commented in a footnote to his Balinese cockfight article that between 40,000 and 80,000 Balinese were killed during the 1965 counterrevolution in Indonesia (Geertz 1973c: 452). As Geertz noted, the cockfight did not "cause" the bloodshed. But one should not isolate cultural form or content from political process. Unfortunately, most readers of Geertz's essay remember the self-effacing character of his description of the police raid on a cockfight or his erudite elucidation of cocks and men. They seldom remember or read the footnotes. My purpose in this book has been to make the political footnote an integral part of the cultural text, to see the politics in culture.

N O T E S

INTRODUCTION

1. For other surveys and commentaries on anthropology and history, see Cohn 1980; 1981; Davis 1981; Medick 1987; Thompson 1972; Recent studies that contribute to an "intersection" of the two disciplines include Behar 1986; Chance 1978; Comaroff 1985; de la Peña 1982; Farriss 1984; Fox 1985; Frykman and Lofgren 1987; Lomnitz-Adler 1982; Mintz 1985; Muratorio 1987; Price 1983; Rosaldo 1980; Roseberry 1983; Sewell 1980; Sider 1986; Smith 1989; Stoler 1985; Trouillot 1988; Vincent 1982; Warman 1981. In my view, the most important recent commentary is an extraordinary essay by Hermann Rebel (1989a; 1989b).

2. My thanks to Lindsay DuBois for noticing this.

CHAPTER 1

1. During the 1980s, commentaries on the Balinese cockfight essay have become quite common, developing, for the most part, in apparent independence (see, for example, Clifford 1983; Crapanzano 1986; Lieberson 1984). At the time the original version of this chapter was published, in 1982, this academic industry was undeveloped. Unlike some of the more recent commentaries, this essay is directed toward a more political understanding of culture.

2. In *Negara,* Geertz seems to take a more cautious stand on cockfights as a major source of public revenue. The book is an analysis of fractionated "theatre states" in precolonial Bali, in which a series of lords and princes is able to build followings but in which the followings themselves are geographically dispersed. Though he analyzes the dispersed tax areas of lords and the activities of the tax

and rent collectors, or *sedahan*, Geertz refers to the cockfight only in a footnote to another section on commerce. There he remarks: "The marketplaces were commonly set up in the space in front of one or another lord's house. . . . And, as with everything else—land, water, people, and so on—the idiom had it that the lord 'owned' the market. In any case, he levied taxes on it, as he did on the cockfights, which, in the afternoon of the market day, were often held in the cockring near the marketplace" (1980: 199).

3. I thank Richard Blot for this point.

4. It should be understood that the difference is not that between text and performance. Such a distinction takes us back to the structuralist opposition between language and speech, to which Geertz would hardly be sympathetic. Rather, the very notion of culture as text must be radically questioned.

5. Marshall Sahlins, who also recognizes the antinomies of anthropological thought and has built his career at both poles of the one between materialism and idealism, makes the opposite criticism of Geertz, seeing Geertz's cultural theory as too closely tied to the social. But Sahlins makes this criticism as part of an argument for the symbolic construction of the social (1976: 106–117; see also Schneider 1980: 125–134).

6. In a reference to the present, Geertz tells us that status cannot be changed in the cockfight and that an individual cannot climb the caste ladder in any case (1973a: 443). Geertz also relates folk tales from the classical period in which cockfighting serves either as a metaphor for political struggle or as a means by which profound political and social changes might occur (ibid.: 418, 441, 442). In one, a king accepts a cockfight with a commoner who has no means to pay should he lose. The king hopes to force the commoner to become his slave should he lose, but the commoner's cock kills the king, the commoner becomes king, and so on (ibid.: 442). Such tales support Geertz's assertion that status differences are a "matter of life and death." They may also provide material for a textual analysis of the sort Taylor and Rebel undertake.

CHAPTER 2

1. For a good analysis of the formation of a "working-class culture" that was *not* "counterhegemonic," that was profoundly conservative in its values and effects, see Jones's (1983: 179–238) examination of late-nineteenth-century London. His study offers an important response to those writers who too quickly and confidently ascribe a semiautonomous space to politics and culture among working-class people. One implication of Jones's work is a reminder that working-class culture, consciousness, and politics are shaped by the same political and economic forces that create working classes (or "a working people that has [yet] to become a class" [Williams 1977: 111]); that "counterhegemonies" are necessarily shaped within a hegemonic *process*. See as well Steedman (1986). For a related, insightful, and suggestive analysis of working-class culture and experiences, as well as a consideration of how histo-

rians and others reconstruct and write about culture and experience, see Popular Memory Group (1982).

CHAPTER 3

1. The field research was conducted in the mid-1970s in the midst of an uneven economic boom due to the rapid expansion of petroleum prices. My knowledge and understanding of Venezuela is very much rooted in my experience of that moment. The symbolic oppositions and the uses and valuations of past and present were active in the political discourse of the mid-1970s. Much has happened since, most importantly the collapse of oil prices and, consequently, of public revenues. The discourse of "development," and of the linkage of democracy and development, has taken on a darker, less confident tone and imagery. The field research was supported by an NSF Graduate Fellowship, a Doherty Fellowship for Latin American Studies, and an NSF Dissertation Improvement Grant.

2. On the petroleum transformation, see Bergquist 1986: 191–273; Córdova 1973; Malavé Mata 1974; Rangel 1970; Tugwell 1975

3. See Baloyra and Martz 1979; Bergquist 1986: 191–273; Ellner 1980; 1981; Levine 1973; Martz 1966; Martz, ed. 1977; Petras, Morley, and Smith 1977

4. For a representative history written from an AD perspective, see Salcedo Bastardo 1972.

5. For a representative socialist history, see Malavé Mata 1974.

CHAPTER 4

1. The reference here is to Marx's observation at the beginning of *The Eighteenth Brumaire:* "Hegel remarks somewhere that all the great events and characters of world history occur, so to speak, twice. He forgot to add: the first time as tragedy, the second as farce" 1974 [1852]: 146). Note as well the observation of the editors to the Random House/Vintage edition that, "It is doubtful whether Hegel ever wrote these words" (ibid.: 146).

2. An early version of this essay was presented to a group of historians at Rutgers University in the spring of 1987, as part of a series of lectures on "cultural empires." I am grateful to John Gillis for prevailing on me to undertake the impossible.

3. See, for example, Redfield 1934; Redfield, Linton, and Herskovitz 1936; SSRC Summer Seminar in Acculturation 1954; Spicer, ed. 1961; Tax, ed. 1952

4. For classic anthropological accounts of this difference, see Benedict 1943; Service 1955.

5. For historical and anthropological accounts of and controversies concerning the creation of indigenous communities, see Cline 1949; Gibson 1964; Rowe 1957; Wolf 1955; 1956b; 1959a. More recent statements can be found

in Farriss 1978; 1984; Gibson 1984; Greishaber 1979; Spalding 1974; Stern 1982; 1983. On demography, see Cook and Borah 1972–79; Sanchez Alborñoz 1974. For an excellent critical survey of the social history of colonial and nineteenth-century Latin America, see Taylor 1985.

6. The best treatment of the association of Mexican liberalism with French intellectual trends can be found in Hale 1968. See as well Hale 1973; Palacios 1983; Safford 1976; 1985.

7. The literature on coffee in nineteenth-and early-twentienth-century Latin America is expanding rapidly. See Bergad 1983; Bergquist 1978; 1986; Cardoso 1975b; 1986; Carvallo and Hernandez 1979; Dean 1976; Font 1987; Gudmundson 1986; Hernandez 1988; Holloway 1980; Love 1980; McCreery 1976; 1983; Palacios 1983; Picó 1979; 1981; Roseberry 1983; Samper 1985; Stolcke 1988. In the fall of 1988, many of these authors met at a conference sponsored by the SSRC and the Universidad Nacional de Colombia to move toward a comparative analysis of Latin American experiences with coffee in the world economy. A volume representing the results of that conference is tentatively scheduled for 1990.

8. For an introduction to this period and to these issues, see Glade 1986; R. F. Smith 1986. Thorp 1986. See as well Lewis 1938; D.C.M. Platt, ed. 1977; Seidel 1972. The bibliographical essay in Volume 4 of the *Cambridge History of Latin America* provides further help.

9. On the liberalism and positivism of this period, see Hale 1986 and the relevant sections of the bibliographical essay in the *Cambridge History of Latin America,* Volume 4. Woodward (1985: 83–207) provides a good discussion of ideology and politics in Central America. For Colombia, see Palacios 1983; cf. Bergquist 1978.

10. See as well *Ariel* (Rodó 1988 [1900]), the quintessential statement of this opposition and rejection (cf. Hale 1986: 414–417).

11. The argument here is Cardoso and Faletto's (1979). For surveys of the experience of particular countries, see González Casanova, ed. 1984; Skidmore and Smith 1984. The essays in Volume 5 of the *Cambridge History of Latin America* offer surveys of the experience of particular countries up to 1930, which are relevant to an understanding of the differential experience of subsequent years. See as well Thorp, ed. 1984 for a survey of the differential experiences of the 1930s, one that challenges many received historiographical assumptions concerning the Depression among ECLA and dependency theorists. The most provocative recent study is Bergquist 1986, which offers a comparative history of twentieth-century Argentina, Chile, Venezuela, and Colombia in terms of their distinct export sectors and the working classes that emerged within them. At the very least, the study gives greater specificity to the types of social groups and experiences lumped together in the phrase "middle classes." More significantly, the study challenges many long-popular historiographical schemes.

12. On the contradictions of import substitution, see Cardoso and Faletto 1979; de Janvry 1981; 1970 Furtado.

13. Cardoso and Faletto 1979; Collier 1979; Johnson 1964; Malloy 1977; O'Donnell 1973; Stepan 1978.

CHAPTER 6

1. As this book was going to press, an important article by Steve Stern appeared that offers an impressive appraisal of Wallersteinian perspectives in the literature on Latin America (see Stern 1988a; 1988b; Wallerstein 1988). Readers interested in the issues raised in this chapter should consult Stern, both for his excellent bibliography and his sophisticated argument.

2. Banaji (1977) refers to two usages, more or less corresponding to the first two mentioned by Cardoso.

3. In this sense, Steward's cultural ecology, though its understanding of economics was limited to something like productive forces, was much more active and dynamic than Harris's cultural materialism. For Steward, humans were not acted upon by nature; they acted upon nature through *work* (Steward 1955; 1978; Murphy 1970; 1978; 1981; Silverman 1979; Wolf 1978).

4. For Althusser, see his 1969; 1971; 1976; and Althusser and Balibar 1970. The best known French follower of Althusser was Poulantzas. His structuralist approach to class and politics can be found in his 1973; 1974; and 1975; but see as well his 1978. For English applications, see Hindess and Hirst 1975; 1977; Taylor 1979. The most stinging criticism came from E. P. Thompson 1978a; but see as well his critics: Anderson 1980; Hall 1981; Hirst 1979; Johnson 1981; Nield and Seed 1979; cf. Thompson 1981. The best history and critique of anthropological structural Marxism in France is Kahn and Llobera 1981.

5. This is one of the areas in which I differ with Rey. Like other structural Marxists, he conceived of modes of production in pure, abstract terms. The presence of apparently anomalous groups within a social formation (e.g., nobility in England, peasants in France) was taken as evidence of the continued existence of prior modes of production. This makes sense in terms of a structuralist logic, but not in terms of much else.

6. See footnote 7, Chapter 4.

7. For related readings of this section of *Capital,* see G. Williams's 1979 criticism of R. Johnson, *and* Johnson 1982.

CHAPTER 7

1. See Deere 1986 for an excellent critical survey of the literature.

2. See Hewitt de Alcántara 1984 for a survey of the literature in Mexico and the many variations on basic positions.

3. This summary mentions only a few aspects of a book that attempts to address a number of theoretical and political issues regarding agrarian structure, poverty, and food production in Latin America. The book's scope is more broad than the question that motivates the present essay, and its content is more rich than a summary and critique of a model can suggest.

4. In addition, his analysis of the removal of peasants from positions as basic commodity producers reflects an aspect of a process that has affected peasants I have studied in Venezuela. And, in considering politics in twentieth-century Venezuela, I reluctantly agree with de Janvry that "the locus of class struggle is increasingly being displaced away from the countryside and into the cities" 1981: 267; cf. Roseberry 1978c; 1982; 1983).

5. Unimodality, which is simply asserted in de Janvry's book, is open to question on other grounds as well. Erik Olin Wright (1978) postulates the generation of "contradictory class locations" as a result of the process of capital accumulation itself rather than as survivals from previously existing modes of production.

6. It does not take us beyond the theme of the book, however. De Janvry considers different class allignments when discussing his model (1981: 40–45) and devotes the last half of the book to agrarian policy.

7. For Morelos, see Martin 1985; de la Peña 1982; Warman 1981; Melville 1979; for Oaxaca, see Taylor 1972; 1974; 1976; Chance 1978; Waterbury 1975; for Yucatan, see Farriss 1978; 1984; Joseph 1986; Patch 1985. I have developed the argument of these paragraphs in a working paper, Roseberry 1987. On the whole subject of regional differentiation of rural social relations in Mexico, the starting point is Katz 1974.

8. Roseberry 1983. Small-scale coffee production was and is important elsewhere in Latin America as well (see Bergquist 1986 and Palacios 1983 on Colombia; Gudmundson 1986 and Samper 1985 on Costa Rica. The final chapter of Gudmundson's book offers an important survey and argument regarding the extent and importance of small-scale production in Latin America's rural history.

CHAPTER 8

1. The connection between an oppositional history (from primitive to civilized, from natural economy to money economy, from use value to exchange value, etc.) and evolutionist thinking is one many latter-day oppositional thinkers might choose to deny. Nonetheless, the basic premises and the epochal approach to history, culture, and politics are quite similar.

2. Interestingly, Marshall Sahlins notes the following while postulating his "domestic mode of production:"

> Interesting that almost all the philosophers who have felt the need to go back
> there—granted not one of them ever made it—saw in that condition a specific

distribution of population. Almost all sensed some centrifugal tendency. Hobbes sent back ethnographic report that the life of man was solitary, poor, nasty, brutish and short. Underline (for once) the "solitary." It was a life apart. And the same notion of original isolation appears ever and again, from Herodutus to K. Bucher, in the schemes of those who dared speculate on man in nature. (1972: 96)

But Bucher's discussion of "independent domestic economy" comes immediately after two chapters on primitive economics and explicitly excludes primitive "man in nature" from the discussion.

3. Despite obvious formal similarities, there were important differences between Marxist and non-Marxist conceptions of natural economy. Non-Marxist oppositions were generally rooted in exchange: natural economy was characterized by a lack of exchange and money economy was characterized by the prevalence of exchange. Although Bucher does not use such terms, the idea is clearly expressed. "The standpoint is none other than the relation which exists between the production and the consumption of goods; or, to be more exact, the length of the route which the goods traverse in passing from producer to consumer" (1967 [1900]: 88–89). For Marxists, however, the emphasis is on production and the *orientation* of production, which may not correspond exactly with the *destination* of the product. Thus, products can be exchanged within natural economy, but as long as production is oriented toward the consumption needs of the direct producer, regardless of whether the product is directly consumed by the producer or placed in exchange for other products to be consumed, the boundaries of natural economy have not been transgressed. Commodity economy, on the other hand, implies a situation in which the product has been objectified through exchange, the product becoming a commodity with a definite exchange value. Exchange can then be oriented not simply toward the consumption needs of the producer but toward the circulation and accumulation of value. Thus, both the product and the producer can become objectified or alienated. Capitalism is seen as a particular kind of commodity economy in which commodity production has so permeated social relations that a value can be attached even to the labor power of the producer.

The basic opposition for the Marxist distinction between natural and commodity economy, then, is not production for use versus production for exchange but production for use value versus production for exchange value. Both distinctions depend, however, upon a consideration of the role of exchange within a society, and the difference is subtle enough to have confused a number of Marxists, some of whom seem to be closer to Karl Bucher than to Marx.

4. Before examining Marx's work in detail, however, it must be pointed out that just as he was subject to common social, political, and intellectual influences of the nineteenth century, he in turn contributed to them, especially in

Germany. Here one might consider, in particular, the work of Toennies and
Weber, but a careful consideration of the influence of Marx on non-Marxist
thinkers is well beyond the scope of this essay.

5. For elaboration on these historical questions, see Roseberry, forthcoming.

6. This discussion of Redfield can also be found in Roseberry 1988.

7. That Redfield was looking critically at the urban end caused some discomfort for those modernization theorists who actually bothered to read him.
Wilbert Moore, for example, commenting on the three results of urbanism
alluded to by Redfield (disorganization, secularization, and individualization),
was most disturbed by Redfield's emphasis on disorganization. He wondered
if Redfield really thought the urban end could never show organization—by
which we might understand "functional integration" (1951).

8. Or at least it is not true in the simple way that Taussig suggests. Many of
the peasants and children of peasants who went into the mines were not from
the Altiplano but from the Cochabamba Valley. As Brooke Larson notes in
her excellent study, a commercially oriented mestizo peasantry had emerged
in the valley by the eighteenth century (1988). Taussig's assertions regarding
indigenous reciprocities and use-value orientations are misplaced. For an excellent study of Bolivian peasant politics over the past thirty-five years, see
Albó 1987.

9. See the *Social Analysis* symposium on Taussig's book (da Matta 1986;
Gregory 1986; McEachern and Mayer 1986; Post 1986; Trouillot 1986; and
especially Turner 1986.) See as well Taussig's bizarre response, 1987.

10. These two problems (the assumption that peasant life is historically
prior to capitalism and the idealization of noncapitalist class relations) are not
unlike the two problems noted in our earlier discussion of some of Marx's
texts: the peasant as starting point and the emphasis on the free peasantry at
the expense of a consideration of serfdom.

11. For example, it can be argued that in England, the classic terrain of
capitalist development, the erosion of peasant communities in the open fields
regions long preceded the process of proletarianization per se. Rather, it was
associated with the demise of serfdom and the responses of peasants and
lords to the demographic collapse of the fourteenth century, in which individual tenants migrated and sought better deals. Individual activity among liberated peasants, then, was central to the emergence both of a new kind of
peasantry and of a proletariat in the enclosure movements (Roseberry, forthcoming).

12. If it is insufficient to *assume* a relationship between class and culture, it
is equally insufficient to assume a lack of relationship, to simply assert the
importance of ethnicity or of other "subcultures" that cross-cut class lines.
Such assertions simply take reified entities ("class," "culture," "ethnicity") and
propose unproblematic relationships (sometimes labeled "dialectical") among

them rather than viewing each of the terms as interconnected within contradictory historical processes. In the process the terms become essences rather than relations. We need to carefully consider *why* in this time and place political communities take a class form while in another time and place they take ethnic or other forms.

13. Fundamental to such processes was an economic transformation that created the basis for a working class—the process of proletarianization in the classic sense. If I have emphasized the heterogeneity and fractionalization of working people—divisions between peasant and proletarian, skilled and unskilled, employed and unemployed, factory and craftshop—it must also be recognized that the economic process creates a kind of heterogeneity at one level and a kind of homogeneity at another level. Despite evident differences there are also evident similarities. All workers are being placed—in England and France in this period—in a common position in relation of capital, and this can serve as a basis for working-class action in classic forms through union, parties, and the like. Thus, even as the economic process dissolves certain kinds of relationships, it creates the basis for other kinds.

R E F E R E N C E S

ADAMS, RICHARD N.
1970   *Crucifixion by Power.* Austin: University of Texas Press.

ADAS, MICHAEL
1980   " 'Moral Economy' or 'Contest State'? Elite Demands and the Origins of Peasant Protest in Southeast Asia." *Journal of Social History* 13: 521–546.

ALBÓ, XAVIER
1987   "From MNRistas to Kataristas to Katari." In *Resistance, Rebellion, and Consciousness in the Andean World, 18th to 20th Centuries,* ed. Steve J. Stern, 379–419. Madison: University of Wisconsin Press.

ALTHUSSER, LOUIS
1969   *For Marx.* New York: Pantheon.
1971   *Lenin and Philosophy and Other Essays.* New York: Monthly Review Press.
1976   *Essays in Self-Criticism.* London: New Left Books.

ALTHUSSER, LOUIS, AND ETIENNE BALIBAR
1970   *Reading Capital.* New York: Pantheon.

AMIN, SAMIR
1976   *Unequal Development.*New York: Monthly Review Press.

ANDERSON, BENEDICT
1983   *Imagined Communities.* London: Verso.

ANDERSON, PERRY
1980   *Arguments within English Marxism.* London: Verso.

ARCHETTI, EDUARDO
1981   *Campesinado y estructuras agrarias en América Latina.* Quito: CEPLAES
          Editores.

ASSADOURIAN, CARLOS SEMPAT, CIRO F. S. CARDOSO, HORACIO CIAFARDINI,
JUAN CARLOS GARAVAGLIA, AND ERNESTO LACLAU
1973   *Modos de producción en América Latina.* Cordoba: Cuadernos de
          Pasado y Presente 40.

BALOYRA, ENRIQUE, AND JOHN MARTZ
1979   *Political Attitudes in Venezuela.* Austin: University of Texas Press.

BANAJI, JAIRUS
1977   "Modes of Production in a Materialist Conception of History."
          Capital and Class 3: 1–44.

BARAN, PAUL A.
1957   *The Political Economy of Growth.* New York: Monthly Review Press.

BARNABAS, JOSEP M.
1984   "The Catholic Church in Colonial Spanish America." *Cambridge
          History of Latin America* 1: 511–540.

BARTRA, ROGER
1974   *Estructura agraria y clases sociales en México.* Mexico, D. F.: ERA .

BASTIEN, JOSEPH
1978   *Mountain of the Condor.* American Ethnological Society Monograph
          #64. St. Paul: West.

BAZANT, J.
1977   *A Concise History of Mexico from Hidalgo to Cardenas, 1805–1940.*
          Cambridge: Cambridge University Press.

BEHAR, RUTH
1986   *Santa María del Monte: The Presence of the Past in a Spanish Village.*
          Princeton: Princeton University Press.

BENEDICT, RUTH
1943   "Two Patterns of Indian Acculturation." *American Anthropologist*
          45: 207–212.

BERGAD, LAIRD
1983   *Coffee and the Growth of Agrarian Capitalism in Nineteenth Century
          Puerto Rico.* Princeton: Princeton University Press.

BERGQUIST, CHARLES
1978   *Coffee and Conflict in Colombia, 1886–1910.* Durham: Duke Univer-
          sity Press.
1986   *Labor in Latin America: Comparative Essays on Chile, Argentina, Venezu-
          ela and Colombia.* Stanford: Stanford University Press.

BOCK, PHILIP K.
1980   "Tepoztlán Reconsidered." *Journal of Latin American Lore* 6(1):
          129–150.

BRADBY, BARBARA
1975   "The Destruction of Natural Economy." *Economy and Society* 4: 127–161.

BUCHER, KARL
1967   *Industrial Evolution*, 3d ed. New York: Burt Franklin.
[1900]

BUECHLER, HANS, AND JUDITH M. BUECHLER
1971   *The Bolivian Aymara*. New York: Holt, Rinehart and Winston.

CABARRÚS, CARLOS R.
1983   *Genesis de una revolución: análisis del surgimiento y desarrollo de la organización campesina en El Salvador*. Mexico, D. F.: Ediciones de la Casa Chata.

CARDOSO, CIRO F. S.
1975a   "On the Colonial Modes of Production of the Americas." *Critique of Anthropology* 4 & 5: 1–36.
1975b   "Historia económica del café en Centroamérica: Estudio comparativo." *Estudios Sociales Centroamericanos* 4(10): 9–55.
1986   "Central America: The Liberal Era, c. 1870–1930." *Cambridge History of Latin America* 5: 197–227.

CARDOSO, FERNANDO HENRIQUE
1972   "Dependency and Development in Latin America." *New Left Review* 74: 83–95.
1973a   "Associated Dependent Development: Theoretical and Practical Implications." In *Authoritarian Brazil*, ed. Alfred Stepan, 142–176. New Haven: Yale University Press.
1973b   "Comentario: Althusserianismo o Marxismo? A propósito del concepto de clases en Poulantzas." In *Las clases sociales en América Latina*, ed. Florestan Fernandes, 137–153. Mexico, D. F.: Siglo XXI.
1977a   "The Consumption of Dependency Theory in the United States." *Latin American Research Review* 12(3): 7–24.
1977b   "The Originality of a Copy: CEPAL and the Idea of Development." *CEPAL Review*, 2d half of 1977, 7–40.

CARDOSO, FERNANDO HENRIQUE, AND ENZO FALETTO
1979   *Dependency and Development in Latin America*. Berkeley: University of California Press.

CARVALLO, GASTON, AND JOSEFINA RÍOS DE HERNANDEZ
1979   *Agricultura y sociedad: Tres ensayos históricos*. Caracas: CENDES .

CHANCE, JOHN
1978   *Race and Class in Colonial Oaxaca*. Stanford: Stanford University Press.

CHAYANOV, A. V.
1966   *The Theory of Peasant Economy*. Homewood, IL: Richard Irwin.
[1925]

CHINCHILLA, NORMA, AND JAMES DIETZ
1981   "Toward a New Understanding of Development and Underdevelopment." *Latin American Perspectives* 8(3 & 4): 138–147.

CLARKE, JULIAN
1981   " 'Capital in General' and Non-Capitalist Relations." *Critique of Anthropology* 16: 31–42.

CLIFFORD, JAMES
1983   "On Ethnographic Authority." *Representations* 1(2): 118–146.

CLIFFORD, JAMES, AND GEORGE MARCUS, EDS.
1986   *Writing Culture: The Poetics and Politics of Ethnography.* Berkeley: University of California Press.

CLINE, HOWARD
1949   "Civil Congregations of the Indians in New Spain, 1598–1606." *Hispanic American Historical Review* 29: 349–369.

COATSWORTH, JOHN
1981   *Growth Against Development: The Economic Impact of Railroads in Porfirian Mexico.* De Kalb: Northern Illinois University Press.

COHN, BERNARD
1980   "History and Anthropology: The State of Play." *Comparative Studies in Society and History* 22: 198–221.
1981   "Anthropology and History in the 1980s. Toward a Rapprochement." *Journal of Interdisciplinary History* 12: 227–252.

COLLIER, DAVID
1979   *The New Authoritarianism in Latin America.* Princeton: Princeton University Press.

COMAROFF, JEAN
1985   *Body of Power, Spirit of Resistance: The Culture and History of a South African People.* Chicago: University of Chicago Press.

CONRAD, JOSEPH
1960   *Nostromo.* New York: New American Library.
[1904]

COOK, SCOTT
1973   "Production, Ecology, and Economic Anthropology: Notes Toward an Integrated Frame of Reference." *Social Science Information* 12(1): 25–52.
1982   *Zapotec Stoneworkers: The Dynamics of Rural Simple Commodity Production in Modern Mexican Capitalism.* Washington, D. C.: University Press of America.

COOK, SCOTT, AND MARTIN DISKIN, EDS.
1976   *Markets in Oaxaca.* Austin: University of Texas Press.

COOK, SHERBURNE F., AND WOODROW BORAH
1972–79   *Essays in Population History: Mexico and the Caribbean,* 3 vols. Berkeley: University of California Press.

COQUERY-VIDROVITCH, CATHERINE
1978   "Research on an African Mode of Production." In *Relations of Production,* ed. David Seddon, 261–288. London: Frank Cass.

CÓRDOVA, ARMANDO
1973   *Inversiones extranjeras y subdesarrollo.* Caracas: Universidad Central.

CRAPANZANO, VINCENT
1986   "Hermes' Dilemma: The Masking of Subversion in Ethnographic Description." In *Writing Culture,* ed. James Clifford and George Marcus, 51–76. Berkeley: University of California Press.

CUEVA, AGUSTIN
1977   *El desarrollo del capitalismo en América Latina.* Mexico, D. F.: Siglo XXI .

DA MATTA, ROBERTO
1986   "Review of Chevalier and Taussig." *Social Analysis* 19: 57–63.

DAVENPORT, WILLIAM
1969   "The Hawaiian 'Cultural Revolution': Some Economic and Political Considerations." *American Anthropologist* 71: 1–20.

DAVIS, NATALIE ZEMON
1981   "Anthropology and History in the 1980s: The Possibilities of the Past." *Journal of Interdisciplinary History* 12: 267–276.

DEAN, WARREN
1976   *Rio Claro: A Brazilian Plantation System, 1820–1920.* Stanford: Stanford University Press.

DEERE, CARMEN DIANA
1986   "The Peasantry in Political Economy: Trends of the 1980s." Paper presented at the Annual Meeting of the Latin American Studies Association. Boston.

DEERE, CARMEN DIANA, AND ALAIN DE JANVRY
1979   "A Conceptual Framework for the Empirical Analysis of Peasants." *American Journal of Agricultural Economics* 61: 601–611.
1981   "Demographic and Social Differentiation among Northern Peruvian Peasants." *Journal of Peasant Studies* 8: 335–366.

DE JANVRY, ALAIN
1981   *The Agrarian Question and Reformism in Latin America.* Baltimore: The Johns Hopkins University Press.

DE JANVRY, ALAIN, AND CARLOS GARRAMON
1977   "The Dynamics of Rural Poverty in Latin America." *Journal of Peasant Studies* 4: 206–216.

DE LA PEÑA, GUILLERMO
1982   *A Legacy of Promises.* Austin: University of Texas Press.

DOBB, MAURICE
1963   *Studies in the Development of Capitalism,* 2d ed. New York: International Publishers.

DONHAM, DONALD
1981 "Beyond the Domestic Mode of Production." *Man* 16: 515–541.

DUPRÉ, GEORGES, AND PIERRE-PHILIPPE REY
1978 "Reflections on the Relevance of a Theory of the History of Exchange." In *Relations of Production,* ed. David Seddon, 171–208. London: Frank Cass.

DURRENBERGER, E. PAUL, ED.
1984 *Chayanov, Peasants, and Economic Anthropology.* New York: Academic.

EDWARDS, RICHARD, MICHAEL REICH, AND DAVID M. GORDON, EDS.
1975 *Labor Market Segmentation.* Lexington, MA: D. C. Heath.

ELLNER, STEVEN
1980 "Political Party Dynamics in Venezuela and the Outbreak of Revolutionary Warfare." *Interamerican Economic Affairs* 34(2): 3–24.
1981 "Factionalism in the Venezuelan Communist Movement, 1937–1948." *Science and Society* 45: 52–70.

ENGELS, FREDERICK
1972 "The Mark." In *Socialism: Utopian and Scientific,* 77–93. New York:
[1882] International Publishers.

EVANS, PETER
1979 *Dependent Development: The Alliance of Multinational, State, and Local Capital in Brazil.* Princeton: Princeton University Press.

FARRISS, NANCY
1978 "Nucleation versus Dispersal: The Dynamics of Population Movement in Colonial Yucatan." *Hispanic American Historical Review* 58: 187–216.
1984 *Maya Society under Colonial Rule: The Collective Enterprise of Survival.* Princeton: Princeton University Press.

FAVRE, HENRI
1977 "The Dynamics of Indian Peasant Society and Migration to Coastal Plantations in Central Peru." In *Land and Labour in Latin America,* ed. Kenneth Duncan and Ian Rutledge, 83–102. Cambridge: Cambridge University Press.

FONT, MAURICIO
1987 "Coffee Planters, Politics, and Development in Brazil." *Latin American Research Review* 22(3): 69–90.

FORMAN, SHEPARD
1975 *The Brazilian Peasantry.* New York: Columbia University Press.

FOSTER-CARTER, AIDAN
1978 "The Modes of Production Controversy." *New Left Review* 107: 47–77.

FOX, RICHARD
1985 *Lions of the Punjab: Culture in the Making.* Berkeley: University of California Press.

FRANK, ANDRE GUNDER
1967   *Capitalism and Underdevelopment in Latin America.* New York: Monthly Review Press.
1969   *Latin America: Underdevelopment or Revolution?* New York: Monthly Review Press.

FRIEDMAN, JONATHAN
1975   "Tribes, States, and Transformations." In *Marxist Analyses and Social Anthropology,* ed. Maurice Bloch, 161–202. London: Malaby.
1987   "Generalized Exchange, Theocracy, and the Opium Trade." *Critique of Anthropology* 7(1): 15–31.

FRYKMAN, JONAS, AND ORVAR LOFGREN
1987   *Culture Builders: A Historical Anthropology of Middle-Class Life.* New Brunswick: Rutgers University Press.

FURTADO, CELSO
1970   *The Economic Development of Latin America,* 2d ed. Cambridge: Cambridge University Press.

GARCÍA MÁRQUEZ, GABRIEL
1983   1982 Nobel Prize Acceptance Speech. *New York Times,* 6 February 1983, OpEd page.

GEERTZ. CLIFFORD
1973a   *The Interpretation of Cultures.* New York: Basic.
1973b   "Thick Description: Toward an Interpretive Theory of Culture." In *The Interpretation of Cultures,* 3–30. New York: Basic.
1973c   "Deep Play: Notes on the Balinese Cockfight." In *The Interpretation of Cultures,* 412–453. New York: Basic.
1980   *Negara: The Theatre state in Nineteenth-Century Bali.* Princeton: Princeton University Press.
1983   "Blurred Genres: The Refiguration of Social Thought." In *Local Knowledge,* 19–35. New York: Basic.

GERMANI, GINO, TORCUATO S. DI TELLA, AND OCTAVIO IANNI
1973   *Populismo y contradicciones de clase en Latinoamérica.* Mexico, D. F.: ERA .

GIBSON, CHARLES
1964   *The Aztecs Under Spanish Rule.* Stanford: Stanford University Press.
1984   "Indian Societies Under Colonial Rule." *Cambridge History of Latin America* 1: 381–419.

GIDDENS, ANTHONY
1971   *Capitalism and Modern Social Theory: An Analysis of the Writings of Marx, Durkheim, and Max Weber.* Cambridge: Cambridge University Press.

GLADE, WILLIAM
1986   "Latin America and the International Economy, 1870–1914." *Cambridge History of Latin America* 4: 1–56.

GODELIER, MAURICE
1972   *Rationality and Irrationality in Economics.* New York: Monthly Review Press.
1977   *Perspectives in Marxist Anthropology.* New York: Cambridge University Press.
1978   "The Concept of the 'Asiatic Mode of Production' and Marxist Models of Social Evolution." In *Relations of Production,* ed. David Seddon, 209–288. London: Frank Cass.

GONZÁLEZ CASANOVA, PABLO, ED.
1984   *América Latina: Historia de Medio Siglo,* 2 vols. Mexico, D. F.: Siglo XXI .

GONZÁLEZ LEÓN, ADRIANO
1967   *País portátil.* Barcelona: Seix Barral.

GORDON, DAVID M.
1972   *Theories of Poverty and Unemployment.* Lexington, MA: D. C. Heath.

GORDON, DAVID M., RICHARD EDWARDS AND MICHAEL REICH
1982   *Segmented Work, Divided Workers.* New York: Cambridge University Press.

GRAMSCI, ANTONIO
1971   *Selections from the Prison Notebooks,* ed. and trans. by Quintin Hoare
[1929–35] and Geoffrey Nowell Smith. New York: International.

GREGORY, CHRIS
1986   "On Taussig on Aristotle and Chevalier on Everyone." *Social Analysis* 19: 64–69.

GREISHABER, ERWIN P.
1979   "Hacienda-Indian Community relations and Indian Acculturation: An Historiographical Essay." *Latin American Research Review* 14(3): 107–128.

GUDMUNDSON, LOWELL
1986   *Costa Rica Before Coffee: Society and Economy on the Eve of the Export Boom.* Baton Rouge: Louisiana State University Press.

GUTMAN, HERBERT
1976   *Work, Culture, and Society in Industrializing America.* New York: Random House.

HALE, CHARLES
1968   *Mexican Liberalism in the Age of Mora, 1821–1853.* New Haven: Yale University Press.
1973   "The Reconstruction of Nineteenth-Century Politics in Spanish America: A Case for the History of Ideas." *Latin American Research Review* 8(2): 53–73.
1986   "Political and Social Ideas in Latin America, 1870–1930." *Cambridge History of Latin America* 4: 367–441.

HALL, STUART
1981   "In Defense of Theory." In *People's History and Socialist Theory,* ed. Raphael Samuel, 378–385. London: Routledge and Kegan Paul.

HALPERIN, RHODA, AND JAMES DOW, EDS.
1977   *Peasant Livelihoods.* New York: St. Martin's.

HARBSMEIER, MICHAEL
1978   "Critique of Political Economy, Historical Materialism and Pre-Capitalist Social Forms." *Critique of Anthropology* 12: 3–37.

HARRIS, MARVIN
1964   *Patterns of Race in the Americas.* New York: Walker and Company.
1968   *The Rise of Anthropological Theory.* New York: Crowell.
1979   *Cultural Materialism: The Struggle for a Science of Culture.* New York: Random House.

HARRISON, MARK
1975   "Chayanov and the Economics of the Russian Peasantry." *Journal of Peasant Studies* 2: 389–417.
1977   "The Peasant Mode of Production in the Work of A. V. Chayanov." *Journal of Peasant Studies* 4: 323–336.
1979   "Chayanov and the Marxists." *Journal of Peasant Studies* 7: 86–100.

HENFREY, COLIN
1981   "Dependency, Modes of Production, and the Class Analysis of Latin America." *Latin American Perspectives* 8 (3 & 4): 17–54.

HERNANDEZ, JOSEFINA RÍOS DE
1988   *La hacienda Venezolana.* Caracas: Fondo Editorial Tropykos.

HEWITT DE ALCÁNTARA, CYNTHIA
1984   *Anthropological Perspectives on Rural Mexico.* London: Routledge and Kegan Paul.

HILTON, RODNEY, ED.
1976   *The Transition from Feudalism to Capitalism.* London: New Left Books.

HINDESS, BARRY, AND PAUL Q. HIRST
1975   *Pre-Capitalist Modes of Production.* London: Routledge and Kegan Paul.
1977   *Mode of Production and Social Formation.* Atlantic Highlands: Humanities Press.

HIRST, PAUL Q.
1979   "The Necessity of Theory." *Economy and Society* 8: 417–445.

HOBSBAWM, ERIC
1959   *Primitive Rebels.* New York: Norton.

HOLLOWAY, THOMAS
1980   *Immigrants on the Land: Coffee and Society in São Paulo, 1886–1934.* Chapel Hill: University of North Carolina Press.

HOLMES, DOUGLAS
1983   "A Peasant-Worker Model in a Northern Italian Context." *American Ethnologist* 10: 734–748.

HUMBOLDT, ALEXANDER VON
1818   *Personal Narrative of Travels to the Equinoctial Regions of the New Continent during the Years 1799–1803.* London: Longman, Hurst, Rees, Orme, and Brown.

JAMESON, FREDERICK
1984   "Postmodernism, or the Cultural Logic of Late Capitalism." *New Left Review* 146: 53–92.

JOHNSON, JOHN
1964   *The Military and Society in Latin America.* Stanford: Stanford University Press.

JOHNSON, RICHARD
1981   "Against Absolutism." In *People's History and Socialist Theory,* ed. Raphael Samuel, 386–396. London: Routledge and Kegan Paul.
1982   "Reading for the Best Marx: History-Writing and Historical Abstraction." In *Making Histories: Studies in History-Writing and Politics,* ed. Richard Johnson, Gregor McLennan, Bill Schwarz, and David Sutton, 153–201. Minneapolis: University of Minnesota Press.

JONES, GARETH STEDMAN
1983   *Languages of Class: Studies in English Working Class History, 1832–1982.* Cambridge: Cambridge University Press.

JOSEPH, GILBERT M.
1986   *Rediscovering the Past at Mexico's Periphery: Essays on the History of Modern Yucatan.* University: University of Alabama Press.

KAHN, JOEL
1981a   "Marxist Anthropology and Segmentary Societies: A Review of the Literature." In *The Anthropology of Pre-Capitalist Societies,* ed. Joel Kahn and Joseph R. Llobera, 57–88. Atlantic Highlands: Humanities Press.
1981b   "Mercantilism and the Emergence of Servile Labour in Colonial Indonesia." In *The Anthropology of Pre-Capitalist Societies,* ed. Joel Kahn and Josep R. Llobera, 185–213. Atlantic Highlands: Humanities Press.

KAHN, JOEL, AND JOSEP R. LLOBERA
1981   "Towards a New Marxism or a New Anthropology?" In *The Anthropology of Pre-Capitalist Societies,* ed. Joel Kahn and Josep R. Llobera, 263–329. Atlantic Highlands: Humanities Press.

KATZ, FRIEDRICH
1974   "Labor Conditions on Haciendas in Porfirian Mexico: Some Trends and Tendencies." *Hispanic American Historical Review* 54: 1–47.

KATZ, NAOMI, AND DAVID KEMNITZER
1979   "Mode of Production and the Process of Domination: The Classi-

cal Kingdom of Dahomey." In *New Directions in Political Economy*, ed. Madeline Barbara Leons and Frances Rothstein, 49–79. Westport, CT: Greenwood Press.

KEESING, ROGER
1987   "Anthropology as Interpretive Quest." *Current Anthropology* 28(2): 161–176.

KIRKPATRICK, JEANNE
1979   "Dictatorships and Double Standards." *Commentary* 68(5): 34–45.

KORSCH, KARL
1971   *Marxism and Philosophy.* New York: Monthly Review Press.
[1923]

LACLAU, ERNESTO
1971   "Feudalism and Capitalism in Latin America." *New Left Review* 67: 19–38.
1977   *Politics and Ideology in Marxist Theory.* London: Verso.

LARSON, BROOKE
1988   *Colonialism and Agrarian Transformation in Bolivia: Cochabamba, 1550–1900.* Princeton: Princeton University Press.

LEACH, EDMUND
1964   *Political Systems of Highland Burma: A Study of Kachin Social Struc-*
[1954]   *ture.* Boston: Beacon.

LEARS, JACKSON
1985   "The Concept of Cultural Hegemony: Problems and Possibilities" *American Historical Review* 90: 567–593.

LEAVIS, FRANK R., AND DENYS THOMPSON
1977   *Culture and Environment.* Westport, CT: Greenwood Press.
[1933]

LEHMAN, DAVID
1982   "After Chayanov and Lenin: New Paths of Agrarian Capitalism." *Journal of Development Economics* 11: 133–161.

LENIN, V. I.
1964   *The Development of Capitalism in Russia.* Moscow: Progress Publish-
[1899]   ers.

LEVINE, DANIEL
1973   *Conflict and Political Change in Venezuela.* Princeton: Princeton University Press.

LEWIS, CLEONA
1938   *America's Stake in International Investments.* Washington, D. C.: Brookings Institution.

LEWIS, OSCAR
1951   *Life in a Mexican Village: Tepoztlán Restudied.* Urbana: University of Illinois Press.

LIEBERSON, JONATHAN
1984   Review of *Local Knowledge: Further Essays in Interpretive Anthropology* by Clifford Geertz. *New York Review of Books* 31: 39–46.

LLAMBÍ, LUIS
1981   "Las unidades de producción campesina en el sistema capitalista: Un intento de teorización." *Estudios Rurales Latinoamericanos* 4(2): 125–153.

LOMBARDI, JOHN, AND JAMES HANSON
1970   "The First Venezuela Coffee Cycle, 1830–1855." *Agricultural History* 44: 355–367.

LOMNITZ, LARISSA
1977   *Networks and Marginality.* New York: Academic.

LOMNITZ-ADLER, CLAUDIO
1982   *Evolución de una sociedad rural.* Mexico, D. F.: Fondo de Cultura Económica.

LOVE, JOSEPH
1980   *São Paulo in the Brazilian Federation, 1889–1937.* Stanford: Stanford University Press.

LUKÁCS, GEORG
1971   *History and Class Consciousness.* Cambridge: MIT Press.
[1922]

LUXEMBURG, ROSA
1968   *The Accumulation of Capital.* New York: Monthly Review Press.
[1913]

MAINE, HENRY
1970   *Ancient Law.* Gloucester, MA: Peter Smith.
[1861]

MALAVÉ MATA, HECTOR
1974   "La formación histórica del antidessarrollo de Venezuela." In *Venezuela: Crecimiento sin desarrollo,* D. F. Maza Zavala, Hector Malavé Mata, Celio S. Orta, Orlando Araujo, Miguel Bolívar Chollet, and Alfredo Chacon, 33–197. Mexico, D. F.: Editorial Nuestro Tiempo.

MALLOY, JAMES, ED.
1977   *Authoritarianism and Corporatism in Latin America.* Pittsburgh: University of Pittsburgh Press.

MANDEL, ERNEST
1978   *Late Capitalism.* London: Verso.

MANNERS, ROBERT
1960   "Methods of Community Analysis in the Caribbean." In *Caribbean Studies: A Symposium,* 2d ed., ed. Vera Rubin, 80–92. Seattle: University of Washington Press.

MARCUS, GEORGE
1986   "Contemporary Problems of Ethnography in the Modern World System." In *Writing Culture,* ed. James Clifford and George Marcus, 165–193. Berkeley: University of California Press.

MARCUS, GEORGE, AND MICHAEL FISCHER
1986   *Anthropology as Cultural Critique.* Chicago: University of Chicago Press.

MARIÑEZ, PABLO
1981   "Acerca de los modos de producción precapitalistas en América Latina." *Estudios Sociales Centroamericanos* 10(29): 121–140.

MARTIN, CHERYL ENGLISH
1985   *Rural Society in Colonial Morelos.* Albuquerque: University of New Mexico Press.

MARTZ, JOHN
1966   *Acción Democrática: Evolution of a Modern Political Party.* Princeton: Princeton University Press.

MARTZ, JOHN, ED.
1977   *Venezuela: The Democratic Experience.* New York: Praeger.

MARX, KARL
1964a   *Economic and Philosophic Manuscripts.* New York: International.
[1844]
1964b   14 March 1868 Letter to Engels. In *Pre-Capitalist Economic Forma-*
[1868];   *tions,* ed. Eric Hobsbawm, 139. New York: International.
1967a   *Capital,* Vol. 2. New York: International.
[1888]
1967b   *Capital,* Vol. 3. New York: International.
[1894]
1970   "Preface." In *A Contribution to the Critique of Political Economy,* 19–
[1859]   23. New York: International.
1973   *Grundrisse.* New York: Random House/Vintage.
[1857–58]
1974   *The Eighteenth Brumaire of Louis Bonaparte.* In *Surveys from Exile,* ed.
[1852]   David Fernbach, 143–249. New York: Random House/Vintage.
1977   *Capital,* Vol. 1. New York: Random House/Vintage.
[1867]

MARX, KARL, AND FREDERICK ENGELS
1970   *The German Ideology.* New York: International.
[1846]

McCREERY, DAVID
1976   "Coffee and Class: The Structure of Development in Liberal Guatemala." *Hispanic American Historical Review* 56: 438–460.
1983   "Debt Servitude in Rural Guatemala, 1876–1936." *Hispanic American Historical Review* 63: 735–759.

McEACHERN, CHARMAINE, AND PETER MAYER
1986   "The Children of Bronze and the Children of Gold: The Apoliti-
          cal Anthropology of the Peasant." *Social Analysis* 19: 70–77.

MEDICK, HANS
1987   "Missionaries in a Rowboat? Ethnological Ways of Knowing as a
          Challenge to Social History." *Comparative Studies in Society and His-
          tory* 29(1): 76–98.

MEILLASSOUX, CLAUDE
1972   "Form Reproduction to Production," *Economy and Society* 1: 93–105.
1978   "The 'Economy' in Agricultural Self-Sustaining Societies: A Pre-
          liminary Analysis." In *Relations of Production*, ed. David Seddon,
          127–157. London: Frank Cass.
1981   *Maidens, Meal and Money.* New York: Cambridge University Press.

MELVILLE, ROBERTO
1979   *Crecimiento y rebelión: El desarrollo económico de las haciendas Azucare-
          ras en Morelos (1880–1910).* Mexico: Editorial Nueva Imagen.

MINTZ, SIDNEY
1953   "The Folk-Urban Continuum and the Rural Proletarian Commu-
          nity." *American Journal of Sociology* 59(2): 136–143.
1973   "A Note on the Definition of Peasantries." *Journal of Peasant Studies*
          1: 91–106.
1974a   *Caribbean Transformations.* Chicago: Aldine.
1974b   "The Rural Proletariat and the Problem of Rural Proletarian Con-
          sciousness." *Journal of Peasant Studies* 1: 290–325.
1978   "The Role of Puerto Rico in Modern Social Science." *Revista/
          Review Interamericana* 8: 5–16.
1979   "Slavery and the Rise of Peasantries." *Historical Reflections* 6:
          213–242.
1982   "Culture: An Anthropological View." *Yale Review* 71: 499–512.
1985   *Sweetness and Power: The Place of Sugar in Modern History.* New York:
          Viking.
1987   "Author's Rejoinder." *Food and Foodways* 2: 171–197.

MINTZ, SIDNEY, AND ERIC WOLF
1950   "An Analysis of Ritual Co-Parenthood (Compadrazgo)." *Southwest-
          ern Journal of Anthropology* 6: 341–368.

MONTOYA, RODRIGO
1978   *A Propósito del carácter predominantemente capitalista de la economía
          Peruana actual (1960–1970).* Lima: Mosca Azul Editores.

MOORE, BARRINGTON
1966   *The Social Origins of Dictatorship and Democracy.* Boston: Beacon
          Press.

MOORE, WILBERT
1951   *Industrialization and Labor.* Ithaca: Cornell University Press.

MORGAN, LEWIS HENRY
1974 *Ancient Society.* Gloucester, MA: Peter Smith.
[1877]

MURATORIO, BLANCA
1980 "Protestantism and Capitalism Revisted, in the Rural Highlands of Ecuador." *Journal of Peasant Studies* 8(1): 37–60.
1987 *Rucuyaya Alonso y la historia social y económica del Alto Napo, 1850–1950.* Quito: Ediciones Abya-Yala.

MURPHY, ROBERT
1970 "Basin Ethnography and Ethnological Theory." In *Languages and Cultures of Western North America,* ed. E. H. Swanson, Jr., 152–171. Pocatello: Idaho State University Press.
1978 "Introduction." In *Evolution and Ecology,* Julian Steward, 1–39. Urbana: University of Illinois Press.
1981 "Julian Steward." In *Totems and Teachers,* ed. Sydel Silverman, 171–206. New York: Columbia University Press.

NASH, JUNE
1979 *We Eat the Mines and the Mines Eat Us.* New York: Columbia University Press.

NERUDA, PABLO
1955 *Canto General,* Vol. 1. Argentina: Losada.

NIELD, KEITH, AND JOHN SEED
1979 "Theoretical Poverty or the Poverty of Theory: British Marxist Historiography and the Althusserians." *Economy and Society* 8: 3–32.

NUGENT, DAVID
1982 "Closed Systems and Contradiction: The Kachin in and out of History." *Man* 17: 508–527.

O'BRIEN, JAY, AND WILLIAM ROSEBERRY, EDS.
Forthcoming "Imagining the Past: Critical Reflections on Anthropology and History." Unpublished manuscript.

O'DONNELL, GUILLERMO
1973 *Modernization and Bureaucratic Authoritarianism: Studies in Latin American Politics.* Berkeley: Institute of International Studies, University of California.

ORLOVE, BENJAMIN
1977 *Alpacas, Sheep and Men.* New York: Academic Press.

ORTNER, SHERRY
1984 "Anthropological Theory since the Sixties." *Comparative Studies in Society and History* 26(1): 126–166.

PALACIOS, MARCO
1983 *El café en Colombia, 1850–1970: Una historia económica, social y política.* Mexico, D. F.: El Colégio de México.

1986   Unpublished Comments. Roundtable Discussion of Coffee in the History of Latin America, Plaza de Cultura, San José, Costa Rica.

PALERM, ANGEL
1976a   *Sobre la formación del sistema colonial en México: Apuntes para una discusión.* Mexico, D. F.: La Casa Chata.
1976b   *Modos de producción y formaciones socioeconómicas.* Mexico, D. F.: Editorial Edicol.
1980   *Antropología y Marxismo.* Mexico, D. F.: Editorial Nueva Imagen.

PATCH, ROBERT
1985   "Agrarian Change in Eighteenth Century Yucatan." *Hispanic American Historical Review* 65: 21–49.

PERLMAN, JANICE
1976   *The Myth of Marginality.* Berkeley: University of California Press.

PETRAS, JAMES, MORRIS MORLEY, AND STEVEN SMITH
1977   *The Nationalization of Venezuelan Oil.* New York: Praeger.

PICÓ, FERNANDO
1979   *Libertad y servidumbre en el Puerto Rico del siglo XIX: Los jornaleros Utuadeños en vísperas del auge del café.* Río Piedras: Ediciones Huracán.
1981   *Amargo café (los pequeños y medianos caficultores de Utuado en la segunda mitad del siglo XIX).* Río Piedras: Ediciones Huracán.

PLATT, D.C.M., ED.
1977   *Business Imperialism, 1840–1930: An Inquiry Based on British Experience in Latin America.* New York: Oxford University Press.

POPKIN, SAMUEL
1979   *The Rational Peasant.* Berkeley: University of California Press.

POPULAR MEMORY GROUP
1982   "Popular Memory: Theory, Politics, Method." In *Making Histories: Studies in History-Writing and Politics,* ed. Richard Johnson, Gregor McLennan, Bill Schwarz, and David Sutton, 205–252. Minneapolis: University of Minnesota Press.

POST, KEN
1986   "Can One Have an Historical Anthropology? Some Reactions to Taussig and Chevalier." *Social Analysis* 19: 78–84.

POULANTZAS, NICOS
1973   *Political Power and Social Classes.* London: Verso.
1974   *Fascism and Dictatorship.* London: Verso.
1975   *Classes in Contemporary Capitalism.* London: Verso.
1978   *State, Power, Socialism.* London: Verso.

PRICE, RICHARD
1983   *First-Time: The Historical Vision of an Afro-American People.* Baltimore: The Johns Hopkins University Press.

QUINTERO RIVERA, ANGEL
1973   "Background to the Emergence of Imperialist Capitalism in Puerto Rico." *Caribbean Studies* 13: 31–63.

RANGEL, DOMINGO ALBERTO
1968   *El proceso del capitalismo contemporaneo en Venezuela.* Caracas: Universidad Central.
1969   *Capital y desarrollo: La Venezuela agraria.* Caracas: Universidad Central.
1970   *Capital y desarrollo: El rey petroleo.* Caracas: Universidad Central.

REBEL, HERMANN
1988   "Why Not 'Old Marie' . . . Or Someone Very Much Like Her? A Reassessment of the Question About the Grimms' Contributors from a Social Historical Perspective." *Social History* 13: 1–24.
1989a   "Cultural Hegemony and Class Experience: A Critical Reading of Recent Ethnological-Historical Approaches (Part 1)." *American Ethnologist* 16(1): 117–136.
1989b   "Cultural Hegemony and Class Experience: A Critical Reading of Recent Ethnological-Historical Approaches (Part 2)." *American Ethnologist* 16(2): 350–365.

REDFIELD, ROBERT
1930   *Tepoztlán, A Mexican Village: A Study of Folk Life.* Chicago: University of Chicago Press.
1934   "Cultural Changes in Yucatan." *American Anthropologist* 36: 57–69.
1940   *The Folk Culture of Yucatan.* Chicago: University of Chicago Press.
1953   *The Primitive World and its Transformations.* Ithaca: Cornell University Press.

REDFIELD, ROBERT, RALPH LINTON, AND MELVILLE HERSKOVITZ
1936   "Memorandum for the Study of Acculturation." *American Anthropologist* 38: 149–152.

Renacimiento, El
1904   Boconó, Trujillo (Venezuela) Newspaper.

REY, PIERRE-PHILIPPE
1975   "The Lineage Mode of Production." *Critique of Anthropology* 3: 27–79.
1976   *Las alianzas de classes.* Mexico, D. F.: Siglo XXI.
1979   "Class Contradiction in Lineage Societies." *Critique of Anthropology* 13 & 14: 41–60.

RIBEIRO, DARCY
1972   *The Americas and Civilization.* New York: Dutton.

RICARD, ROBERT
1966   *The Spiritual Conquest of Mexico.* Berkeley: University of California
[1933] Press.

RODÓ, JOSE E.
1988   *Ariel.* Austin: University of Texas Press.
[1900]

ROSALDO, RENATO
1980   *Ilongot Headhunting, 1883–1974: A Study in Society and History.* Stanford: Stanford University Press.

ROSEBERRY, WILLIAM
1978a   "Historical Materialism and *The People of Puerto Rico.*" *Revista/ Review Interamericana* 8: 26–36.
1978b   "Peasants in Primitive Accumulation: Western Europe and Venezuela Compared." *Dialectical Anthropology* 3: 243–260.
1978c   "Peasants as Proletarians." *Critique of Anthropology* 11: 3–18.
1980   "Capital and Class in Nineteenth Century Boconó, Venezuela." *Antropológica* 54: 139–166.
1982   "Peasants, Proletarians, and Politics in the Venezuelan Andes, 1875–1975." In *Power and Protest in the Countryside,* ed. Robert Weller and Scott Guggengeim, 106–131. Durham: Duke University Press.
1983   *Coffee and Capitalism in the Venezuelan Andes.* Austin: University of Texas Press.
1986a   "Hacia un análisis comparativo de los paises cafetaleros." *Revista de Historia* 14: 25–30.
1986b   "The Ideology of Domestic Production." *Labour, Capital and Society* 19: 70–93.
1987   "Household and Community Structure in the History of Mexican Peasantries." Paper presented at the Annual Meeting of the American Ethnological Society.
1988   "Domestic Modes, Domesticated Models." *Journal of Historical Sociology* 1(4): 423–430.
Forthcoming   "Potatoes, Sacks, and Enclosures in Early Modern England." In *"Imagining the Past: Critical Reflections on Anthropology and History,"* ed. Jay O'Brien and William Roseberry. Unpublished manuscript.

ROSEBERRY, WILLIAM, AND JAY O'BRIEN
Forthcoming   "Introduction." In *Imagining the Past: Critical Reflections on Anthropology and History,* ed. Jay O'Brien and William Roseberry. Unpublished manuscript.

ROWE, JOHN
1957   "The Incas Under Spanish Colonial Institutions." *Hispanic American Historical Review* 37: 155–199.

RUBIN, VERA, ED.
1960   *Caribbean Studies: A Symposium,* 2d ed. Seattle: University of Washington Press.

RUDÉ, GEORGE
1964   *The Crowd in History*. New York: Wiley.

SAFFORD, FRANK
1976   *The Ideal of the Practical: Colombia's Struggle to Form a Technical Elite.* Austin: University of Texas Press.
1985   "Politics, Ideology, and Society in Post-Independence Spanish America." *Cambridge History of Latin America* 3: 347–422.

SAHLINS, MARSHALL
1972   *Stone Age Economics*. Chicago: Aldine.
1976   *Culture and Practical Reason*. Chicago: University of Chicago Press.
1981   *Historical Metaphors and Mythical Realities: Structure in the Early History of the Sandwich Islands Kingdom*. Ann Arbor: University of Michigan Press.
1985   *Islands of History*. Chicago: University of Chicago Press.

SALCEDO BASTARDO, J. L.
1972   *Historia fundamental de Venezuela*. Caracas: Universidad Central.

SAMPER KUTSCHBACH, MARIO
1985   "La especialización mercantil-campesina en el noroeste del Valle Central: 1850–1900. Elementos microanalíticos para un modelo." *Revista de Historia*, Número Especial, 49–87.

SANCHEZ ALBORÑOZ, NICOLÁS
1974   *The Population of Latin America: A History*. Berkeley: University of California Press.

SANOJA, MARIO, IRAIDA VARGAS
1974   *Antiquas formaciones y modos de producción Venezolanos*. Caracas: Monte Avila Editores.

SCHNEIDER, DAVID
1980   *American Kinship: A Cultural Account*, 2d ed. Chicago: University of Chicago Press.

SCOTT, C. D.
1976   "Peasants, Proletarianization and the Articulation of Modes of Production: The Case of Sugar-Cane Cutters in Northern Peru, 1940–69." *Journal of Peasant Studies* 3: 321–342.

SCOTT, JAMES C.
1976   *The Moral Economy of the Peasant*. New Haven: Yale University Press.
1977   "Protest and Profanation: Agrarian Revolt and the Little Tradition." *Theory and Society* 4: 1–38; 211–246.
1985   *Weapons of the Weak: Everyday Forms of Peasant Resistance*. New Haven: Yale University Press.

SCUDDER, THAYER
1962   *The Ecology of the Gwembe Tonga*. Manchester: Manchester University Press.

SEIDEL, R. N.
1972   "America's Reformers Abroad: The Kemmerer Missions in South
            America, 1923–1931." *Journal of Economic History* 32(2): 520–545.

SERVICE, ELMAN
1955   "Indian-European Relations in Colonial Latin America." *American
            Anthropologist* 57: 411–425.

SEWELL, WILLIAM
1980   *Work and Revolution in France: The Language of Labor from the Old
            Regime to 1848.* New York: Cambridge University Press.

SHANIN, TEODOR
1972   *The Awkward Class.* Oxford: Oxford University Press.
1979   "Defining Peasants: Conceptualizations and Deconceptualiza-
            tions—Old and New in a Marxist Debate." *Peasant Studies* 8(4):
            38–60.
1983   *Late Marx and the Russian Road: Marx and the Peripheries of Capital-
            ism.* New York: Monthly Review Press.

SIDER, GERALD
1986   *Culture and Class in Anthropology and History: A Newfoundland Illustra-
            tion.* New York: Cambridge University Press.

SILK, MARK
1987   "The Hot History Department." *New York Times Magazines,* 19
            April, 42–63.

SILVERMAN, SYDEL
1979   "The Peasant Concept in Anthropology." *Journal of Peasant Studies*
            7: 49–69.

SISKIND, JANET
1978   "Kinship and Mode of Production." *American Anthropologist* 80:
            860–872.

SKIDMORE, THOMAS, AND PETER SMITH
1984   *Modern Latin America.* New York: Oxford University Press.

SMITH, CAROL A., ED.
1976   *Regional Analysis,* 2 vols. New York: Academic.

SMITH, GAVIN
1979   "Socio-Economic Differentiation and Relations of Production
            among Rural-Based Petty Producers in Central Peru, 1880–
            1970." *Journal of Peasant Studies* 6: 176–206.
1989   *Livelihood and Resistance.* Berkeley: University of California Press.

SMITH, ROBERT FREEMAN
1986   "Latin American, The United States, and the European Powers,
            1830–1930." *Cambridge History of Latin America* 4: 83–119.

SOMBART, WERNER
1967   *The Quintessence of Capitalism.* New York: Howard Fertig.
[1915]

SPALDING, KAREN
1974 *De indio a campesino: Cambios en la estructura social del Peru colonial.* Lima: Instituto de Estudios Peruanos.

SPICER, EDWARD H., ED.
1961 *Perspectives in American Indian Culture Change.* Chicago: University of Chicago Press.

SSRC SUMMER SEMINAR IN ACCULTURATION
1954 "Acculturation: An Exploratory Formulation." *American Anthropologist* 56: 973–1002.

STAVENHAGEN, RODOLFO
1975 *Social Classes in Agrarian Society.* Garden City: Doubleday/Anchor.
1978 "Capitalism and the Peasantry in Mexico." *Latin American Perspectives* 5: 27–37.

STEEDMAN, CAROLYN KAY
1986 *Landscape for a Good Woman: A Study of Two Lives.* New Brunswick: Rutgers University Press.

STEPAN, ALFRED
1978 *The State and Society: Peru in Comparative Perspective.* Princeton: Princeton University Press.

STERN, STEVE J.
1982 *Peru's Indian Peoples and the Challenge of Spanish Conquest: Huamanga to 1640.* Madison: University of Wisconsin Press.
1983 "The Struggle for Solidarity: Class, Culture, and Community in Highland Indian America." *Radical History Review* 27: 21–45.
1988a "Feudalism, Capitalism, and the World-System in the Perspective of Latin America and the Carribean." *American Historical Review* 93: 829–872.
1988b "Reply: 'Ever More Solitary.'" *American Historical Review* 93: 886–897.

STEWARD, JULIAN
1955 *Theory of Culture Change.* Urbana: University of Illinois Press.
1978 *Evolution and Ecology.* Urbana: University of Illinois Press.

STEWARD, JULIAN, ROBERT MANNERS, ERIC WOLF, ELENA PADILLA, SIDNEY MINTZ, AND RAYMOND SCHEELE
1956 *The People of Puerto Rico.* Urbana: University of Illinois Press.

STOLCKE, VERENA
1988 *Coffee Planters, Workers, and Wives: Class Conflict and Gender Relations on São Paulo Plantations, 1850–1980.* New York: St. Martin's.

STOLER, ANN LAURA
1985 *Capitalism and Confrontation in Sumatra's Plantation Belt.* New Haven: Yale University Press.

STRICKON, ARNOLD
1965   "Hacienda and Plantation in Yucatan." *América Indígena* 25 (1): 35–63.

TAUSSIG, MICHAEL
1980   *The Devil and Commodity Fetishism in South America.* Chapel Hill: University of North Carolina Press.
1987   "The Rise and Fall of Marxist Anthropology." *Social Analysis* 21: 101–113.

TAYLOR, JOHN
1979   *From Modernization to Modes of Production.* Atlantic Highlands: Humanities Press.

TAYLOR, PETER, AND HERMANN REBEL
1981   "Hessian Peasant Women, Their Families, and the Draft: A Socio-Historical Interpretation of Four Tales from the Grimm Collection." *Journal of Family History* 6: 347–378.

TAYLOR, WILLIAM
1972   *Landlord and Peasant in Colonial Oaxaca.* Stanford: Stanford University Press.
1974   "Landed Society in New Spain: A View from the South." *Hispanic American Historical Review* 54: 387–413.
1976   "Town and Country in the Valley of Oaxaca, 1750–1812." In *Provinces of Early Mexico: Variants of Spanish American Regional Evolution,* ed. Ida Altman and James Lockhart, 63–95. Los Angeles: UCLA Latin American Center Publications.
1985   "Between Global Process and Local Knowledge: An Inquiry into Early Latin American Social History, 1500–1900." In *Reliving the Past,* ed. Olivier Zunz, 115–190. Chapel Hill: University of North Carolina Press.

TAX, SOL, ED.
1952   *Heritage of Conquest.* Glencoe, IL: Free Press.

TERRAY, EMMANUEL
1971   *Marxism and "Primitive" Societies.* New York: Monthly Review Press.
1974   "Long Distance Trade and the Formation of the State." *Economy and Society* 3: 315–345.
1975   "Classes and Class Consciousness in the Abron Kingdom of Gyaman" In *Marxist Analyses and Social Anthropology,* ed. Maurice Bloch, 85–135. London: Malaby.
1979   "On Exploitation: Elements of an Autocritique." *Critique of Anthropology* 13 & 14: 29–39.

THOMPSON, E. P.
1963   *The Making of the English Working Class.* New York: Pantheon.
1967   "Time, Work-Discipline, and Industrial Capitalism." *Past and Present* 38: 56–97.

1971 "The Moral Economy of the English Crowd in the Eighteenth Century." *Past and Present* 50: 76–136.

1972 "Anthropology and the Discipline of Historical Context." *Midland History* 1(3): 41–55.

1974 "Patrician Society, Plebian Culture." *Journal of Social History* 7: 382–405.

1978a *The Poverty of Theory and Other Essays.* New York: Monthly Review Press.

1978b "Eighteenth-Century English Society: Class Struggle Without Class?" *Social History* 3(2): 133–165.

1981 "The Politics of Theory." In *People's History and Socialist Theory,* ed. Raphael Samuel, 396–408. London: Routledge and Kegan Paul.

THORP, ROSEMARY

1986 "Latin America and the International Economy from the First World War to the World Depression." *Cambridge History of Latin America* 4: 57–81.

THORP, ROSEMARY, ED.

1984 *Latin America in the 1930s: The Role of the Periphery in World Crisis.* New York: St. Martin's.

TOENNIES, FERDINAND

1957 *Community and Society (Gemeinschaft und Gesellschaft).* East Lansing:
[1887] Michigan State University Press.

TOKEI, FERENC

1966 *Sur le mode de production Asiatique.* Paris: CERM .

TROUILLOT, MICHEL-ROLPH

1986 "The Price of Indulgence." *Social Analysis* 19: 85–90.

1988 *Peasants and Capital: Dominica in the World Economy.* Baltimore: The Johns Hopkins University Press.

TUGWELL, FRANKLIN

1975 *The Politics of Oil in Venezuela.* Stanford: Stanford University Press.

TURNER, TERENCE

1986 "Production, Exploitation, and Social Consciousness in the 'Peripheral Situation.' " *Social Analysis* 19: 91–115.

VENEZUELA, BANCO CENTRAL

1971 *La economía Venezolana en los últimos treinta años.* Caracas.

VENEZUELA, MINISTERIO DE FOMENTO

1971 *X censo de población y vivienda: Resumen general.* Caracas.

VINCENT, JOAN

1982 *Teso in Transformation: The Political Economy of Peasant and Class in Eastern Africa.* Berkeley: University of California Press.

1989 *Anthropology and Politics: Visions, Traditions and Trends.* Tucson: University of Arizona Press. In press.

WAGLEY, CHARLES, AND MARVIN HARRIS
1955   "A Typology of Latin American Subcultures." *American Anthropologist* 57: 426–451.

WALLERSTEIN, IMMANUEL
1974   *The Modern World-System: Capitalist Agriculture and the Origins of the European World Economy in the Sixteenth Century.* New York: Academic.
1979   *The Capitalist World-Economy.* New York: Cambridge University Press.
1988   "Comments on Stern's Critical Tests." *American Historical Review* 93: 873–885.

WARMAN, ARTURO
1981   *We Come to Object: The Peasants of Morelos and the National State.* Baltimore: The Johns Hopkins University Press.

WASSERSTROM, ROBERT
1983   *Class and Society in Central Chiapas.* Berkeley: University of California Press.

WATERBURY, RONALD
1975   "Non-Revolutionary Peasants: Oaxaca Compared to Morelos in the Mexican Revolution." *Comparative Studies in Society and History* 17: 410–422.

WILLIAMS, GAVIN
1979   "In Defense of History." *History Workshop* 7: 116–124.

WILLIAMS, RAYMOND
1960   *Culture and Society.* New York: Columbia University Press.
1961   *The Long Revolution.* New York: Columbia University Press.
1973   *The Country and the City.* New York: Oxford University Press.
1977   *Marxism and Literature.* Oxford: Oxford University Press.
1979   *Politics and Letters.* London: New Left Books.
1980   *Problems in Materialism and Culture.* London: New Left Books.
1982   *The Sociology of Culture.* New York: Schocken.

WOLF, ERIC R.
1955   "Types of Latin American Peasantry: A Preliminary Discussion" *American Anthropologist* 57: 452–471.
1956a   "San José: Subcultures of a 'Traditional' Coffee Municipality." In *The People of Puerto Rico,* Julian Steward, Robert Manners, Eric Wolf, Elena Padilla, Sidney Mintz, and Raymond Scheele, 171–264. Urbana: University of Illinois Press.
1956b   "Aspects of Group Relations in a Complex Society: Mexico." *American Anthropologist* 58: 1065–1078.
1957   "Closed Corporate Communities in Mesoamerica and Central Java" *Southwestern Journal of Anthropology* 13: 1–18.
1959a   *Sons of the Shaking Earth.* Chicago: University of Chicago Press.

1959b   "Specific Aspects of Plantation Systems in the New World: Community Subcultures and Social Class." In *Plantation Systems of the New World*, ed. Vera Rubin, 136–147. Washington, D. C.: Pan American Union.

1966   *Peasants*. Englewood Cliffs: Prentice-Hall.

1969   *Peasant Wars of the Twentieth Century*. New York: Harper and Row.

1978   "Remarks on *The People of Puerto Rico*. " *Revista/Review Interamericana* 8: 17–25.

1981   "The Mills of Inequality." In *Social Inequality: Comparative and Developmental Approaches*, ed. Gerald Berreman, 41–58. New York: Academic.

1982   *Europe and the People Without History*. Berkeley: University of California Press.

WOLF, ERIC, AND SIDNEY MINTZ
1957   "Haciendas and Plantations in Middle America and the Antilles." *Social and Economic Studies* 6: 386–412.

WOODWARD, RALPH LEE, JR.
1985   *Central America: A Nation Divided*. New York: Oxford University Press.

WRIGHT, ERIK OLIN
1978   *Class, Crisis and the State*. London: Verso.